Successful Marketing Strategy for High-Tech Firms

Second Edition

For a complete listing of the *Artech House Technology Management and Professional Development Library,* turn to the back of this book.

Successful Marketing Strategy for High-Tech Firms

Second Edition

Eric Viardot

Artech House
Boston • London

Library of Congress Cataloging-in-Publication Data
Viardot, Eric.
    Successful marketing strategy for high-tech firms / Eric Viardot. — 2nd ed.
        p.   cm. — (Artech House professional development library)
    Includes bibliographical references and index.
    ISBN 0-89006-854-2 (alk. paper)
    1. High technology—Marketing.   2. Technological innovations—
Marketing.   I. Title.   II. Series.
HC79.H53V5   1998
620'.0068'8—dc21   98-19225
                                                                   CIP

British Library Cataloguing in Publication Data
Viardot, Eric.
    Successful marketing strategy for high-tech firms. — 2nd ed.
    1. High technology—Marketing   2. High technology industries—
Marketing
    I. Title
    620'.00688

    ISBN 0-89006-854-2

Cover design by Lynda Fishbourne

International Standard Book Number: 0-89006-854-2
Library of Congress Catalog Card Number: 98-19225

10 9 8 7 6 5 4 3

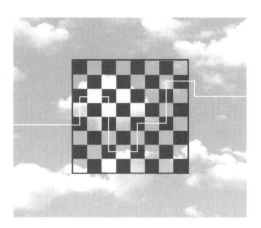

Contents

Acknowledgments

This book is dedicated to all the marketing managers at high-tech companies who agreed to share with me their professional experiences. I would like to thank the employees at the following companies for their cooperation.

- ATOCHEM
- BAIN AND COMPANY
- BASF FRANCE
- BAY NETWORKS
- BOSTON CONSULTING GROUP
- CISCO
- DASSAULT SYSTEMES
- DIGITAL EQUIPMENT

- FRANCE TELECOM
- GSI
- HEWLETT PACKARD
- IBM
- ICI
- L'AEROSPATIALE
- McKINSEY
- MICROSOFT

- MOTOROLA
- ORACLE
- RHONE POULENC
- ROCKWELL TELECOMMUNICATION
- ROUSSEL UCLAF

- SAT
- SGN
- SLIGOS
- STAUBLI
- TEXAS INSTRUMENTS
- THOMSON SINTRA

Introduction

This book is based on a simple observation: successful high-technology companies do not necessarily have the best product, but they do have the best marketing strategy.

In order for a new technological innovation to make a significant impact, it should identify and satisfy a specific human need in a new and cost-effective way. After all, Marconi invented the technology for wireless communication, but it was in the 1920s while leading RCA that David Sarnoff, an untaught immigrant, imagined how the new technology could be applied to transmit news, music, and other kinds of entertainment.

Many companies consider their product to be the absolute best around. For example, France has specialized in manufacturing technological gems for which there is no need. Consider the Concorde—a technological wonder that has suffered a bitter failure and owes its survival to the generosity of French and British taxpayers who have amply participated in financing the deficit caused by the project's financial disaster.

On the contrary, the Airbus, another plane, is probably one of the most profitable examples of a successful marketing policy. The founders of Airbus Industries identified a market need for medium-range aircraft as well as a relative weakness of American aircraft manufacturers in this market. They launched a suitable product of which the market approved. Airbus continues to market its planes successfully.

The case of EMI, one of Britain's leading defense companies, provides another classic example of how a high-tech firm can blunder. In the early 1970s, it discovered the computer tomography technology that was the basis for a revolutionary medical tool, the CAT scanner. EMI was strong in electronics and in innovation, and it also employed G. Hounsfield, the inventor of tomography and later the recipient of the Nobel Prize.

EMI's research and development (R&D) strength did not pay off because the main result of its research, mathematical algorithms for the computerized evaluation of X-rays, had been published in scientific journals, allowing competitors like General Electric, Ohio Nuclear, and other major suppliers of medical equipment to adapt the technology on their own and to enter the market. General Electric, for example, had an efficient service organization and used superior marketing to develop strong connections with hospitals, the chief users of the technology. Further, General Electric was able to produce this medical tool at lower cost. Meanwhile, between 1977 and 1979, EMI made cumulative loss on computer tomography equipment and eventually withdrew from the market, selling its CAT scanner business to General Electric.

A McKinsey study identified four success factors for high-technology companies. These companies market two or three times as many new products as their competitors, incorporate two to three times more technical innovations into each new product, and introduce their products to the market two times faster than their competitors. In addition, the geographical size of their markets is double that of their competitors [1].

Overall, this study shows that these companies make marketing their main objective. Their main concern is the market and not the product; this is the key to their success. All research and development activities, manufacturing, sales, and after-sales services aim to satisfy the customers better and faster.

Marketing plays a fundamental role in this process. Actually, its goal is to determine the needs of the market and to assure that the products manufactured by the company correspond precisely to these needs.

Some claim that high-technology products are so specific that the classic rules of marketing used for selling detergents or yogurt cannot be applied. In reality, this argument is often used to justify the absence of actual strategies oriented toward markets and customer needs. For certain companies, blinded by the mirage of technological innovation, it is easier to continue manufacturing a technical masterpiece even on the brink of bankruptcy.

Moreover, marketing managers of high-technology companies stress that there is not a large difference between marketing traditional products and high-technology products. They contend that the customer philosophy remains the same and that only the specific features of a high-technology product shape its marketing and give it a distinctive twist.

This work is based on consulting experiences with companies in the high-technology sector as well as on comments from numerous professionals. It is addressed to all who wish to understand, set up, or better apply marketing principles in order to succeed in this fascinating world of high technology.

Finally, a point of clarification: the word "product" is used extensively in this book. A high-tech product is considered to be not only a good, but also a service. A good is a physical entity one can touch, while a service provides intangible benefits to customers. Today many high-tech services, from communication services to multimedia networks, are available. Some high-tech services firms such as EDS in the United States or Cap Gemini Sogeti (CGS) in Europe are among the major worldwide corporations. CGS, for instance, offers customers a wide range of services including information technology consulting, customized software, education and training, systems integration (all-in-one working package that, for example, will automate a factory or computerize a billing process), and facilities management.

References

[1] Nevers, M., G. Summe, and B. Uttel, "Commercializing Technology: What the Best Companies Do," *Harvard Business Review*, May–June 1990.

1

What Is High-Tech Marketing?

The term "high-tech marketing" often hides confusion. First, consider the term "marketing." Regis MacKenna, a leading marketing specialist who works with numerous high-tech companies, claims that "Marketing is every one's job, marketing is everything, and everything is marketing" [1]. This overall view of marketing does not simplify the task of managers who feel the need (some strongly, others vaguely) to develop an efficient marketing policy.

Secondly, the term "high tech" or "high technology" refers to technology that stretches from stoves to nuclear power plants and from razor blades to satellites. The term has been used both appropriately and inappropriately and sometimes is nothing more than an empty phrase. SGN, the biggest European nuclear engineering company and a true high-tech firm, has even amended their advertisements to promote themselves as an "advanced-technology engineering" firm rather than a "high-technology engineering" firm.

1

For the sake of clarity, we first recall the meaning of the term "marketing" and review its objectives before defining a high-technology product. We then explore the differences between the marketing of advanced technology products and that of traditional products.

1.1 What is marketing?

The definition of the word "marketing" can be found in its etymology. Marketing means "putting on the market." Therefore, the purpose of marketing is to act in such a way that a company places on the market products that correspond to demand and satisfy the needs and wants of customers at an acceptable return.

Marketing's philosophy reverses the traditional perspective toward the company, its needs, and its production capacity. Marketing considers its main task to be "determining the needs and wants of the appropriate markets and to profitably produce the desired product or services by being more efficient than the competition" [2]. The following, more detailed definition has been developed by the *American Marketing Organization* (AMA): "Marketing is the process of planning and executing the conception, pricing, promotion, and distribution of ideas, goods, and services to create exchanges that satisfy individual and organizational goals" [3]. Marketing focuses on making the product available at the right place, at the right time, and at a price that is acceptable to customers [4].

Given this perspective, marketing complements or replaces short-term views that give greater importance to the product, the manufacturing process, or the selling method (see Table 1.1).

Every company that believes that customers will buy its products if they are "good" (of good quality and with good performance) automatically has a product orientation. This implies that customers are able to recognize the product's quality and that they are possibly willing to pay more if the product justifies it.

This viewpoint is even stronger for high-technology companies that favor product development based on performance or state-of-the-art features that are often far from the customer's needs. From supercomputers

Table 1.1
From a Product Orientation to a Marketing Orientation

Orientation	Customer Purchasing Criteria	Assumptions	Objectives	Department Involved
Product	Quality	Customers buy products for themselves	Find "good" products	R&D
	Product technology	Customers are able to identify a product's advantages	Produce quality products	Design
		Customers are willing to pay more if justified by the product	Explain product functions	Production
Production	Availability and reasonable prices		Produce sufficient quantities	Production
			Optimize logistics and distribution	Logistics sales
Sales	Stimulation of interest	Customers only purchase what is needed	Increase product and company awareness	Sales
		Customers can be encouraged to buy more due to sales techniques	Encourage product purchase	Marketing
Marketing	Response to needs and motivations	Customer point of view is of utmost importance in long-term sales exchange	Know customer needs	Marketing
		Customer interest in a product depends on the product's ability to solve a problem or satisfy a need	Satisfy customer needs	All departments

to supersonic jetliners, some companies have conceived technological wonders at such a high cost that their markets never materialized.

Production orientation refers to the belief that if an acceptable product is available at a reasonable price, it will be purchased. In other words, if a sufficient quantity is produced and the logistics department distributes and supplies the product, the customers will do the rest. This philosophy, which is usually related to an excess of demand (common in postwar Europe and today's developing countries), can also be found in the high-tech sector.

Actually, this infatuation with new technology can be beneficial to a company that is capable of immediately flooding the market with large quantities of its product(s). Such a company, however, should beware of the day when the product no longer pleases the customers and sales suddenly start to plunge. The production-capacity surplus—the cost of inventory and distribution—can kill a company. Several firms in the microcomputer business have witnessed or struggled with this problem (for instance, Thomson with TO7, Apple with Lisa, and Digital Equipment with Rainbow).

In order to sell products to customers, other companies have adopted a third approach, namely, the sales orientation. According to this approach, for the customer to make a purchase, his or her interest in the product must be stimulated through price reductions and special large-scale sales promotions, using gifts and contests or other more aggressive sales techniques such as high-pressure selling. The objective is to sell quickly by encouraging the customer to buy a product immediately, even if it does not correspond exactly to his or her requirements.

This approach is effective for only a short period of time. By selling products that do not really meet an actual need, a company risks sacrificing its credibility. The product quickly disappears to a shelf, and the disappointed customer promises never to be taken again. This approach is even worse for services because if a service is oversold in the first place, it will never be used again.

The sales orientation is not very common in high-tech companies due to the extreme technical, rather than sales, environment. Nevertheless, in periods of overproduction and slowing of demand, some companies (or their distributors) do not hesitate to increase sales. This was the case for microwave ovens and portable computers.

The danger of these three approaches is clear. They focus on the company and forget that the sales exchange involves two parties. Without customers to purchase products, there is no justification for production. On the contrary, the marketing philosophy centers on the customer; it emphasizes that the key element of a product lies in the value that it provides to the user. A company that concentrates too much on the physical attributes of a product, its logistics, or financial profit risks forgetting that the customer purchases a product only as a means to resolve a problem.

This customer orientation involves all the departments of a company because customer satisfaction on all levels, from the product design to its (after-sale) maintenance, is the final measure of success for the company as well as its long-term promise of success.

Being tuned in to customers in order to satisfy them better is more than a philosophy. It is a discipline that requires an organized and responsive company as well as everyone's involvement. All members of the organization, from researchers to CEOs, including switchboard operators and production workers, are involved and responsible for the quality of customer relations.

When the company's organization is turned upside down, the customer becomes the sturdy base of a long-lasting exchange relation between the company and its customers (see Figure 1.1). This

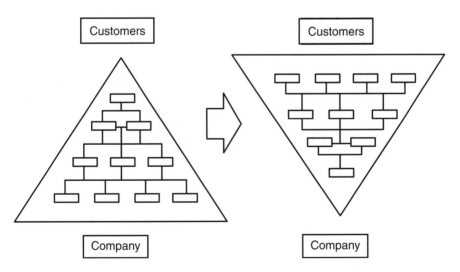

Figure 1.1   Marketing state of mind: the inverted pyramid.

management philosophy was made popular by Jan Carlzon as CEO of Scandinavian Airlines (SAS) in the beginning of the 1980s. As SAS was losing money while facing a bigger competitor, Carlzon asserted that the company had lost its focus on customers' needs: management was placing too much attention on the technicalities of flying airplanes and not enough on the quality of the customers' experiences.

Carlzon said, "We used to think our biggest assets were aircraft, overhaul stations, and technical resources. But we have only one real asset, and that is a satisfied customer prepared to come back to SAS and pay for our costs once more. That's why assets in our balance sheet should show the number of satisfied customers who flew SAS during the year and not the number of airplanes that are not worth one single cent as long as there is no secondhand market in the world for used aircraft and nobody wants to pay for a flight in those airplanes" (for more details on Carlzon at SAS, see [5]).

His philosophy has not lost its validity and has survived other short-lived management theories. In the high-tech sector, companies such as Silicon Graphics, Oracle, Télémécanique, and Canon have been giving customers the attention they deserve for a long time. These companies have built their own success on this state-of-mind marketing.

1.2   What is a high-tech product?

The term "high-technology" is a catch-all category that includes any product manufactured with some type of an advanced technology, from razor blades or athletic shoes, to sports cars, to long-range missiles. The literature on this subject contributes to the continuation of a certain confusion because it rarely gives a clear definition for high-tech products. In any case, technology is not the only characteristic and discriminating feature of these products.

Today's technology can be found everywhere; microprocessors are part of washing machines and cars, and a new enzyme called bifidus has revolutionized the world of yogurt. Yet, a product does not automatically become "high-tech" just by incorporating a certain technical dimension into its production. A definition for high-tech products must take into account not only the particular industry but the product's characteristics as well.

1.2.1 The high-tech sector

Before defining advanced or emerging technological products, we must determine the purpose for which they are used. High-tech products are closely related to the fields of biology, materials, computers, and energy (atomic or solar). These four main branches have gone through extraordinary advancements that have led to the development of numerous high-tech products and that will lead to many more such developments in the future.

Biotechnology is widely used in the manufacturing of simple chemical compounds such as lysine and glutamate or more complex compounds such as antibiotics (microbiologists have discovered more than 5,000 substances with antibiotic activities), enzymes, vitamins, or hormones. New genetic engineering techniques also allow new chemical products to enter into agricultural (agrochemicals, seeds) and pharmaceutical fields.

In the materials sector, high-performance plastics have progressively replaced more traditional materials (that were derived from metals) in the aeronautics and automotive industries. Even highly fire-resistant resins have replaced heavier, more expensive, and less effective metals.

In information processing, high-tech products are the most visible of all industries. According to the *Fortune* magazine's yearly ranking of the 500 global biggest companies, in 1996 the sales figures of the major companies in computers, telecommunications, and electronics were superior to those of the automotive industry: $1,594 billion versus $1,178 billion. In the United States, according to a survey by the American Electronic Association, the electronic sector is the first economic sector to generate $686 billion dollars, that is, more than 6% of the Gross National Product, and to employ 4.3 million salaried people; it is also the first manufacturing job provider with 1.9 million workers. These figures reflect the growing demand for more abundant, more flexible, and more adapted communication and information. At the same time, successive technological revolutions have led to constant improvements in the price-performance ratio.

Even the general public owns products as diverse as personal computers, laser disks, cable television, portable telephones, and pagers. Many companies use large computers with computer-aided design (CAD) software, artificial intelligence (AI), and relational databases (RDs). Many of these computers are connected to networks that will eventually communicate with robots, programmable tools, and sophisticated measuring instruments.

The energy sector has witnessed the development of nuclear power plants but is now familiar with recycling and nuclear reprocessing as well as the treatment of uranium. Closer to the final consumer, the first equipment using solar energy (for heating and road signals) has slowly started to appear.

Every technological breakthrough seems conceivable nowadays. In each particular field, large investments are being made: chemists and pharmaceutical companies in biotechnology, aeronautics and computer industry in materials management, and oil-producing companies in non-conventional hydrocarbons and photovoltaic materials.

1.2.2 Characteristics of high-tech products

When asked about the main characteristics of high-tech products, marketing managers are mostly concerned with four distinctive characteristics that pertain specifically to high-tech products (see Figure 1.2).

First of all, these products incorporate the latest scientific results of a sophisticated technology. Examples of these complex technologies are protein engineering, plasma techniques, multiprocessor computer architecture, and the recycling of nuclear combustibles. These technologies are still being developed but have already led to true high-tech products: interferon, super minicomputers, and a reprocessing plant in La Hague, France.

Second, these products are developed and replaced at a high rate. A typical example deals with microprocessors. "Moore's Law," named after one of Intel's founders, clarifies the development of product performance: the number of transistors per memory circuit doubles every 18 months (see Figure 1.3). In 1970, each circuit had more than 10,000 transistors; in 1990, the most advanced chips contained between three and six million transistors. The goal is to reach between 100 and 200 million transistors per chip and to execute two billion instructions per second before the end of the decade. The limit on how many transistors can be squeezed on to the surface of a silicon chip recently was raised in 1988. Engineers at Intel managed to store twice as much binary data in a single-flash memory chip, while researchers at IBM discovered a way to

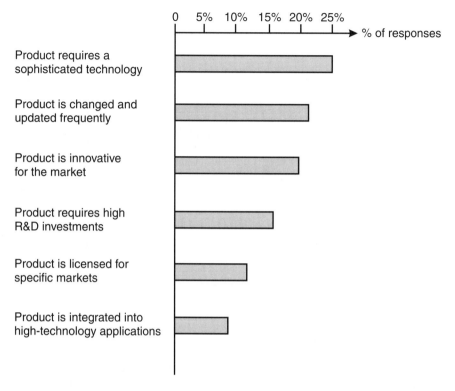

Figure 1.2 Characteristics of high-tech products according to high-tech marketing managers. Tabulation of responses to the question "How would you define a high-technology product?" (*Source:* Interviews by Eric Viardot.)

replace aluminum conductors in microchips with copper, which is faster and cheaper. In addition, another researcher has managed to create a prototype with a data storage capacity that is 300 times more powerful than the average chip using a bacterium that lives in a salty environment, the bacteriorhodopsin. In a surprising twist, biotechnology is encountering information technology.

The third characteristic of a high-tech product is its innovative quality; it should bring a (usually) radical change to a market where one new product will drive away others. Every need is satisfied by a technology that has a "life cycle," characterized by introduction, growth, maturity, and decline. The need to communicate led to primitive arts, writing, printing, typewriters, and computers (which also meet the need to

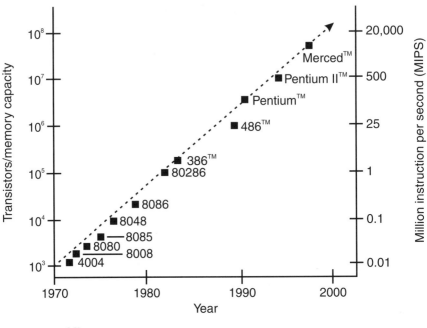

■ Microprocessor

Figure 1.3   Evolution rate of memory capacity of Intel microprocessors. (*Source:* Intel annual reports and press reports compiled by Eric Viardot.)

count). The need to know about space led to Assyrian temple-planetariums, then astronomic telescopes, and currently satellites and other space rockets.

Every technology gives rise to products that then have their own life cycles with the same phases (introduction, growth, maturity, and decline). The product life cycle is the mirror image of the changing needs that the product satisfies and reflects customer diffusion of the innovation curve. At its introduction, a product attracts people who like innovations. Then, as the product grows in popularity, a larger majority is interested in the product. Sales increase until a late majority adopt the product. Then the level of sales stabilizes, while decline is sped up by the arrival of a new technology (see Figure 1.4).

In the consumer goods area, televisions in the 1940s, calculators in the 1960s, and microwave ovens in the 1980s introduced a breakthrough

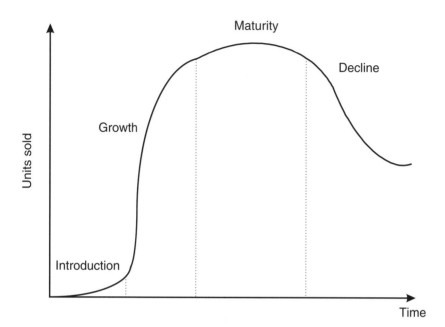

Figure 1.4 The concept of a life cycle for products and technology.

in consumption, banishing the radio, multiplication tables, and traditional ovens, which are now almost forgotten.

For industrial products, the case of electronics is characteristic: in the 1950s the input medium for information processing was first performed by vacuum tubes. These vacuum tubes were then replaced by transistors in the 1960s. Striving toward miniaturization, manufacturers of electronics introduced integrated circuits, before they were replaced by microprocessor technology in the beginning of the 1980s. In each case, an innovative technological development chased its predecessor. Today it seems that microprocessor technology has arrived at certain limits (such as the balancing speed of gate arrays or the internal clock frequency of processors) related to its input medium, silicon. However, it won't be impossible to go beyond these limits in the future with new technology like supraconducting materials at ambient temperatures (see Figure 1.5).

Similarly, in the pharmaceutical business, biotechnologies are replacing more traditional technologies to make new drugs. According to a recent study made by Lehman Brothers, in the year 2000, 5 of the

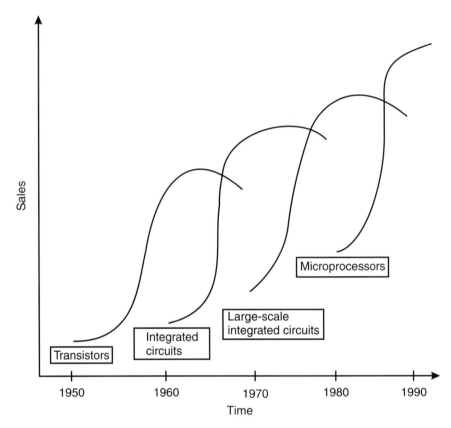

Figure 1.5   Technology succeeding technology.

17 best-selling drugs will come from biotechnology. A biotech-drug such as Epogen from Amgen, which helps to treat anemia by increasing the amount of red cells in human blood, could top today's worldwide best-seller Zantac from Glaxo-Wellcome. Zantac, a drug used to treat ulcers, will soon lose its proprietary rights and face direct competition from generics.

Major or breakthrough innovations—like electricity, transistors, or machine tools in the past and computers, networks, and robots, nowadays—are diffusing throughout the economy. They often provide the basis for the emergence of new industries that create major new markets. Once computers were introduced and accepted, it made sense to expand their power, offer new application software, and connect them.

Once they were connected, online services and electronic commerce naturally made their way into the economy and consumers' behavior.

One of the main reasons why firms bring innovation and new products to the market is out of necessity, that is, of retaining their competitiveness. One leading German electronics manufacturer drew about 70% of its revenues in the late 1970s from products that were better than those of its competitors. Five years later, that share had fallen to 35%; 10 years later, the company did not have a single superior product and was losing market share.

More generally, in a survey of 102 electronics firms worldwide made by the consulting firm McKinsey, innovation provided the majority of growth for the top third of the companies, in terms of profitability and increase in sales. From 1991 to 1993, new product introduction helped them to increase their sales by 37%, despite an 11% sales reduction for older products; while the bottom third saw a decrease of 10%.

Innovative products and processes also appear to be critical in achieving cost competitiveness; according to the McKinsey survey, they contribute for approximately two-thirds of all unit cost reduction.

All these reasons translate to the fact that the fourth characteristic of a high-tech product is the requirement of high investments in research and development. These investments finance large teams of successful and knowledgeable researchers, which is very costly! For example, the research budget of Aerospatiale, one of the major European aerospace companies and the biggest in France, is equivalent to the sales figures for the 129th company in France. According to Ernst and Young, in the biotech industry, 1,287 U.S. companies are investing $5.6 billion in research and development each year, and their 716 European competitors are spending $1.33 billion.

Nevertheless, the ratio of R&D expenses to sales figures is considered a more significant indicator for a company producing advanced technology products than the total amount spent. Opinions differ on which research investment figure to use when classifying a company as a manufacturer of advanced technology products, but the average percentage ranges from 4 to 5%. For instance, in the top 20 French companies ranked by research and development expenditures, the companies that spend more than 5% of their sales figures on R&D are all in the high-technology sector; the same percentage applies in the United States [6].

A certain number of marketing managers also indicate that when dealing with an advanced technology product, specific markets should be approached first, particularly, markets that consider performance to be the most important criterion when purchasing a product. This is valid for several industries from aeronautics to defense; they are always looking for innovations to improve performance or spur the development of new features.

This is true as well for products for the general public, such as personal computers, cellular telephones, and laser disks. The group of customers that is first and foremost interested in these products consists of people who are interested in innovation and in increased performance for calculations, communication, or sound, whatever the price.

As we will see later, however, these specific markets only represent part of the potential target market. Even though this characteristic is significant, it is not discriminating enough to distinguish high-tech products.

1.2.3   Government involvement in the high-tech sector

Since technology can become a dangerous weapon in the competition between nations, countries cannot afford not to be interested in technology. The industrial policies of MITI in Japan, the Department of Defense in the United States, the XIII Direction in the EEC, and the Ministry of Industry in France seek to influence certain technological choices and to further their national industries.

Consequently, government involvement is also another characteristic of certain high-technology products that respond to the needs of the state, either directly, through governmental research programs such as Eureka and Jessi in the EEC and SDI in the United States, or indirectly, through the manufacturing of military equipment.

Military organizations worldwide are always searching for better overall performance from technologies ranging from genetic experiments, to exploring the use of new materials in fighter jets, satellites, or tanks; and from controlling nuclear energy, to optimizing information management for attack systems (missile guiding systems, smart bombs), defense systems (optronics, antimissile missiles), and battlefield coordination (satellite spotting, battlefield communication). The superiority of high technology in modern-day warfare was exhibited during the Iraqi conflict; it underlined the importance of high-tech products in military markets, including products as common as microcomputers.

Nevertheless, the occasional government support of commercial R&D developments is not a necessary condition nor sufficient for success.

1.2.4 Product diversity in high technology

Finally, it should be noted that all high-tech products are not identical by nature. First, components should be distinguished from systems. Components are just raw materials that contribute to the building of other products. This is the case with components that are integrated in washing machines, automobile engines, and children's toys. Systems are finished products in which the technology is clearly obvious and that are sold directly to the final user. Examples include robots and AI programs.

Second, standard products should be distinguished from differentiated products, which are adapted to the customer's wants. Standard products are defined by a limited number of precise characteristics and, therefore, allow for mass production. Examples include computer memories, microcomputers, standard application software (spreadsheets, word processing), and laser disc readers.

Differentiated products allow for flexibility in order to satisfy changing demands. These demands could be for sophisticated resins that produce separation membranes for gases, fire-resistant materials, specialized robots (specifically assembled and programmed for each customer), or specific software developed for the particular needs of a customer.

This distinction between the different types of high-technology products is of importance for a company's marketing method, which will be explained in Chapter 9.

1.3 What is high-tech marketing?

Outside of its strong technical content, its quick development, and its innovative aspects, a high-tech product is first and above all a product that can satisfy a need or a want.

Some high-tech products are consumer products that are produced in large quantities. Examples include portable phones, over-the-counter medications, multimedia software, and microcomputers. Other high-tech goods are industrial products such as robots, fire-resistant fibers, ceramics, supercomputers, nuclear project engineering, and computer-related services (development and production of programs, integration of complex plans).

The "high-technology" dimension is only an extra layer on a product and is defined by its tangible or service aspect and the nature of its consumer or industrial market. The marketing of high-tech products is no more than a subset of marketing consumer goods; of industrial marketing; or of services marketing, whichever the case.

Marketing managers agree with this analysis and emphasize that their objectives are not very different from those of their colleagues who work with more traditional products (see Figure 1.6). Both types of managers seek to increase their market share with higher profits while optimizing their available resources according to the product range, the price, the promotion, and the distribution.

Even if the ingredients of the marketing recipe do not change, their composition and respective importance will have to take into account the distinctive characteristics of high-tech products. First, technology generally has a tendency to worry many customers—some are intimidated by the task of learning how to use a high-tech product, some are risk-averse to any novelty, and others are afraid that the current technology available will become obsolete quickly; all are always postponing their decision. Second, the short product life cycle requires efficient time management (development of schedules, marketing time limits). Third, product innovation requires direct cooperation with research and development and

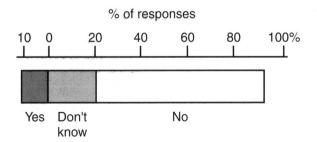

Figure 1.6 Tabulation of responses to the question "Do you believe that your objectives are different from those of a marketing manager for more standard, traditional products?" (*Source:* Interviews by Eric Viardot.)

other services. Finally, sometimes technology will drastically change the conditions of a market by creating an exceptional attraction for a product.

The traditional marketing tools should be adapted to the specific requirements imposed by high-tech products. This adaptation also applies to the marketing strategy (Chapters 2 to 5), its application (Chapters 6 to 9), and the organization of the marketing department (Chapter 10).

1.4   Chapter summary

The purpose of marketing is to act in such a way that a company puts products on the market that correspond to demand, that is, satisfy the needs and wants of its customers. This approach complements and replaces short-term approaches that favor the product, the manufacturing method, or the sales method. By relying on long-term customer satisfaction and by allowing the company to organize itself so that it can respond to this long-term satisfaction, marketing contributes to the company's success and its longevity.

Marketing managers in high-tech companies confirm that marketing plays this role and emphasize that their objectives are not different from those of their colleagues who work with less technologically sophisticated products in both mass consumption and in industrial goods and services. The differences appear mainly in the operational management of marketing and, in addition, in risk evaluation due to the specific characteristics of high-tech products.

These products are characterized by sophisticated technology and a high rate of development and improvement (i.e., a short life cycle), as well as a high innovation value for the market. For this reason, high-tech products require large research and development investments and are often intended for specific markets. These products cover four large industries: biology, materials, computers, and energy. Products should also be differentiated as simple components or complex systems and according to their degree of standardization or customization. In any case, the technological dimension is only an addition (to its value); a high-tech product is above all—depending on the case—a consumer good, an industrial product, or a service.

References

[1]   MacKenna, R., "Marketing Is Everything," Harvard Business Review, January–February 1991.

[2]   Kotler, P., *Marketing Management: Analysis, Planning, Implementation and Control*, 6th ed., Englewood Cliffs, NJ: Prentice Hall, 1988.

[3]   Bennet, P. D. (ed.), *The Dictionary of Marketing Terms*, Chicago, IL: American Marketing Organization, 1988.

[4]   Dibb, S., L. Simkin, W. M. Pride, and O. C. Ferrell, *Marketing, Concepts and Strategies*, Boston, MA: Houghton Mifflin Company, 1994.

[5]   Sasser, W. E., C. Hart, and J. L. Heskett, *The Service Management Course*, New York: The Free Press, 1991.

[6]   Davis, L., "Technology Intensity of U.S. Output and Trade," Report of the Office and Trade and Investment Analysis, International Trade Administration, U.S. Department of Commerce, Washington, DC, 1982.

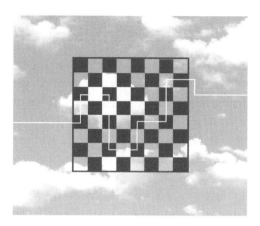

Corporate and Marketing
Strategy in the
High-Tech Industry

2

The goal of a marketing strategy is to respond to the needs and wants of customers, but this strategy is only one part of a company's corporate strategy, which aims to link its objectives and resources with the market's opportunities. The development of a marketing strategy must, therefore, lie within the framework of a company's corporate strategy.

2.1 Corporate strategy in the high-tech industry

Generally, the planning process of a company's corporate strategy consists of four phases. The first phase deals with the company's mission, which is defined by its skill (What is our business?), its market segments (Who are our customers?), and its added value (What do we do for our customers?).

This process leads the company to determine the strategic segments in which it wants to play a major role. A company usually selects strategic segments according to their significance and the competitive position that a company can attain within these strategic segments.

The third step leads the company to allocate resources among different strategic segments in order to attain a lasting competitive advantage with regard to its competitors.

The last phase consists of filling the gap between the expected results and the strategic objectives by forming a development plan of new business activities. This plan will be based on either the company's resources that it wishes to develop (internal growth) or external expertise that it is going to buy (external growth).

This general concept does not need to be changed for a high-technology company. However, the specific characteristics of high-tech products—sophisticated technology, a high rate of change, and a significant degree of innovation—lead to an adaptation of these four phases.

2.1.1   The company's mission

Successful companies know their mission in a continuously changing environment, and this knowledge gives them the necessary discipline and efficiency with which to focus their efforts on correctly serving the identified customers. High-tech companies are not exempt from the need for a defined mission.

However, high-tech companies must be careful not to define their mission in terms of the product ("we are an advanced robotics company") or the technology ("biotechnology is our specialty"). They must instead focus on the market and the customers because products and technologies will pass but the needs and wants of the customers will continue to exist. Therefore, for instance, a company's mission is not to manufacture computers, resins, or lasers but to offer the possibility of faster calculations, increased fire resistance, or a more precise cut of steel.

2.1.2   Strategic segments: definition and choices

Upon establishing a definite mission for a company, its managers will select the company's strategic segments. Strategic-planning specialist D. F. Abell defined a strategic segment according to three dimensions: customer group, functional use for the customer, and the appropriate technology (see Figure 2.1).

Thomson Sintra, a defense contractor and member of the French group Thomson, serves 40 large national navy organizations in the world (its clients) to assure an efficient antisubmarine battle (the customer's function) with the help of its ultraperfection sonars (its technology).

Sligos, a major European software firm, has also defined nine preferential strategic segments. One of them contains large European companies (customers) looking for specific products that respond to their need

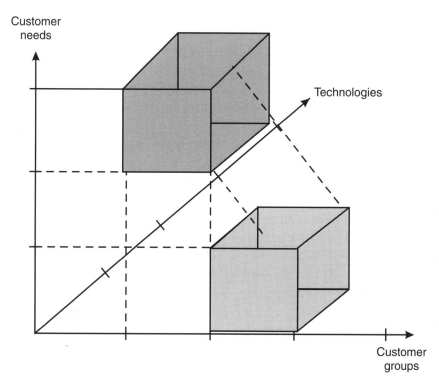

Figure 2.1   Three dimensions of a business domain.

for management information processing (function for the customer) with the use of sophisticated computer programs such as relational databases or AI systems (technology). Another strategic segment consists of small-to medium-sized companies that seek simpler, more standard, and less expensive programs for payroll or traditional bookkeeping purposes.

Once the different attainable strategic segments are identified, selecting a unit depends on the company's skills and its ability to manage the key success factors of the unit in order to attain a lasting competitive advantage when compared with competitors.

Aerospatiale, one of the aerospace giants, defines three main key success factors for its helicopter business unit: a high rate of penetration in foreign markets, a high level of innovation, and an excellent cost management due to a solid network of suppliers and competitive subcontractors.

The third dimension of the strategic segments definition, technical know-how, is extremely important in the high-tech sector. Technology can be used as a powerful tool to differentiate between competitors. Since technology continuously generates new products and applications, it can move the battlefield to less saturated and more favorable markets.

Consider the example of Novell, the leading company in Local Area Network (LAN) solutions for businesses. In 1985, LAN hardware sales represented 70% of its revenues. However, to better serve its customers' needs, Novell decided to focus exclusively on software and to divest its LAN hardware business. This decision reduced concerns of its customers that it might use its network operating system unfairly to benefit its hardware business. As a side effect, Novell's decision gave new entrants opportunities to participate in the emerging LAN business and develop solutions (hardware and software) around Novell's LAN software. Between 1986 and 1994, Novell increased its market share in LAN software from 40 to 75%, and its revenues rose from $120 million to $2 billion. More recently, however, Novell has faced increased competition in its core market from Microsoft, whose operating system Windows NT is seen as more sophisticated and easy-to-use than Netware from Novell.

All managers (but especially marketing managers) must know the extent of the available technological possibilities in a company. Only an extensive inventory of a company's technological assets can lead to an efficient operation of its market opportunities.

2.1.2.1   The technology life cycle

In marketing, the most frequently used concept today is that of the technology life cycle. It characterizes the development of technology by correlating the efficiency of its applications and the invested resources (see Figure 2.2) in a way that is similar to the evolution of organisms. Various forms branch out at the beginning; then the rate of branching declines, extinction sets in, and only a few major alternative forms persist at the end.

In the startup phase, when the company invests heavily, the earnings are slow and not very significant. In the growth phase, the accumulation of knowledge and competence leads to significant earnings (this is now the case for superconductivity research). At this stage, one may find a wide range of early experiments with radically different designs aimed at improving the technology.

As better designs are found, it becomes progressively harder to make further improvements, so variations become more modest, leading to the next phase, the maturity period. During this period, the growing returns undergo a constant improvement of performance (this is now the case for microprocessors in the computer industry or 35-mm film in light-proof canisters in the photography industry). As product characteristics are

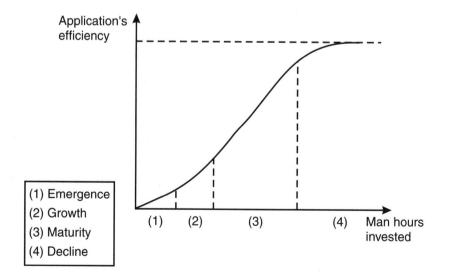

Figure 2.2   Technology life cycle.

agreed upon by producers and customers, and as the market expands, a transfer might occur from product to process innovation. As an industry becomes more stable, greater confidence is placed on the use of specialized and expensive equipment. This is the case for PCs in the 1990s, where the challenge for firms is to build faster and cheaper and to produce a larger volume of hardware boxes with a limited number of features selected by the customer. Dell Computer, Gateway, and, more recently, Compaq appear to be the champions in mastering the so-called "build-to-order" manufacturing process. The last phase, a decline or saturation, arises when the physical limits of a technology have been reached and/or when additional spending and efforts in R&D do not increase penetration or sales.

As seen in Chapter 1, the technology life cycle is similar in phasing to the product life cycle; however, it is different because a product is an output of technology at a given time. This translates to the fact that in each step of a given technology there may be various products with their own life cycles. For instance, the microprocessor technology is at the beginning of its maturity stage; but within this stage there have already been various products: in June 1994, the Intel 386 microprocessor was declining, the Intel 486 was arriving at maturity, and the Pentium was in the growth stage, while the PowerPC chip from the Apple–IBM–Motorola consortium was at the introduction level.

More than an absolute physical limit, a technology's relative limit compared to other technologies should be evaluated. In general, competing technologies are linked together along a growing spiral, which indicates that a new technical procedure requires a higher investment but with a starting performance much closer to the maximum that it replaces (see Figure 2.3).

This positioning of different technologies is not always easy to carry out. Emerging technologies are often difficult to identify, and performance levels cannot be determined easily because the products still are not well known. On the other side, the competitive pressure of a new technology tends to provoke a vigorous improvement in the old technology. Everyone knows that wooden sailing ships enjoyed a renaissance between 1860 and 1880, shortly after the invention of the iron hulls and compound steam engines that were to supersede them by the beginning of the twentieth century. Similarly, the gas lamp for interior lighting was

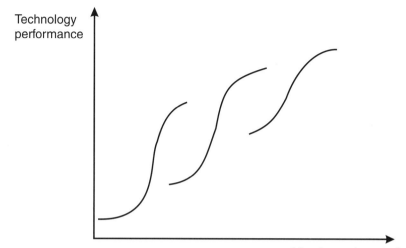

Figure 2.3   Competitive evolution of technologies.

enhanced tremendously just after the appearance of the incandescent electric light bulb.

More recently, in telecommunications, some improvements often achieved with only minor modifications have produced order-of-magnitude gains that have effectively postponed the introduction of a new generation of transmission technology. Time-division multiplexing, for instance, now allows a pair of wires to carry 24 voice channels instead of just one; consequently, this made fiber optics and cable more expensive and less attractive as a solution for local and low-volume connection.

Similarly, in the 1980s the prospects for communication satellites declined in Europe with the introduction of a new generation of fiber optics, which offered a massive and secure increase in channel capacity at a transmission rate of 500 megabytes per second (versus 50 megabytes per second at the end of the 1970s). However, it is important, for a marketer and for a company, not to believe in the invulnerability of a technology's life expectancy on the supply side.

2.1.2.2   The company's technological assets

Technological resources are a fundamental wealth for companies that produce high-tech goods. These technological resources must be managed similarly to human, marketing, or financial resources and with a long-term perspective.

Every company must protect these assets with the use of patents and licenses. A company can guarantee a product's quality and advantage by investing in research and development and by capitalizing on technological sharing.

An inventory must be made of all techniques currently used in a company's various activities as well as of the possible technological applications of which a company is aware but has not yet used for manufacturing purposes.

This inventory is not a means to an end. It allows a company to evaluate the competitive impact of various technologies by identifying the strengths and weaknesses of its competitors.

In order to make an inventory of technological assets, Arthur D. Little, a consulting firm, distinguishes the following three general categories of technologies:

- Basic technologies allow a company to launch a product or a service of which the competitive impact is weak in the current market. These basic technologies are readily available on the market and can be used by competitors.

- Key technologies offer a significant advantage over current competitors. These technologies belong exclusively to one particular company and are usually patented. This technological knowledge is a key success factor for the industry.

- Emerging technologies are still being developed and are in a beginning implementation stage; their future is unsure. Some will become key technologies, while others will never be used.

For example, computer-aided design and manufacturing (CADM) can create models and prototypes of products by using computers. This technology allows for the fast completion of thousands of calculations that play a part when an engineer modifies one element of a product. CADM also allows for a quick visualization on the screen of a terminal; this process previously took industrial designers tens to hundreds of hours.

CADM was introduced in the 1970s in the aeronautics industry for productivity reasons; for all airplane manufacturers, it is now a basic technology. In the automotive industry, CADM is a key technology because it considerably reduces the time required to produce new models of automobiles and quickens the marketing process. The majority of car manufacturers are now equipped with CADM systems. The same holds true for computer manufacturers, who are using CADM heavily for designing and manufacturing their integrated circuits and printed circuit boards.

In the textile industry, CADM is an emerging technology that is well on its way to becoming a key technology. At Benetton, CADM can immediately develop a new design into a multitude of different sizes. These designs are then sent by a telecommunication network to digital control machines that initialize automatically and wait for orders. Furthermore, Benetton's raw material is of a neutral beige color. When stores send their orders by way of the network, the clothing is cut and dyed accordingly. With this system, Benetton is able to respond to the changes in their customers' preferences with greater accuracy and speed than its competitors who are less automated [1].

Titanium-based materials are common for aeronautics; the lightness, toughness, and anticorrosiveness are qualities that are preferred by airplane manufacturers. These titanium-based materials are key for defense contractors, especially in the manufacturing of deep-sea submarines. These materials are just emerging in architecture (the first titanium roof is under construction at the Suma Aquarium in Japan), medicine (for use in prosthetics), and jewelry (like the Brietling Aerospace watch); a successful future is in store for these new applications of a technology.

To get a complete vision of the technological business activities portfolio of a firm, one can match the competitive impact of various technologies with the company's degree of expertise. This comparison allows for an evaluation of a company's technological assets. For example, in the case of the position of a major telecommunication firm versus three available key technologies, one is basic, X25, while the two others are emerging, VSAT and ATM. Figure 2.4 shows a discrepancy between the mastering by the firm of the last two technologies and their potential impact on the market if they are introduced by the competitors.

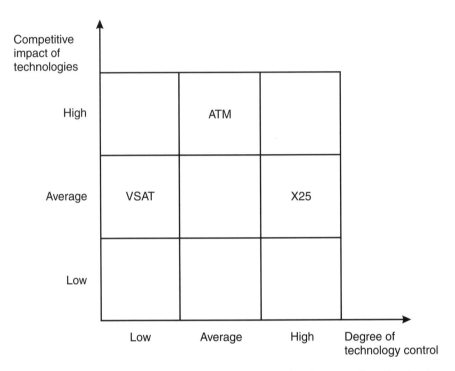

Figure 2.4 Technology portfolio. The competitive impact of technologies can be evaluated by a cost-efficiency ratio, a value-addition ratio, or by a more qualitative index of differentiation potential.

2.1.2.3 Why are companies usually unable to anticipate the market impact of technologies?

It seems that very frequently people are unable to anticipate the future business impact of auspicious innovations, even after their technical feasibility has been confirmed.

The inventor of the radio, Marconi, believed it would mainly be used by steamship companies, newspapers, and navies needing to transmit private messages over long distances where communication by wire was impossible. None thought originally to communicate to a large audience of listeners rather than to a single point. The first public broadcast conceived was the transmission of Sunday sermons—the sole event where one individual would address a mass public [2].

Similarly, at the end of the 1940s, the computer was considered useful only for carrying out rapid calculation in limited scientific and data-processing contexts. The dominant judgment, shared even by Thomas Watson Sr., then the president of IBM, was that world demand could be met by a very limited number of computers.

At the same time in 1947, when the transistor was invented, it was first proposed that this new device might be used to develop better hearing aids for the deaf. None envisaged the future connection with computers.

Likewise for the laser, another major innovation of the twentieth century, whose range of uses has expanded in so many directions since its invention. Lasers are used for precision cutting in the textile, metallurgy, and composite materials industries as well as in various surgical procedures. They produce high-quality sound in compact disc players and high-quality text and drawings through laser printers.

Furthermore, combined with fiber optics the laser has revolutionized telecommunications. In the 1960s, the best transatlantic phone cable could carry only 140 conversations concurrently. In 1988, the first fiber-optic cable could convey 40,000 conversations concurrently. The most recent cable can carry nearly 1.5 million conversations [3]. In 1997, CNET, the research and development laboratory of France Telecom, the French telecommunication carrier, failed to saturate the transmission capacity of the last generation of fiber-optic cable, meaning that the transmission capacity is almost limitless.

Despite this achievement, the patent lawyers at Bell did not apply for a patent to the laser, believing it could not attract interest in the telephone industry.

All of these examples, among many others, of failure to foresee the future business impact of technological innovations tell of our inability to beat the uncertainties associated with new technology. This failure can be explained by four factors.

First, very often new technologies come into the world in a rudimentary condition, and it is not always easy to predict the trajectory of future progress in performance, size, price, and economic consequence. The first electronic digital computer, the ENIAC, was unreliable and consisted of more than 18,000 vacuum tubes that filled a huge room. It was difficult to imagine in the 1940s that one day a computer more powerful than the ENIAC would be the size of a laptop (or even smaller). Similarly, when the transistor was invented, few people would have believed that one day the integrated circuit, a component in itself, would eventually become a computer with the creation of the microprocessor in 1970.

Second, identifying uses for new technologies is difficult and takes time, especially when they emerge from pure scientific research. Faraday discovered the principles of electromagnetic induction in 1831, but it took many decades to find applications for electricity.

In medical diagnostics, it also takes a long time to translate a new visualization technology into a clinically functional capacity. This was the case of computerized axial tomography (CAT) scanners and magnetic resonance imaging (MRI) before they became standard tools for anatomical observation. The new positron emission tomography (PET), however, is still at an early stage of development. PET scanners provide quantitative analysis of certain physiological functions (like the efficacy of drug therapy in the treatment of brain tumors), but their applications in neurology, cardiology, and oncology have been restrained by the pitfall of translating measurements of physiological functions into meaningful clinical interpretations.

One must note that medical innovations are especially arduous because of the complexity and the heterogeneity of human bodies, which make the identification of a causal relationship very difficult.

The third reason why it is difficult to beat the uncertainties associated with new technology is that, frequently, the impact of an innovation relies on complementary inventions, which contribute to a full system solution that will add to its performance and, consequently, its demand.

For instance, Edison's system of incandescent lighting required the simultaneous development of lamps, generators, sockets, and wiring.

Similarly, the telephone has existed for more than a hundred years, but only recently has its performance been improved by facsimile transmission, voice mail, conference calls, data transfer, and online services, for example.

In the telecommunications industry, the laser was useless on its own. Associated with fiber optics, however, lasers are revolutionizing telephone transmissions.

Though optical fiber was available in a primitive form in the 1960s when the first lasers were developed, it took many years to discover that fiber-optic technology allow a tremendous augmentation in bandwidth because the light spectrum is a thousand times wider than the radio spectrum. In addition, fiber-optic technology provides a better quality of transmission because of its lack of electromagnetic interference.

The recent explosion of demand for PCs has been fueled by network system add-ons like modems, LANs, and connections to the Internet as well as by the integration of various application software in one package, like Office by Microsoft or Smartsuite by IBM.

The development time for these complementary innovations can fluctuate very significantly. For example, after the dynamo was invented in the early 1880s, electrolytic techniques were created contiguously, giving birth to a prosperous electrochemical industry; but it took more than half a century to see the arrival of the electric motor.

Similarly, the transistor and, later, the integrated circuit were introduced into computers years behind their invention to transform the computer industry. Ultimately, the integrated circuit itself became a computer with the advent of the microprocessor in 1970.

One must note that the development of such interconnected innovations integrated into a system solution creates barriers to aspiring competitors because of the complexity of the offer to build. As we will see later, the existence of complementary inventions intensifies the need for technological standards and alliances.

The fourth reason that makes predicting the uses of a new technology difficult is that many inventions proceed to solve a specific problem but often turn out to have unexpected uses in unexpected conditions.

Consider the role of the computer in the car industry. Computers are used:

■ For the aerodynamic research and design of cars and components;

■ For manufacturing through robots and automatic assembly lines;

■ For the activity in the car (such as the braking system, fuel consumption monitoring, and maybe someday the automatic pilot);

■ For determining optimal driving paths;

■ For ticketing and controlling access to highways;

■ For monitoring traffic lights (and minimizing traffic jams) in major cities.

2.1.2.4 Technology and competence

One must note that major innovations come very often from outsiders. Edison had no experience in the lighting industry, just as Gemplus had little relevant experience when it created the first "smart card," namely, a plastic card with an engraved microprocessor intended for use for telecommunication or electronic payment.

The main explanation for the unwillingness of existing firms to adopt new technology as it appears comes from the fact that innovations require new competencies, which compete and may destroy existing competencies. Sometimes, however, they may enhance existing competencies.

Usually, competency-enhancing innovations come from established firms and outsiders alike. General Electric moved from manufacturing incandescent lights to making vacuum tubes for radio and televisions but had difficulty switching from tubes to transistors. Kodak successfully made the transition from photographic movie film to videotape. Microsoft advanced from a proprietary technology to an Internet-based offering of solutions. In each case, the innovations were competency enhancing and backed by top management. On the contrary, competency-destroying innovations always come from outsiders.

Building new competencies and recruiting new talents in anticipation of future developments is a key element of long-term business success. Eastman, the founder of Kodak, was one of the successful innovators who understood this necessity. When color film began to appear in European laboratories, Kodak had no know-how, but Eastman recognized the importance of building the know-how and did so. Today, however, electronic digital technology, developed and introduced by Japanese firms like Sony, lead the industry and Kodak has been trying to catch up.

Similarly, the founder of Digital Equipment (DEC), Ken Olsen, foresaw the importance of the local networking computer and developed the resources to make Digital one of the major vendors of telecommunication hardware in the 1980s. Unfortunately, he later failed to understand the growing acceptance of the PC by the market in place of the minicomputers DEC was selling; Olsen delayed the development of new competence in this field and was ultimately ousted because DEC was no longer in tune with the markets.

2.1.3 Identifying competencies: the value chain analysis

Value chain analysis helps to describe the various separate activities within a firm and to assess their performance when combined into a system in producing value for money solutions.

According to the now-traditional model introduced by M. Porter [4], there are five categories of primary activities.

- Inbound logistics receive, store, and distribute the inputs.

- Operations transform inputs into the final product or service through manufacturing, assembly, and packaging.

- Outbound logistics store and physically distribute the solution to the customer.

- Marketing and sales make customers aware of the solution and provide them with the way to buy it.

- Services maintain or increase the value of the solution through installation, maintenance, or training.

Each of those essential activities are linked to support activities of four different kinds.

- Procurement, whose mission is to acquire all the primary resources according to processes like purchasing;

- Technology development, which may concern either product development or process development;

- Human resources management, to recruit, manage, and develop firm personnel;

- Infrastructure, which sustains the organization and the firm culture, including departments like accounting and finance, legal, quality control, or information management system.

This model helps top managers pinpoint key firms activities and their interrelations with others to yield maximum value for customers in comparison with competitors. It allows them to identify the core competencies required to perform in a given business.

For instance, let us consider the value chain model for two major European telecommunication carriers in the beginning of the 1990s: France Telecom and British Telecom (see Figure 2.5). As a public monopoly, France Telecom was significantly concerned with the technical value of the solutions offered to its customers. Consequently, its main competencies were technology development and operations (production). On the one hand, France Telecom had one of the best R&D centers in the world, the CNET; moreover, France had the highest share of digitized telecommunication exchanges of any major country because of the optical fiber digital network installed by France Telecom.

On the other hand, France Telecom was very weak in marketing and services, the two core competencies of British Telecom. Facing competition on its home market after the deregulation in 1984, British Telecom adopted the new motto "putting the customer first" and structured its organization around customer-centered divisions years before France Telecom or Deutch Telekom. Similarly, British Telecom put in place a direct marketing relationship program toward small business customers (called "Telephone Account Management") in 1986, while France Telecom launched a similar program 10 years later. British Telecom, however, had to catch up with technology and modernize its network.

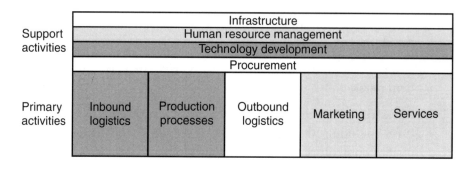

Figure 2.5   The value chain of British Telecom and France Telecom in the early 1990s.

The value chain analysis is also a useful tool for top management when it has to decide if it must make or buy a given competence. In some high-tech industrial markets with high growth but short product life cycle it is very often the lack of resources, rather than profitable opportunities, that is the bottleneck for growth.

Some aggressive companies consequently use external resources rather than develop everything internally in order to minimize fixed investment. For instance, when Cirrus Logic, a peripheral chip manufacturer company, decided to enter the data fax modem chip market, it bought Crystal Semiconductor to quickly get the necessary integrated design. Then it bought Pixel Semiconductor in order to gain an immediate entrance into the full motion video multimedia market.

On the other side, to ensure the maximum value a company may decide to internally build a core competence and then defend from competitors. This was the case with Intel. Facing competitors like Motorola and IBM, it decided not to license its technology for the Pentium microprocessor. This sole provider strategy, coupled with its leadership in design technology, has kept its competitors at bay while generating huge margins.

2.1.3.1 The virtual value chain

We are now increasingly living in a world of information, sometimes called the *marketspace,* where products and services exist as digital information and can be delivered through information-based channels like phone lines, cables, TV, or Internet. This is the world of electronic commerce where the raw material is information that can be turned into new services.

However, the value chain model treats information as a supporting element in the value adding process, not as a source of value in itself for the customer. To create value with information, top managers need to build a virtual value chain model that mirrors the physical value chain.

First, firms must view physical operations more effectively through large-scale information systems, which coordinate activities in the physical value chains. The second step is to substitute virtual activities for physical ones, thus creating a parallel value chain in the marketspace.

For instance, when Rockwell developed its new K56 modem, it moved one key element of the value chain—product development—into the marketspace. Rather than create national product teams, Rockwell established a virtual team to develop the modem, located in three different locations, communicating and working together through a highly powerful and sophisticated CAD/CAM global network.

In the virtual world, the design team can transcend the limitations of time and space that characterize management in the physical world. They build and test prototypes, share design and data with colleagues around the world over a computer network 24 hours a day, and receive customer feedback from the other side of the world.

Developing prototypes for airplanes, cars, satellites, or molecules on computer rather than with physical prototypes is another way to add virtual value.

To get the maximum yield, information must be processed systematically. It has to be gathered, organized, and selected according to its value and then synthesized and distributed to users or potential customers. For example, digitally captured product designs can be converted or adapted as multimedia software for PC or video game stations.

It is important to understand that information-based solutions obey different rules than physical solutions. Most notably, they allow radical economies of scale because, unlike physical assets, information is not depleted by their consumption; it can be duplicated at almost nil variable cost and thus has been offered through an almost infinite number of transactions.

Furthermore, the transaction costs keep decreasing steeply as the processing capacity per unit of microprocessors doubles every two years. Today, it costs less than one cent to keep information about a single customer as compared to about $1 per customer in the mid-1960s.

Consequently, creating value with digital assets allowed small companies to hit a low unit cost for products and services in markets dominated by major firms. In information-based businesses, intellectual properties and copyrights are much more important than the sheer size and capacity of mass production.

Finally, a firm is usually part of a bigger value system, where various suppliers and distributors are also involved in making and delivering a solution to the final customer. Value chain analysis positions the firm within the total value process according to its current competencies as well as its influence on the other components of the industry value chain.

For instance, in the multimedia markets, contents are more important than containers as key resources. Firms that control exclusive rights over movies, sports, text, fundamental information, or uncommon talent have a strong competitive advantage in the multimedia value chain. Accordingly, they are in the best position to get the maximum value from other firms. The importance of content explains why some multimedia containers or carrier firms are buying content producers, like Viacom's acquisition of Paramount or Time Warner's purchase of Turner Corporation.

2.1.4 Allocation of resources

After determining its mission and analyzing the strategic business, a company must define the best possible use for its resources, in cash and competencies, in order to develop those businesses.

2.1.4.1 Portfolio analysis

When dealing with the optimum allocation of resources, traditional strategic analysis models (such as those by the Boston Consulting Group and McKinsey) take into account first the degree of attractiveness of each business for the firm, and second the current company's competitive position on each strategic segment, because the main issue of strategy is to beat the competitors. Without actual adversaries, there is no need for such a strategy as long as a demand exists.

In the high-tech field, these choices of allocation of resources must be made not only according to those two strategic criteria but also in consideration of the technological criteria. The high degree of innovation that characterizes the high-tech sector enables certain companies to completely change a market and to quickly upset long-term competitors. Therefore, an evaluation of a company's range of business activities must take into account this characteristic. Unfortunately, in the traditional strategic analysis models, the technological factors are lost in the middle of many other criteria when determining a company's competitive position.

For every strategic analysis, a high-tech company's technological advantage should be estimated and included. A technological advantage is a company's level of expertise regarding key technologies that could have major competitive impacts.

Accordingly, the different business activities of a high-tech company can be evaluated according to three criteria.

- Value of the business, or the growth capacity, which is indicated by the growth rate of the market or the life cycle of the business;

- Market coverage of the company, which is measured by its relative market share, penetration rate, or awareness;

- Technological position, which is measured by the degree of expertise in key technologies, according to Arthur D. Little's research. This technological position corresponds to the importance of a company's technology from a competitive standpoint.

The resulting model contains eight categories of business (see Figure 2.6) whose situation can help management determine the optimal allocation of necessary resources. The first four are businesses with a strong technological position, while the last four have a weak technological position.

1. A star business activity must be nurtured; the company must strengthen its place on the market, continue its technological lead, and promote the business's development by investing.

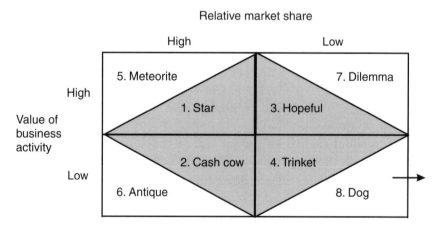

Figure 2.6 Business portfolio of a high-tech company. The shaded area represents a strong technological position; the nonshaded area represents a weak position.

2. A cash cow business activity must free up a maximum amount of cash in order to pursue hopefuls and to expand the stars by limiting investments and by planning to transfer technological capacity toward areas with high potential.

3. A hopeful represents a limited risk because it is based on a solid technological base. A company must aim to develop its market by using its own resources or by associating with another company that has a good marketing coverage. If investing is not preferred, selling the technology can free up cash.

4. A trinket is a business activity in which the company has no significant competitive position and that no longer has significant business value. The company must take maximum advantage of its acquired technological capabilities either by using these trinkets in other markets with a better potential or by selling them to other companies.

5. A meteorite takes up a strong position in a potential market; it requires the immediate acquisition (generally outside of the company since time is an essential factor) of necessary technological skills in order to capitalize on the advantage that the company enjoys on the market.

6. An antique is similar to a cash cow; both generate a maximum of cash. An increasing investment in technology is only justified if the product is profitable in the short run.

7. A dilemma must either become the object of important investments (to improve the company's technological expertise and its market force) or be abandoned.

8. A dog is a business similar to a trinket, but one that has no technological advantage. Accordingly, it can be sold or terminated, unless it does provide some external leverage to the other businesses, for instance, by sharing some costs or competencies.

For example, Figure 2.7 shows the range of business activities of Roussel Uclaf according to these criteria.

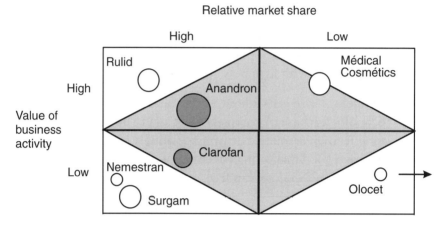

Figure 2.7 Range of business activities of Roussel-Uclaf. (*Source*: Roussel-Uclaf, DAFSA 90.)

Such a model is useful in evaluating the value of a portfolio of various businesses at a given time. However, it does not explain why and how, in an emerging high-technology industry, some companies like Microsoft, Intel, Netscape, Cisco, L'Air Liquide, or America Online have created new markets with few, if any rivals, and are able to keep their competitive advantage for a long time. Such an understanding can be found in the economics of increasing returns.

2.1.4.2   The law of increasing returns

Traditional theory states that industries are inclined to diminishing returns as a result of competition between firms for scarce resources. However, according to the law of increasing returns, returns from marginal investments go up rather than down. As some firms continue investing, their profitability grows, and eventually one or two firms end up dominating the market because the other firms are unable to match their level of investment.

Archetypal examples of increasing returns are utilities, which are consequently regulated as de facto monopolies. Still, the law of increasing returns plays a large role in the high-technology and knowledge-based industries of today for various reasons.

First, increasing returns occur because, as many knowledge-based products such as software, information, or drugs have a marginal cost of production that is almost nil, any additional market share has a tremendous impact on profit. For example, the first product by Netscape was a browser based on the Mosaic Technology developed by one of the company's founders at the University of Illinois, and it exploited the vast (free) resources available on the Internet. This allowed Netscape in designing its controversial strategy to enter the market quickly by giving the browser away, which soon won it a market share of 75%.

Second, in our global economy, increasing returns follow the firms that penetrate one large geographical market after another. In the software industry, the swift growth of Computer Associates relied on the increasing acceptance of its Unicenter control software as the governing standard for managing business software applications programs in various part of the western world.

Third, increasing returns happen when competitors are unable to match each other's investments, like in the microprocessor industry or in the software industry. In the first case, Intel recently bought the semiconductor business of Digital because of Digital's inability to get more than 1% of the market despite significant investment. In the second case, one thinks immediately of Microsoft, whose investment capacity is dwarfing its competitors in the operating and application software for PCs. Less widely known is the case of Oracle, which stands alone in the database business for exactly the same reason.

Finally, increasing returns turn up because in the high-tech sector firms tend to work together to ensure the success of a joint product or service by forming a business net. The addition of more firms to a group creates an incentive for other firms to join, thus providing the necessary momentum and critical installed base to make a technology successful enough to become a de facto standard and wipe out other competitors' technology. Wintel (the alliance of Intel and Microsoft), SAP, Lotus, and more recently IBM have made and forged an entire industry around their solutions, namely Windows, R/3, and Notes, with application developers, system integrators, trainers, and hardware companies working together to provide solutions to end users. Similarly, the regrouping of various aircraft companies like Aérospatiale, British Aerospace, MBB, and Casa within the Airbus consortium has provided the critical size and the credibility to convince airline companies to buy Airbus aircrafts. Success leads to success, and Airbus has managed to develop its customer installed-base constantly. In 1997, for the first time in its 30 year history, Airbus received as many orders as its arch rival Boeing—425 new planes.

2.1.4.3 Strategies for establishing a technological standard

The value to a customer of many high-tech solutions is a function of the availability of complementary solutions, like software applications for a PC, or the coverage of the telephone network for a cellular handset. In order for all those complementary solutions to work well together, compatibility is essential.

In the personal computer industry, compatibility is required to ensure that computers, software, modems, printers, and other peripherals interface easily. In the cellular telecommunications market, compatibility demands a common set of technological standards for the design of cellular base stations, digital switches, and handsets to ensure maximum geographical coverage for users. The larger the coverage, the greater the value for customers and the bigger the future demand, leading more customers to invest in the expansion of the network.

This explains why some telecommunication carriers like AT&T Wireless in the United States, Orange in the United Kingdom, or Cegetel in France have devoted so much money to building a seamless nationwide wireless network based on a common technological standard, time division multiple access (TDMA) in the United States for AT&T Wireless, and GSM (Global System for Mobile Communications) in the United Kingdom and France.

Similarly, in the telecommunication hardware industry, the Swedish company Ericsson is championing the use of TDMA technology as the standard for cellular telephone systems while Qualcom is championing an alternative standard known as code division multiple access.

As shown in Figure 2.8, mastering a technical standard generates increasing returns on investments. Accordingly, it is a key success factor in many high-tech industries where the winner usually takes all.

On the Internet, standards have recently emerged around basic foundation technologies (but not yet, for sound, graphic, video, and animation software) as connectivity protocols like TCP/IP offer more flexibility at far lower cost than equivalent nonstandard technologies. One must note that TCP/IP won over Open System Integration (OSI), which likewise is a technical standard but too costly to introduce widely.

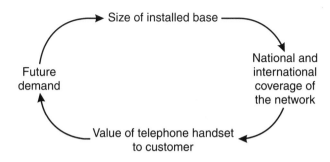

Figure 2.8 Increasing returns in the cellular phone industry.

Key players in the online service business like Prodigy and AOL are migrating to those foundation technologies, while late entrants such as Microsoft and AT&T adopted those standards after initially pursuing a nonstandard strategy.

Experience shows that in markets where two or more incompatible increasing-return technologies compete, any modification, even a small one, in the original situation may help one technology secure a lead big enough to eventually lock in the market and become the de facto industry standard. Consequently, competing technologies are locked out even if the dominant technology is clearly inferior.

A classic example of a market locking out an inferior technology is the QWERTY format for typewriter (and now computer) keyboards. The QWERTY format was originally developed in the 1860s to slow down typing speed by separating keys whose letters frequently appeared next to each other in words. This design helped to diminish the inclination of type bars to collide and jam when keys were struck rapidly, which was a persistent problem on the first generation of typewriters.

The technical problem of type-bar jamming was fixed in the 1890s, and new keyboard formats were developed for faster typing. However, they were a flop on the market because the first touch typists had been trained on QWERTY keyboards and did not want to change even for better keyboards. By the 1910s, the QWERTY keyboard was locked in as the standard and still is at the end of this century!

A long catalogue could be filled with the list of firms that developed a superior technology but failed to establish it as a standard. In the lone field of PCs, one may think of Apple, IBM, and Next, which have lost a battle against the so-called Wintel alliance. However, such a contest for establishing new standards is still going on around the Internet-based market, with dogfights between Netscape and Microsoft over different types of browsers, or Microsoft and Sun Microsystem competing on programming languages, or even between Wintel and Oracle-Sun-IBM competing for the next generation of PCs. To win this fight, the ownership of a key platform technology is necessary. In the beginning of the 1980s, IBM decided to create an attractive standard for the desktop computer by offering an open architecture. IBM relied on Microsoft and Intel to provide the core technology and mobilized various firms behind it, but failed to hold ownership of this platform technology and lost its ability to control the evolution of standard to Microsoft and Intel.

Keeping a proprietary technology exclusive is a must but is extremely difficult. Some firms have managed to build powerful patent and/or copyright walls around their original technology coupled with aggressive legal enforcement to prevent copy by potential competitors such as Xerox did with its proprietary dry-toner xerographic technology or Intel with its X86 and Pentium microprocessor series.

However, in many industries patents can be quickly turned away and invented around thanks to the use of reverse engineering techniques. As a rule, patents ordinarily delay but do not stop competition. They may even push efficient competitors to invent in-house technology that may be better, like in the photocopier business where Xerox's competitors developed their own liquid-toner xerographic technology.

The second condition of success is a marketing one. It lies in the willingness to open the business to expand opportunities for other participants. For instance, when Novell made the decision to divest its LAN hardware business and to focus exclusively on software, it opened opportunities for other companies to launch products and lessened worries that it might use its network operating system unfairly to benefit its hardware business. As a consequence, the LAN business exploded and Novell increased its revenues from $120 million in 1986 to $2 billion in 1994. Novell's revenues declined, however, to $1 billion in 1997, after Microsoft entered the competitive arena with Windows NT.

Similarly, by choosing to license its operating system to a large number of vendors, Microsoft has grown the personal computer business to a size of more than $66 billion (although it captures only 4% of the total, it has expanded its revenues from $3.75 billion in 1993 to $11.4 billion in 1997). In the same time, Apple, which refused to license its operating system to a large extent, has seen its market share decline dramatically.

In the jet-engine business, CFM International, the joint venture between General Electric and Snecma, managed to make its CFM-56 engine a success story by enlarging its market constantly. The first sales were small and difficult: the first customers were the United States and French armies in the late-1970s. CFM worked hard to improve its technology and, in 1981, Boeing made the decision to equip all of its B737 airplanes with CFM engines exclusively. Next, CFM developed a new version of the engine to be installed on the Airbus A320 and A321, and then the A340, constantly improving the ratio cost/quality through an aggressive management of the experience curve. As a consequence, the growing number of customers provided a de facto monopoly position for the CFM engine in the medium-sized aircraft range. By the early 1990s, CFM received more than 6,000 orders from 160 different airline companies.

Likewise, in the aerospace business, Arianespace, the European rocket launcher company, built its success partly on the reliability and regularity of its satellite launching and partly because its rockets, Ariane 3 and then Ariane 4, were exactly in line with the needs of its customers, namely, to carry medium-sized satellite. Over the last 10 years, Arianespace has managed to achieve a leading 60% market share in the satellite-launching business.

The lesson is clear: in high-tech industries where increasing returns exist and standards are important, the guideline for success is to maximize the installed base of users by offering them solutions to fit their needs. To achieve such a goal, market-oriented firms are definitely better positioned than technology-oriented firms.

The expected profits of existing business activities can prove to be insufficient for the realization of a company's growth objectives as set by management. However, one must note that firms with little practice in developing new business in high tech often have unrealistic expectations, especially big firms in grown industries holding business units with yearly revenues of $500 million or more, like some major computer vendors or certain big pharmaceutical companies. Top managers of those firms might expect a new business to grow within three years to $100 million in revenues and within six years to at least $600 million in revenues at margins greater than 12%.

But even the fastest growing high-technology firms would be unable to meet such ambitious expectations. Six years after its founding, Genentech had annual revenues of $26 million, Silicon Graphics's revenues were $87 million, and even Microsoft was making only $350 million!

Actually, as for any new high-technology business, the value creation of those firms and the stock market's perception of this value is as important to consider as revenues and earning goals. For instance, the market value of Genentech in 1990 was set at more than $4.2 billion. When Roche bought 49% of the equity stake in Genentech, it had to invest $2.1 billion. Similarly in 1997, Amgen, the leading biotechnology firm, had a market value of more than $16 billion, representing 8 times its turnover of $1.94 billion and 30 times its net income of $538 million.

However, this gap between expectations and reality calls for the implementation of a development plan.

2.1.4.4   The importance of cost control and productivity

In many high-tech industries of today, like in the electronics industry for instance (see Table 2.1), product costs—measured by the cost of goods sold (COGS)—are critical to profitability because of their weight in the

Table 2.1
Cost Structure of a High-Productivity Electronics Company as a Percentage of Revenues. (*Source:* McKinsey, companies' reports compiled by Eric Viardot.)

Industry/ Cost Structure	Computers/ Communication	PCs	Consumer/ Small Products
Profit before taxes	12	3	4
Other expenses	0	2	2
Operation expenses	30	23	18
Cost of goods sold	58	72	76

total revenues. Most of the differences in profitability between the more and the less successful companies come from COGS rather than operating expenses. A 5% savings on the COGS may have a positive impact of between 50 and 600% on the profitability before tax.

Furthermore, it is estimated that about 60% of manufacturing costs are dictated by product design. However, when making decisions about the allocation of resources, the managers of high-tech firms cannot trade quality for cost. They must consider both simultaneously in the product design as well as in the manufacturing process.

Let us consider the success of Kodak in the photography industry. One may wonder how a small provincial American firm became the global market leader instead of the mighty German firms that were mastering the sciences and technologies of optics, fine chemicals, and camera design. A likely explanation lies in the fact that German products frequently were very expensive and hence manufactured in small quantities, while Eastman, the founder and president of Kodak, targeted his resources on an international mass market, with a large-volume production at low cost. So, for example, he did not hesitate to substitute his original camera with what would be his famous No. 1 model because the former's shutter system was too onerous to produce.

In a striking replay of history, in 1997 Kodak had to initiate a massive cost-cutting reorganization to boost productivity because the huge investment in the new digital technology launched by its new CEO, G. Fisher, previously at Motorola, was not enough to restore a flinching profitability.

Another example comes from the PC industry where, in 1991, Hewlett-Packard (HP) ranked seventeenth in worldwide market share. Two years later, it had risen to eleventh place with annual sales climbing from 70,000 units to over 600,000 while augmenting profitability. Today HP is standing as the fifth PC vendor on the worldwide market. HP got there by:

- Cutting its staff by 40%;

- Reducing its plants from 12 to 2;

- Decreasing price premium by 30%;

- Narrowing its product range;

- Reducing new product development time from 18 months to 6;

- Maintaining its quality and, hence, its tremendous image as a high-quality vendor.

2.1.5   Development plans for new business activities

In order to develop new business activities, every company must find new markets, develop new products, or diversify based upon internal resources or on external competencies. The latter can be acquired in a variety of ways as listed in Figure 2.9, according to the complexity of the operation and its value addition to the competence of the firm.

The uniqueness of high-tech companies influences the development possibilities of new technologies. The possible choices are as follows:

Relabeling is the purchase of finished products or components that are then sold under the company's brand name. This is how Grundig buys its consumer camcorders from Sony and Panasonic. The main component of compact photo cameras comes from one factory—Samsung in Korea; IBM buys monitors for its PS2 microcomputers from Samp and Goldstar; and "bubble jet" Apple printers are actually the Canon BJ-10E model.

Licensing allows for the use of technologies developed by another company. New business can be created through the selling of licenses like Matsushita did with the VCR when it licensed its VHS technology to other consumer electronic enterprises including Hitachi, Sharp, Mitsubishi, and Philips NV, and formed an original equipment manufacturer (OEM) agreement with GE, RCA, and Zenith. In doing so, Matsushita

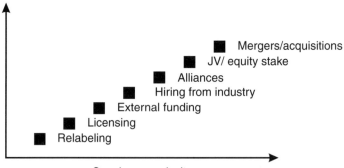

Figure 2.9   External source of market development.

put together a big network of firms eager to push the same technological solution to the end-user, while Matsushita continued to compete against these companies in the final market place under the JVC brand name. Consequently, it managed to win over its main competitor, Sony, whose product was based on a different technology called Betamax.

A successful licensing strategy helps increase returns by decreasing customer perplexity, leading to bigger market acceptance for a given technology. So, when Philips NV settled on licensing the VHS videocassette recorder format from Matsushita rather than continuing to pursue its own V2000 technology, it decreased the number of technologically incompatible VCR formats from three to two. Further, this move contributed significantly to the growing approval of the VHS format by the market as well as the manufactures of complementary products.

However, licensing a technology may be risky if later on, one licensee manages to modify the technology in such a way that it can replace the licenser's technology and stop paying royalties to the licenser. Intel had such an argument with AMD for the K5 microprocessor, AMD's clone of Intel's Pentium microprocessor. Intel affirmed that K5 was derived from its own technology, originally licensed to AMD for the production of the 80286 microprocessor, but AMD answered that K5 utilized a microcode developed in-house and was consequently not related to any former contract.

Naturally, a licenser can draft a contract that requires the licensee to pay royalties despite any posterior changes they might make in the core technology. In practice, however, it is impossible to extensively define all the technological conditions that legally protects a licenser. A well-drafted contract may decrease the risk, but it cannot eliminate it. Recently, Sun Microsystems was in dispute with Microsoft about Java, a new programming language for Internet-based applications. In order to make Java a new technological standard, Sun has been extensively licensing its new program to various developing companies under the condition that it be made open to any computer architecture. However, Microsoft had bought the license to include Java in its own proprietary Windows NT environment, thus making Java a non-open-standard program.

When a company enjoys a technological monopoly, licensing agreements may generate less profit than doing business on one's own because it increases the number of suppliers in the final market. Consequently, prices may drop below the rate that would exist in a monopoly situation, since royalty rates are usually a fixed percentage of sales revenues. This may explain why Intel gradually stopped the licensing of its microprocessor technology: Intel licensed 12 firms to produce its 8086 microprocessor, 4 to produce its 80286 microprocessor, one (IBM) to produce its 80386 microprocessor, and none to produce its 80486 and Pentium microprocessors.

Purchase of licenses allows for the use of technologies that were developed by other companies. When Sagem noticed a decline in the market for telex machines (its sales figures decreased from $1 billion to $300 million in less than five years), it ventured into the facsimile machine market by acquiring a license from Murata, a Japanese company.

External research contracts exist when technical development is contracted out to a research laboratory, research consultants, or a university. In the United States, 49% of all companies finance research in universities where (on the average) four times as many patents are generated as in industrial research. In France, the Technological University of Compiègne participates in 20 research contracts with industrial partners, 14 of which are French.

Hiring from the industry was one solution Hughes Electronics' DirecTV used to enter the "direct-to-home" broadcast market, an emerging market very different from its traditional business of communication satellites. To be successful, Hughes Electronics had to buy programming content, manufacture and distribute home satellites dishes, manage the customer billing, and set up and run a customer service network.

However, DirecTV also made an early *alliance* with firms such as Thomson for manufacturing and distribution, DEC for billing systems, and Matrixx Marketing for customer service. Each partner had to invest significantly in its part of the business, but the returns relied on the success of the whole project.

Alliances (instead of cooperation agreements) are two or more parties agreeing to change how they do business by integrating and jointly controlling some part of their common business system while sharing together the profit.

As in many traditional businesses, alliances are conceived as a means for major manufacturers to reduce supplier costs. For example, before

McDonnell Douglas was bought by Boeing, its alliance with Rolls Royce and BMW for engines and with Halla Engineering and Heavy Industries of Korea for wings aimed at producing and selling its new MD95 for a third less than a comparable Boeing and Airbus model.

Today, the lessons learned from allying with suppliers are being applied to alliances with peer companies, channels, and customers to gain market share at a lesser cost. For instance, Allen Bradley, the world leader in automation control solutions, has more than 80 alliances, not only with suppliers, such as Motorola for microprocessors, but also with peer companies and primary distributors. In the telecommunications industry, the primary motivation behind the alliance of Sprint, Deutsch Telekom, and France Telecom is clearly to gain access to each other's markets.

An alliance is more and more frequently also seen as a way to achieve increasing returns by constructing a technology-oriented alliance around a technological standard. This approach works even for small firms like Netscape, a startup company commercializing various technological tools designed to implement commerce on the Internet. In less than two years, Netscape has quickly mobilized other companies to support and implement its technology, including such major hardware providers as IBM, DEC, Silicon Graphics, Sun Microsystems, and Apple and such network providers as AT&T, Worldcom, and France Telecom. Leading content providers such as News Corporation are also adopting Netscape server software as a platform for their web sites on the Internet.

Technology-based alliances spring from the confusion created by uncertainty and change. They distribute and decrease risks, augment flexibility, improve innovation capacity, and decrease complexity, which can be too high and too costly for individual firms.

In the electronic commerce industry, General Magic is a good example of a technology-based alliance for innovative products. Apple, AT&T, Matsushita, Motorola, Philips, and Sony are teaming up to devise an easy-to-use communications program, called Magic Cap, and to conceive handheld personal communications devices that provide electronic shopping, message exchanging, and other services to consumers.

Likewise, Sun Microsystems, which holds Internet server technology, and Netscape, which owns Internet browser technology, are allying to quickly achieve the technology necessary to develop a new, easy-to-use Internet programming language, Javascript. Thus, they hope to influence evolving industry standards and get wider control and market share in the Internet business.

Other recent examples of technology-based alliances include:

- The Verifone and Netscape alliance to develop software for accepting credit cards over the Internet;

- The 3Com, Newbridge, and Siemens alliance to develop a new technology, called "Carrier Scale Internetworking," for increasing the speed of electronic data interchanges through standard public telecommunication networks;

- The Eli Lilly and Centocor alliance to produce and market biotechnology-based pharmaceuticals;

- The alliance between Eastman Kodak Company and Heidelberg Druckmaschinen, a German printer maker, to create, manufacture, and market a new digital small-sized color printer for business customers;

- The alliance of Motorola, Lockheed, Raytheon, Comdev, Siemens, Sprint, Oftel, and Korea Mobile telecom—all members of the "Iridium" consortium—to launch Low Earth Orbit (LEO) satellites used for transmitting mobile phone communications;

- Its main competitor, the "Globalstar consortium," an alliance of Loral Space and Communication, Qualcom, Aerospatiale, Alcatel, Daimler-Benz, Finnemeccanica, Hiundai, Telitall, Ericsson, France Telecom, Vodafone, Air Touch Communications, and Dacom.

Technology-based alliances have replaced the vertical integration of companies. For example, in the desktop computing business, the fully integrated firms of the eighties, like IBM, have made room for such alliances (see Table 2.2). Today, some companies provide silicon as raw material for other firms who make microprocessors and semiconductors; others manufacture printed circuit boards or peripherals, while some develop operating system software, and yet others application software.

Table 2.2

Technology-Based Alliances in the Desktop Computing Business

Component Provided in the Alliance	Major Players
Silicon/raw material	MMC, Walker, Shinetsu
Microprocessing Unit	Intel, AMD, Toshiba, NEC
Peripherals	Seagate
Operating system	Microsoft, IBM, Apple
Application software	Novell, Microsoft, Lotus

Another group of firms in the industry specialize in offering integrated computing systems and consulting, while other firms provide training or after-sales services. Other alliances have been carved around Novell's PC networking systems and SAP's integrated application software solutions for manufacturers.

The online services industry is another example of the substitution of technology-based alliances for integrated firms as a key to achieving success in a new field. When Prodigy (IBM + Sears) entered the business in the early 1990s, it had to build a vertically integrated business that covered content creation and packaging, network and server design and operation, as well as billing and network operating systems. This business model blew up later as specialized providers sprang to supply every component of an online service technology platform.

Likewise in the aircraft manufacturing business, while Boeing is still mostly vertically integrated, its competitors have adopted a similar model within the Airbus alliance; each member is in charge of making one key module of a plane (see Table 2.3).

Technology-based alliances also improve the climate for innovation because they connect various resources in creativity. The first spreadsheet product from Visicalc originated from the technological net of small firms created by Apple for the Apple II platform. Later, the first desktop publishing software rose from the alliance set up around the Macintosh platform. One can wonder if they would have occurred had the innovation remained only within Apple.

Table 2.3

Technology-Based Alliances in the Aircraft Manufacturing Business: The Case of Airbus

Component Provided in the Alliance	Company
Nose	Aerospatiale
Body	MBB
Wings	British Aerospace
Tail	CASA
Final assembly	Aerospatiale

One may estimate that a firm can manage about five to 10 technology-based significant alliances, but not more. Though they may have positive effects, too many such alliances will slow new solution development because of the pressure they put on a company's financial and managerial resources.

To maximize the investment, some firms carefully scrutinize their alliances to learn more about the process instead of only the outputs. For instance, managers at HP hold a debriefing after an alliance is formed with all the participants. They consider the original goals and their implementation, figuring out the reasons for success or failure. All this information is entered into an alliance database.

In any case, one must always remember that whenever an industry begins to expand, cooperation comes less easily than competition between firms. Furthermore, the rise of a predominant design can increase the importance of a given technology provided by a partner and change the relative bargaining power of participants. Hence, companies should first decide what technology is important to them from a strategic standpoint and then make sure that they are fully assimilating this technology from the alliance. They must ensure that they are not simply buying it, like IBM did with Intel and Microsoft in the desktop computing business.

Joint ventures are another powerful medium for entering and developing new markets. For instance, when Corning ventured into the optical fiber technology business, it created a joint venture with companies such as Siemens and Plessey to expand its own manufacturing, marketing, and selling capacities. Today, Corning is a leading worldwide supplier of optical fiber.

Acquisition of a company is the last way to develop a new business by directly buying market share and innovation competencies. Examples are numerous in various high-tech industries. Lately, IBM bought strategic stakes in several niche innovators and extended its product range by acquiring Lotus Corporation in 1995 for $3.5 billion. Similarly, in 1997, Compaq bought Tandem for $3 billion in order to expand its range of solutions up to powerful fault-tolerant mainframe computers. It also acquired Digital in January 1998 for $9.6 billion—a deal that gives it access to Digital's large account customers as well as Digital's know-how and expertise in computer and telecommunication services.

In the data networking business, Cisco System has managed to grow extensively from zero when it was created in 1994 to a $6.5 billion firm in 1997 via a significant number of acquisitions. Cisco bought 33 firms between 1994 and 1997, including 17 during 1997 alone. Recent acquisitions include two direct competitors, Stratacom in April 1996 and Granite Telecom in September 1996; Telesend in April 1997 (ISDL technology); Global Internet Software Group (firewall technology) and Ardent Communication (data compression technology) in June 1997; and Light Speed International (speech recognition and automatic translation) in December 1997.

In one of the biggest takeovers in the telecommunication sector, Worldcom acquired MCI in the telecommunications sector for $30 billion in 1997 to become the fifth largest telecom operator in the world.

In the biotechnology business, some major "traditional" pharmaceutical firms have bought biotechnology firms to enhance their competencies in this new and promising sector. In 1990, Roche acquired 49% of Genentech for $2.1 billion and in 1997 made the decision to buy the rest of the stock before the year 2000. Likewise, Ciba took control of Chiron, a leading American biotech company, for $2 billion in order to expand its offerings into diagnosis tools and vaccines.

Acquisitions are riskier than alliances. For example, facing the convergence of both telecommunication and computer technologies, AT&T bought NCR in 1990 in order to gain the control of computer technology. The acquisition did not pay off because of poor management and shifting technology demands. Eventually, after having lost billions of dollars, AT&T spun off NCR in 1996. One may think that AT&T would have been better off in teaming with NCR to obtain technology.

Inhouse development of expertise usually requires large investments and long waiting periods but give a company the greatest independence. The CEO of Air Liquide had this in mind when he created a special team for the development of noncryogenic procedures for air separation purposes. IBM entrusted a small team, independent from traditional research teams, with the development of its first microcomputer.

Usually however, relying only on its own capacities and neglecting external leverage can be dangerous in the high-technology business. For example, Apple refused for years to license its Macintosh operating system; in doing so, it was able to maximize its revenues in the short term but did not realize that it was growing less rapidly than the whole PC market. Apple ended with a shrinking market share that led to its arch rival Microsoft taking a stake in its equity.

Dornier, a German firm, had a similar experience. Using the ultrasonic shock wave technology it had previously developed for military material destruction applications, Dornier created the first lithotripter, a medical instrument used in the treatment of kidney stones and gallstones.

Dornier's new medical business expanded fast and soon reached a point where it competed against possible new products from GE and Siemens. Dornier's senior management decided to stay on its own and not enter into licensing agreements or partnerships because potential candidates had already invested in their own product development. As a consequence, when revenues began to drop sharply, leading to huge losses, Dornier was trapped with a failing stand-alone business and ultimately settled on closing it.

Another well-known example is the case of Sony when it entered the video camera recorder market in the 1980s with its Betamax technology. Sony held its license as proprietary and rested on a limited number of dedicated sales channels. As seen previously, despite the admitted technical superiority of its product and significant price-cutting, Sony lost the VCR market to its main competitor Matsushita, which had licensed its VHS technology to other consumer electronic enterprises.

The lesson was not lost on Sony when it launched the 3.5-in computer disk drive. First, Sony sold or licensed its new technology to leading PC producers, including IBM, Apple, Compaq, and NEC. Consequently, the 3.5-in disk drive quickly became a worldwide standard in this global industry and Sony achieved a 50% market share.

Similarly, in the consumer business, Sony made an alliance in 1981 with Philips NV to commercialize the digital audio technology developed by Philips in the 1970s for audio compact disc players. The impact of this alliance was to boost support for the Philips-Sony standard. By the end of 1981, more than 30 firms had signed contracts to license the Philips-Sony technology, and the two other competitors, Telefunken and Matsushita, removed their own incompatible competing prototype.

In any case, the choice between these different types of development plans should not only take into account technological criteria but also the company's overall position in all of its business activities.

The marketing manager plays an important role in the strategic development process because he or she can supply information about customers, the environment, and competitors.

The marketing manager's role is even more essential in the high-technology industry because different requirements such as performance requirements, forecasting, the company's reaction capability, and innovation demand a continuous strategic re-evaluation; the high-tech-product world looks more like a raging ocean than a calm river.

When this work is completed, the marketing manager can define a marketing strategy that will, of course, be included in the more general framework of the company's strategy.

2.2   What are the marketing strategy and the marketing plan for high-tech products?

The marketing strategy represents the framework on which the company's sales activities are based. The marketing strategy is developed by the marketing manager and is then used to complete an annual marketing plan. Every company has its own way of drawing up a marketing plan, but the following four steps are essential.

The situation analysis aims to identify market opportunities as well as the company's constraints. This analysis allows for quantitative forecasting about the potential of various markets.

The marketing strategy statement introduces the marketing objectives, sales figures, amount of profit (and the calculation method), and then the target markets. For every market, the marketing manager defines the company's proposal in terms of the four Ps—product, price, promotion, and place (distribution)—or marketing mix.

The main tasks associated with a product include developing and testing new products, modifying or eliminating existing products, managing the product range, formulating a brand name, and creating a product guarantee and associated services. With regard to the price, pricing policies must be formulated, competitors' prices and customers' sensitivity to price (elasticity) evaluated, and prices and discounts set. Promotion activities include setting promotional objectives, selecting the adequate promotional media, designing the message, developing the advertising message, and creating sales promotion leaflets and programs. At the distribution level, the marketing manager must, among other responsibilities, select appropriate distribution channels, design an effective program for the distributors, set up inventory controls, and minimize total distribution costs [5].

Action programs correspond to the implementation of each element of the marketing mix by market. These action programs indicate which steps must be taken, their responsibilities, their deadlines, and their available financial resources and budgets.

Monitoring procedures plan an evaluation schedule for the progress of the action programs as well as of the results of the marketing strategy in terms of the sales and profit figures.

The specific characteristics of high technology, however, will impose on each of these four categories certain adjustments of which the marketing manager must be aware when making his or her marketing plan.

2.2.1 Situation analysis

On one hand, a situation analysis must take into account the existing and future life cycle of a technology. This analysis is essential for making good evaluations of market opportunities as well as competitors' positions.

On the other hand, the study of a company's strengths and weaknesses must inevitably include an evaluation of the cooperation between the marketing and the research and development departments. This relationship is very important for the successful development of new products that the market expects within certain time limits.

2.2.2 Target market and marketing mix analysis

Three peculiarities must be considered at this stage of the marketing plan. First, due to the specific characteristics of high-tech products certain segmentation techniques to target markets must be specifically designed, as we will see in Chapter 5. Second, the marketing mix for a high-tech product is dominated by the product variable. New high-tech products are more often introduced to the market than traditional, non-high-tech products. Finally, selecting a distribution and sales system is often very difficult. The distribution channels do not change as quickly as the products. This constraint is very important for managers of high-tech products.

2.2.3 Action programs

Since the environment changes very quickly in the world of high technology, action programs must be developed according to a relatively flexible format so that they can easily be reviewed and modified. Budgetary procedures must especially be open to change so that they can follow the movements of a rising and falling market. A truly efficient action program must be short and flexible; otherwise it will simply become an administrative exercise, contrary to the objectives it seeks to meet. The monitoring procedures should be designed according to the same principle.

2.2.4 Monitoring procedures

The evaluation process must serve as a reference point for the marketing manager, who then has the opportunity to correct the company's marketing strategy. The evaluation process should not, however, become a restraining device that will keep it from adapting itself to the market. Bureaucratic companies do not survive in the high-tech industry.

With all the turbulence and uncertainties in a high-tech environment, certain authors suggest adding a fifth phase, called a "contingency plan," to the marketing plan [6]. If a threat such as the entrance of a new competitor or the disappearance of a market segment occurs, a ready-to-use contingency plan is very useful. With such a plan, a company can react instantly and with much greater efficiency than if it were completely taken by surprise.

A marketing plan is very useful because it allows for a more complete understanding of the competitors' market as well as of the company's strengths and weaknesses. It is also useful in documenting the main strategic marketing decisions that can then be discussed or adopted using clear and precise information. This information facilitates quick decision making as well as communication among the company's different departments. Finally, the marketing plan must be approved by the executive board of directors, which emphasizes the importance of the marketing department.

Figure 2.10 summarizes the marketing manager's role in the general framework of the company's strategy. A marketing manager contributes to the collection of necessary information on markets and the environment to facilitate decision making with regard to the strategic segments (or business activities). For each of the selected strategic segments, the marketing manager establishes a marketing strategy and supplies a marketing plan, which is used by the executive board to allocate the available resources among different departments.

The marketing department implements its plan depending on the allocated financial resources. Ultimately, these plans are regularly evaluated by the executive board, which allows the marketing manager to make new recommendations.

2.3　Chapter summary

As is the case for every company, marketing in a high-tech company is part of the overall framework of the strategy that is instituted by the executive board to make the company's objectives and resources correspond to the market's opportunities.

The specific characteristics of high technology, however, lead to the use of additional tools in the development of a strategy. The definition of a company's mission is not treated any differently. However, the identification of strategic sectors takes on a certain technological importance. Selecting sectors requires an evaluation of a company's technological assets and its positioning according to the technology life cycle. This

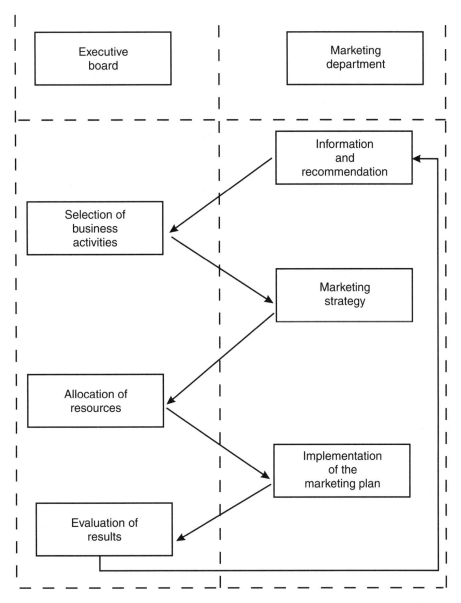

Figure 2.10 The role of the marketing department in corporate strategy.

evaluation is necessary for the verification of market synchronization and has become necessary due to the fast-changing environment of high technology. The innovative quality of high technology requires the evaluation of its technological advantage; the degree of control over future key technologies will have an important competitive impact.

Finally, the development of new business activities in order to fill the gap between objectives and expected results always requires that new technologies be mastered.

When the overall strategy of a company is approved, the marketing manager develops a marketing strategy for the marketing activities. This process is similar to processes used by traditional companies, but it must integrate the specific characteristics of the high-technology industry in each of its elements.

References

[1] Bower, J. L., and T. M. Hout, "Fast Cycle Capability for Competitive Power," *Harvard Business Review*, November–December 1988.

[2] Martin, J., *Future Developments in Telecommunication*, Englewood Cliffs, NJ: Prentice Hall, 1977.

[3] Briston, W. B., *The Twilight of Sovereignty*, New York: Charles Scribner's Sons, 1992.

[4] Porter, M., *Competitive Advantage*, New York: The Free Press, 1985.

[5] Dibb, S., L. Simkin, W. M. Pride, and O. C. Ferrell, *Marketing, Concepts and Strategies*, Boston, MA: Houghton Mifflin Company, 1994.

[6] Macinnis, M., and L. A. Heslop, "Market Planning in a High-Tech Environment," *Industrial Marketing Management*, Vol. 19, February 1990.

Knowing Customers and Markets

3

A marketing manager who aims to put products on the market that satisfy customers' needs and wants must be tuned in to the market; he or she must know the customer's expressed or latent needs before these needs can be transformed into a company's products and technology. The requirement for success in high technology is understanding customer value.

For example, the need for a higher quality of sound has been materialized by laser discs and the use of digital sound technology. The need to communicate has been transposed into wireless networks and satellite connections. The need for greater reliability and performance in the assembly of automobiles has been materialized by the use of robots for welding, painting, and assembly purposes.

According to the manufacturers of electronic measuring instruments, three out of four of their innovations come directly from customers' insights. In the semiconductor and printed circuit board industry, it is two out of three.

However, the high-technology sector is also characterized by an abundance of technical processes derived from research and development laboratories or individual researchers. In this case, a marketing manager must therefore be able to help transform these new ideas into products that are suited to the needs of the customer and the market. This preliminary step is necessary in assuring the maximum amount of success when launching new products as a result of a newly developed technique in the company.

In both cases, a marketing manager must know how to estimate the level of market demand. He or she must have an understanding of the buying behavior of a company's actual and potential customers in order to know better the needs of the market, find ideas for new products, or test the compatibility between the applications of a new technology and the customers' needs.

3.1 Determining the customer's buying behavior

The analysis of the principal purchasing factors for high-technology products is not different from the analysis performed by a marketing manager in a more traditional company. The guidelines that are used in performing such an analysis already exist and are used as much in the consumer goods and services sector as in the industrial goods and services sector.

However, the particular characteristics of high-tech products, especially their newness, which makes their value often difficult to determine for potential customers, lead to a specific analysis of customers' attitudes regarding innovation and risk.

3.1.1 Purchasing factors for high-tech consumer products

When someone buys a high-tech good or service for personal use, he or she is influenced by four classes of factors: sociocultural, psychosocial, personal, and psychological (see Figure 3.1). This influence is illustrated using a high-definition television (HDTV) as an example, but it applies to

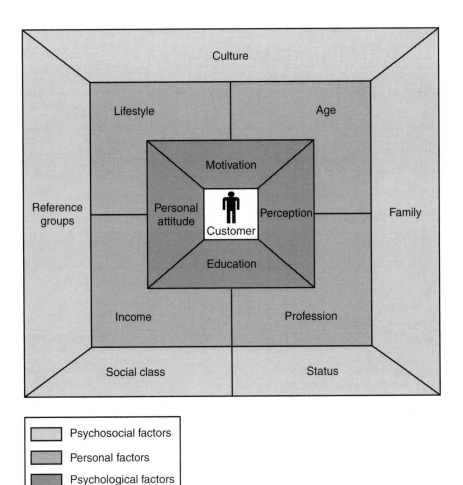

Figure 3.1 Purchasing criteria groups for high-tech consumer products. The lightest shaded areas represent psychosocial factors, the darker shaded areas represent personal factors, and the darkest shaded areas represent psychological factors.

any high-tech consumer product, like Digital Video Disc (DVD), digital cameras or camcorders, cellular phones or pagers, GPS, or WebTVs.

3.1.1.1 Sociocultural factors

The interest in HDTV sets only exists because our culture values images and because we have owned TVs for a long time. The product does not have the same attraction for consumers who live in cultures in which TV and technology are relatively unfamiliar.

Consumption choices vary according to nationality, religion, race, and national origin. The Japanese, for example, buy new TVs every three years, whereas Europeans buy a new set about every ten years.

The social environment also plays an important role: someone who belongs to a fairly high class spends more money on leisure activities and could be specifically targeted for a new high-tech product.

3.1.1.2 Psychosocial factors

Reference groups (such as family, neighbors, friends, and colleagues) have a strong influence on purchases of high-tech products. Purchasing an HDTV can be influenced by family pressure, impressionable neighbors and friends, or colleagues who have already bought and are very happy with one. Furthermore, an HDTV can be perceived as a status symbol that appeals to all consumers who buy products for social status reasons.

3.1.1.3 Personal factors

Age is an important determining factor. An HDTV is mainly of interest to age groups that heavily invest in their leisure activities: singles or young couples without children as well as older couples ("empty nesters").

An HDTV also attracts professionals who work with images, from TV directors to retail sales clerks in TV and stereo stores. These professionals can quickly determine the advantage of such a product (for example, digital sound, improved picture, and its compatibility with computers) as compared to a traditional TV set.

The consumer's financial status (level of income and debt) is also important in the decision to purchase a high-tech product with a price that is initially high because the research and development costs must be recovered.

Lifestyle also determines consumption choices. According to the lifestyle definitions by CCA, a major French market research company specializing in consumers' lifestyles analysis, an HDTV more often attracts forerunners, who are interested in new technologies and have an adventurous mind, than the traditionalists, who glorify the past.

3.1.1.4 Psychological factors

Many psychologists, the most famous of which are Sigmund Freud, Abraham Maslow, and Frederick Herzberg, have stressed the importance of motivation. Their conclusions have important ramifications for the marketing of high-technology products.

Freudian theory emphasizes the psychological dimensions of a product: that outside of its functional aspect, a buyer of an HDTV takes into consideration more than just the product's performance. An HDTV buyer is sensitive to other aspects of the product: its size, shape, weight, color, and even the aesthetic quality of its buttons. These elements are capable of activating emotions that will reinforce a customer's attraction to a product or, on the contrary, will keep him or her from purchasing an HDTV. Therefore, all exterior aspects (such as packaging) must be carefully considered during a product's design and manufacturing phases.

Maslow developed an analysis grid that is divided into five categories of needs: physiological, safety, love, esteem, and self-actualization. The purchase of an HDTV can therefore respond to many motives, which correspond to diverse needs such as reassurance and belonging to a group (by imitating people who already own HDTVs), being respected (by differentiating from others who cannot afford an HDTV), or treating oneself (by buying a high-performance item).

Herzberg differentiates between the two states of satisfaction and dissatisfaction that exist in each person. The practical consequence is that a company must absolutely avoid dissatisfying elements and must carefully list the satisfying elements for the consumer so that these elements can be added to the product. Therefore, a European HDTV set that cannot be connected to an American VCR already owned by the user will bring about dissatisfaction. On the other hand, an extraordinarily sharp picture can provoke the consumer's satisfaction and enthusiasm and lead him or her to purchase the product.

The purchase of a product also depends on the perception that people have of the product. Someone who wants to buy an HDTV will notice all the advertising for HDTVs but ignore advertising for microcomputers. Also, such a person will pay more attention to HDTVs in stores than to new VCRs on display.

Perception is complicated by two phenomena: selective distortion and selective retention. Selective distortion makes someone "adjust" information so that it corresponds to his or her wants. In Europe, someone who likes Thomson products will have a tendency to idealize the advantages and reduce the disadvantages when examining a Thomson HDTV (in the United States, the example would apply to RCA products since Thomson owns the RCA brand in the United States).

Selective retention leads the customer to better remember information that reinforces his or her beliefs. A Thomson advocate will more easily remember the advantages of a Thomson HDTV and the disadvantages of a Sony HDTV than vice versa.

Past experiences also play a large role in the purchasing decision process. These experiences can be ascribed to behavioral learning. Someone who is unhappy with a high-tech product after purchasing it will have a future tendency to turn away from this type of product and instead consider more traditional products. In addition, a buyer who is satisfied with his or her Thomson TV and VCR will most likely prefer a Thomson HDTV. This preference goes to a brand with which a customer is already familiar.

Finally, one's attitudes toward a product are important. Opinions and tendencies lead or curb certain behaviors. Everyone has a certain attitude toward almost every element of society: politics, art, education, food. These attitudes allow for a coherent response to many diverse subjects. An attitude creates a positive or negative environment for a product. Someone who believes that Europeans have greater technical expertise than the Japanese and that "Thomson always has top-of-the-line products" has an attitude that reinforces his or her intentions to purchase a Thomson HDTV.

Finally, a consumer who chooses to buy a high-tech product for personal use is influenced by many factors. Accordingly, a marketing manager must identify all the factors that lead to a purchase and should take these factors into account during product development, price setting, distribution selection, and sales promotion.

3.1.2 Purchasing factors for high-tech goods and services in business-to-business activities

Typically, high-tech industrial markets are smaller than consumer markets. In 1995, the worldwide market for photoresist, a chemical material used in manufacturing semiconductors, was $500 million while the market for semiconductors was over $140 billion. Similarly, the market for the plasma material used in the flat panel display (FDP) was only $300 million while the global FDP market was over $5 billion. As a consequence, the limited size of business-to-business markets make them easier to identify, analyze, and understand. The purchase of industrial goods and services rarely depends upon a single person but rather usually on a group. In such a group, there are the following participants: the user, who needs a good or service and prepares the specifications; the go-between, who puts the user in contact with an outside supplier; the adviser, who is usually the subject specialist (for example, in computers and robotics); the purchasing agent, who chooses the suppliers; and the decision maker, who signs the purchasing contract.

The price of a particular high-tech product strongly determines the number of participants in a purchasing group. A computer workstation, worth thousands of dollars, can be bought directly by a development engineer, but an investment in robotics equipment for a manufacturing line with a total value near several million dollars will be carefully scrutinized before a member of the executive board signs the purchasing contract.

Therefore, a marketing manager must analyze the principal determining factors for industrial purchases. These factors can be divided into three classes according to their relation to the environment, to the organization of the purchasing company, and to the decision maker (see Figure 3.2).

3.1.2.1 Environmental factors

Environmental factors that can be found outside of business customers are political context, economic situation, demand level, competition, and technological evolution. This last dimension is, of course, fundamental in the high-technology sector.

So, for instance, when the marketing manager of Arianespace analyzes the needs of some of its clients, such as the telecommunication companies, he or she must evaluate the position of rocket launchers in relation to other technologies, such as radio links, electromagnetic waves, or fiber optics, that will strongly determine the demand for satellite launching.

He or she must also study the position of competitors (for example, "Will the Chinese government continue to sell its long-range launcher at a low price?" and "At which price will the Japanese offer their new H2 rocket?"); the overall economic situation (for example, "What impact will

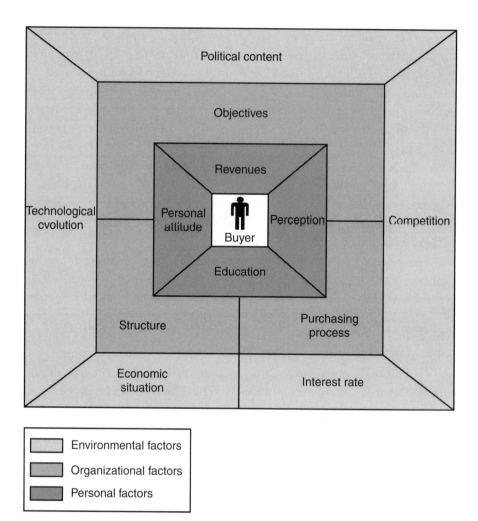

Figure 3.2 Purchasing criteria groups for high-tech industrial products. The lightest shaded areas represent environmental factors, the darker shaded areas represent organizational factors, and the darkest shaded areas represent personal factors.

rising interest rates have on the projects of the Turkish government regarding the launching of nonmilitary satellites?"; and the political situation (for example, "Will the deregulation in the United States, which opened the American market to foreign launchers, risk a challenge by the United States Senate?").

3.1.2.2 Organizational factors for the purchasing company

As for all industrial products, the client's organizational dimensions must be taken into account in order to make a high-tech product a marketing success.

Every company has its centralized or decentralized organizational structure, its procedures, its objectives, and its politics that can influence the success or failure of a product. The sales force plays a fundamental role in pushing the product through the decision-making system of the purchasing company. The marketing department is able to supply the sales force with useful reference points.

The marketing department can point out changes in the decision-making process for a particular sector or a type of customer. For example, in the information technology business, MIS managers are no longer always the ultimate decision makers when choosing computers and software; the general management and the users often make these decisions, even in the case of purchasing a large mainframe or a big database software.

The marketing manager must also urge the sales force to establish early business relations with potential clients. Actually, certain high-tech products require an extremely long courtship, for example, extending up to 10 years for a rocket launcher or a supercomputer and even 15 years for certain chemical molecules. These time periods are longer when the products are more specific.

The customer must be approached at the moment when a need develops. The sales force must have a firm control of the relationship in order to offer products that satisfy the company and to work with the company regarding the development of the product. If this is not the case, competitors take control.

Another very important case is for purchases that are made by a bidding process, a frequently used procedure for high-tech products in civilian and military industrial markets. Here, a prospect company must be approached very early on, as soon as it shows a need, in order to present the company with a preliminary draft of the solution and to establish a specifications list that will be used as a source document during the bidding process. When this specifications list officially appears, it is already too late to react; for example, Hewlett-Packard will have trouble responding to these specifications if the demanded product resembles a Bull computer, and Aerospatiale will not be able to offer a satellite if the characteristics are almost an exact copy of the model manufactured by Spar, the Canadian company.

3.1.2.3 Personal factors

The individual characteristics of each decision maker and participant in industrial purchasing groups must also be very carefully taken into account. The personal factors for consumer good purchases also play an important role in industrial purchasing.

However, different studies show that the intangible characteristics of the solution (the supplier's credibility, service, and long-term commitment to support the product) matter more than its physical characteristics (for example, performance and speed) when the minimum performance level has been reached.

The importance of psychological factors is still too often neglected in the industrial high-tech product sector. The marketing department's explication can often be of considerable help to the sales force and lead them to a better understanding of the representatives.

However, there is often a tendency to focus on the functional characteristics of the product instead of on the needs that should be satisfied. As we will see later, experience shows that many buyers are often dazzled by the complexity of the technology and choose the solution that reassures them the most.

The marketing department must therefore carefully analyze the importance of different purchasing factors and take these factors into account during all product stages from design, to introduction to the market, and to further development.

3.1.3 Specific purchasing criteria for high-tech products

For a consumer, buying the latest laser-video disc player is riskier than buying a traditional hi-fi sound system. For an industrial purchaser, buying the first robot with six degrees of freedom (for manufacturing purposes) that just appeared on the market is riskier than buying a robot with three degrees of freedom and with technology has already been in use for a long period of time.

Therefore, because buying a high-tech product as compared to a traditional product often means taking the risk of experiencing the initial problems of a new product, two additional purchasing criteria should be considered: the customer's attitudes toward innovation and risk.

3.1.3.1 Attitude toward innovation

Many studies have been carried out on the new product adoption process (for example, [1]). The results of these studies can be adapted to the world of high-tech products, which is often characterized by a high degree of innovation.

These studies show that not all customers (individuals or organizations) react to new products in identical ways. Certain customers will buy new products immediately, while others will buy them much later.

We can distinguish between six classes of customers and characterize them using psychological traits:

- Innovators enjoy trying new products and are adventuresome. They are those leading-edge customers who are not afraid of the "bleeding edge" of any new technology.

- Forerunners are often respected opinion leaders who are more careful than innovators.

- Mainstream users like to analyze a product before buying it.

- Followers are skeptics who go along with the majority but much later.

- Traditionalists are conservatives who do not buy a product until it has become part of tradition.

- Finally, the rebels will always reject a product because of its very nature.

For simplification, all six classes can be theoretically divided along a normal distribution curve (see Figure 3.3), though in reality their distribution may vary significantly according to the very nature of each market. For instance, in the case of U.S. cable TV pay-per-view services, 20% of households account for 80% of all purchases. Similarly, in the cases of U.S. and U.K. video rentals, 20% of households with VCRs generate 80% of the total demand.

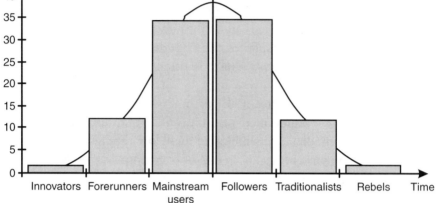

Figure 3.3   Market sensitivity to innovation (segmentation according to attitude).

The attitude toward innovation may also vary from one country to another. Consider, for example, the case of the penetration rate of cable TV in various western European countries. Satellite and cable networks have achieved different rates of adoption across western Europe. In France, Italy, the United Kingdom, and Spain, less than 10% of households are equipped with cable TV (emerging markets); in Scandinavia, Austria, Germany, and Ireland, the adoption rate is between 25 and 60% (maturing markets); and in Benelux and Switzerland over 80% of households use cable TV (mature markets). Satellite network adoption is even lower, surpassing cable penetration only in the United Kingdom.

This analysis is important when marketing innovative products with a possibly short life. In fact, to optimize the introduction of a new high-tech product, innovators and forerunners should first be identified. These two groups of potential customers will give the product its acceptance and win over other customer groups. Identifying innovators and early adopters is not easy, but it will be a guarantee of success.

For example, before introducing the Macintosh computer, Apple carefully   prepared   its   potential   market   by   building   fruitful relationships with six different types of people: third-party developers; dealers; financial analysts; trade, business, and general press; most critical Apple customers; and "luminaries." This last group represented about 50 creative people and decision makers such as Ted Turner, Lee Iacocca, and Andy Warhol. These famous people were all opinion leaders who were ready to make the Macintosh a new phenomenon and would pass on their passion for the Macintosh computer to an audience of "up-to-date" innovators and early adopters.

The importance of understanding the needs of innovators and forerunners is illustrated by another example in the online services business, where first users seem to value networks' communication abilities rather than their content. However, when Prodigy entered the online services business, its management postulated that its central value would be to give consumers access to various kinds of published content—such as news, weather reports, sports scores, and economic data—as and when required. Very soon subscribers appeared to be much more interested in communicating with one another. Unfortunately for Prodigy, its architecture was designed to ease access to published content rather than connection among users.

That flaw left a window of opportunity for America OnLine. It developed a different architecture that allowed users to communicate either in real time through chat rooms or at any time through bulletin boards where they could post and get messages. While Prodigy's growth stagnated, users rushed to AOL, especially after its introduction of specialized chat rooms and bulletin boards for users who shared a particular interest or a similar lifestyle, like teenagers.

Targeting first innovators is also a sound business-to-business marketing strategy because they may create a snowball effect that will expand in the whole market.

For instance, Shinko, a Japanese semiconductor packaging manufacturer, decided to target Intel as a key customer because of Intel's leadership in the semiconductor business. Shinko managed to meet Intel's packaging design requirements for different chip forms and became its first supplier.

When other semiconductor manufacturers such as Texas Instruments and IBM switched to the same technology as Intel's, Shinko was already there to provide leading-edge solutions. As a result, Shinko increased sales at an annual growth rate of 18% from $68 million in 1980 to $726 million in 1994.

Similarly, Hashimoto Chemical first targeted Sony as a customer and managed to achieve a 90% market share by establishing a de facto standard in electrolyte-related materials for lithium ion batteries. Another Japanese chemical company, Tanaka Chemical, first targeted Matsushita and ultimately won an 80% market share of the nickel metal hydride battery cathode active material.

Furthermore, studies show that the more complex an innovation is, the more time it will take for the innovational product to be accepted (see, for example, [2]). For any new product, the more important the extensive retraining required, the higher the risk to be rejected. A classic example is the QWERTY typewriter keyboard that has persisted as a standard for years, despite the availability of superior alternatives; a contemporary example is the de facto Lotus 1–2–3 standard for spreadsheet software due to the proliferation of the electronic spreadsheet in the workplace and the extended period of training needed to use them efficiently [3]. In the mid-nineties, Excel replaced 1–2–3 as a best seller, but one must note that it adopted a similar design to 1–2–3 in order to ease the switch for 1–2–3 users. Even popular products such as Windows 95 or the Pentium microprocessors are not as widely adopted as one would imagine, given their image of being the "standard" solution. A recent survey in June 1997 credits the Pentium as used by only 40% of the American households equipped with PCs ,while the other 60% rely on x86-based computers (or even older). Similarly, only 48% of the American PC household users use Windows 95; the others use older operating systems.

As a consequence, the market penetration of a new product can be accelerated by informing and educating as many potential customers as possible so that they will know the product, are able to measure its superiority over other existing products, and can describe the advantages of the innovation to other people.

Long before introducing the Macintosh to the market, Apple had already informed the six aforementioned reference groups about the product so that these people would be inclined to make favorable comments because they already knew the product well. Apple gave almost 60 individual seven-hour presentations to financial analysts and journalists in the computer industry, 16 demonstrations for groups of

10 people or less, and training sessions for 40,000 retailers in the three months before introducing the Macintosh to the market. Microsoft used the same strategy on an even larger scale when launching Windows 95, and Microsoft currently has its new operating system, code-named Memphis, being tested by more than 10,000 users (see also Section 6.3.1).

Another reason why innovation may take many years to replace an established technology is because of the investments made in the previous technologies that can be still productive. A classic example is the introduction rate of electricity on the American industrial market. In 1910, only 25% of U.S. factories used electric power mostly for new plants or new activities. In more mature industries, the replacement of water or steam by electricity as the source of power had to await the depreciation of existing plants. Twenty years later, 75% of firms were using electricity. This trend is not confined to businesses; it exists also with consumers. For instance, the market success of the Digital Video Disc is largely correlated to the consumers' value of their current VCR system. The higher the value, the less they will be inclined to invest in a new image recording system.

3.1.3.2   Attitude toward risk

Having confidence in the company that offers a solution is an extremely important factor. According to marketing managers, this trust is an even more important purchasing factor than the technology used and is equal to the price of the product (see Figure 3.4).

In the high-technology industry, customers are often faced with a technically complex solution, the elements of which they do not understand. These customers, however, do realize that this solution is likely to change quickly over time and can suddenly become obsolete. Finally, innovation can often be disturbing for buyers.

With this in mind, customers prefer security. They choose a company they can trust and that they know will be around for a sufficient length of time to guarantee the durability of the solution. This was the strength of IBM in the computer industry of the 1970s—no one was ever fired for selecting an IBM product.

Arianespace's marketing director Ralph-Werner Jaeger expresses this same idea: "In our business, there is a development toward criteria of trust and reliability of service. All our activities are ultimately

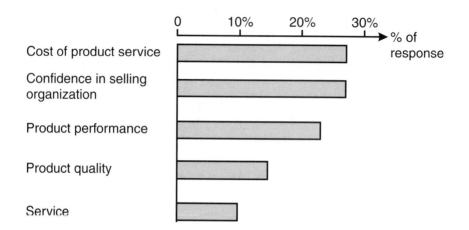

Figure 3.4 Purchasing criteria for high-technology goods and services. Tabulation of responses to the question "Which are the deciding factors that influence your customers in a purchasing decision?" (*Source:* Interviews by Eric Viardot.)

materialized in about 30 minutes, after a three-year waiting period and million dollar investments...customers prefer that we spend more so as to supply an extremely reliable product."

The same reaction can be found concerning high-tech consumer products. Faced with a complex and changing supply, consumers prefer either the least expensive brand or the most prestigious brand, which is the rule for the electronic calculator market.

The marketing strategy for large companies should include improving their image and reputation. Smaller companies must rely on recommendations that reassure their potential customers, on a selling style that can establish confidence, and on a long-term support commitment for the solutions that these smaller companies offer.

In any case, according to marketing managers, technology is not a necessary and satisfactory element for convincing the market. The marketing manager must understand the client's needs in terms of performance but also in terms of psychological expectation. He or she must also try to reduce the risk aversion that inhibits the behavior of many buyers (final consumers or businesses) toward a high-tech product.

3.2 Estimating demand

When estimating demand, marketing high-tech products is significantly different than marketing standard products because the marketing of high-tech products must create markets rather than battle for market share like in the consumer goods business, for instance.

The French marketing manager of Oracle, a large database software company, recently remarked that "Today, out of 2,500 large French companies, 4% have a database management system. Our market consists of the other 96%."

Similarly, John Sculley compares his experiences at Pepsi Company and Apple: "One of the major differences between computers and soft drinks is that the soft-drink business is a large industry where the major competitors fight over fractions of market share. In personal computers, the growth was so phenomenal that early market share gains were not nearly as important as making sure Apple was properly positioned in areas that were going to be significant in the longer term" [4].

Another PepsiCo marketer, Steve Case, the founder of America Online, defines its markets as "everybody else" and was quoted as, "we want (AOL) to be the Coca-Cola of the online world." AOL had only 200,000 members in 1992, but surged to 1 million in 1994, 4 million in 1995, and 8 million in January 1997, aiming at 25 million by 1998.

Furthermore, a precise evaluation of demand is not easy to accomplish when markets are exploding, which is often the case for high-tech products. Measuring a product's market share is always risky when the market grows 60 to 80% per year and the competitive positions change with incredible speeds, showing sales curves that more often bring to mind Swiss mountains instead of gently sloping Irish hills.

Nevertheless, the purpose of marketing is to understand the customer in order to better respond to his or her needs. An analysis of future demand is needed, especially for new innovative products of which the market acceptance rate should be tested. The high amount of investments ($100 million for the development of a sophisticated processor or the one single production of HDTV) also requires multiple forecasts in order to estimate the return on investments and to measure the customer's reactions. At this price only, marketing catastrophes should be avoided.

Therefore, marketing research is conducted. The American Marketing Association defines marketing research as the "function that links the consumer, customer, and public to the marketer through information—information used to identify and define marketing opportunities and problems; generate, refine, and evaluate marketing actions; monitor marketing performance...Marketing research specifies the information required to address these issues; designs the method for collecting information; manages and implements the data collection process; analyzes the results; and communicates the findings and their application" [5].

Marketing research is mainly used for studies of usership and attitudes, product testing, advertising and corporate image evaluation, retail audit, consumer/customer panels, customer satisfaction measurement, concept evaluation, and distribution/price checks [6].

The typical steps of an effective marketing research process are: formulating the problem to be solved, determining a research hypothesis, designing a sample, collecting data through various methods (such as readings, field surveys, store checks, concept tests, and focus groups), analyzing and interpreting the data, and finally reporting the research findings (for more details, see [7]).

Hence, there are certain traditional marketing research tools that are used to estimate future demand, all the more because all high-tech products introduced on the market are not always revolutionary. The majority of these products consists of nothing but innovative improvements on already existing products of which the market can be identified. These identifying tools can be divided into four categories: concept tests and prototype tests, opinions of experts, sample groups and test markets, and quantitative analysis.

3.2.1 Concept tests and prototype tests

Performed on existing or potential groups of customers, concept and prototype tests allow for a conceptual evaluation of a new product or a prototype and its features. These tests measure the product's appropriateness in relation to needs, the perceived degree of its advantages, the ease with which these advantages can be understood, the provoked interest for the product, and the possible inclination to purchase the product.

Concept tests can be performed in two ways. In a focus group, a number of individuals are brought together in a room to talk about some topic of interest to the focus group sponsor. The discussion (which is taped for further analysis) is directed by a moderator, who follows a rough outline of issues while simultaneously entertaining comments made by each person of the group.

Focus groups are used very often in marketing research because they have proved to be very effective in generating hypotheses that can be tested further quantitatively, generating information for structuring consumer questionnaires, providing background information on a product category, and securing impressions on new product concepts.

Concept tests can also occur in creative workshops according to, for example, the method of Turtlebay Institute, a New York–based market research company. In this case, customers are asked to fill out long questionnaires; the information is not as valuable as that of a focus group, but it is better organized and therefore easier to analyze.

The development of concept tests is based upon classic survey techniques that are used to measure a customer's reactions to global concepts and their characteristics, but it is also based upon more sophisticated methods such as multidimensional scaling analysis and conjoint analysis or tradeoff analysis. The experience survey attempts to tap the knowledge and experience of those familiar with the general subject being investigated. The aim is to obtain insight into the relationship between variables, not the exhaustive statistics of the profession. Thus, a selected sample of respondents must be chosen. The survey can be conducted through interviews, structured or loosely structured, or questionnaires. In multidimensional scaling analysis, the respondents are asked to make judgments about the relative similarities of products or brands. In conjoint analysis (or tradeoff analysis), the respondents are asked to make judgments about their preferences for various attribute combinations (that is, features) of products or brands; for example, conjoint analysis played a key role in AT&T's entry into the data-terminal market by facilitating an estimate of the total demand for data terminals and AT&T's market share [8].

In regard to prototype tests, innovators and early adopters as well as important customers, who might be interested and to whom the company wants to show its long-term commitment, should ideally be part of a group test. These presentations should always be performed in strict secrecy.

For the development of its Docutech Systems program, Xerox initially chose 25 carefully selected test customers. Xerox then heedfully took into account their suggestions for improving the prototype before introducing it to the market. Metravib, a French research company, also used concept test and brainstorming techniques to perfect motion detectors in the intelligent suspension of the Safrane, Renault's top-of-the-line car.

Similarly, Boeing worked closely with United Airlines in developing its new line of 777 jets to decrease the likelihood of a product miss. In the consumer market, Microsoft relies heavily on prototype tests. More than 10,000 worldwide customers tested its Windows 95 operating system before its ultimate launching; 7,500 worldwide customers tested its fifth-version DOS operating system before marketing; and more than 10,000 customers tested its new operating system, Windows 98—code-named Memphis—which will replace Windows 95. In the telecommunication business, Viacom, TimeWarner, and Comcast are currently running a test market of interactive-TV in Orlando, Florida, involving more than 50,000 households, to evaluate their needs and behaviors when able to choose from a menu of shopping catalogs, news, networks, and movies, for example. In a similar test involving 200 homes in the Denver area, ATT and TCI found that viewers ordered an average of only 2.5 films per month, roughly the same consumption as ordinary moviegoers, which is a clear indication that technology does not drive needs on its own.

It is also very useful to perform concept and prototype tests on retailers. Retailers are close to the market and, hence, more likely to consider its marketability than simply a single technical feature.

3.2.2   The opinions of experts

Another interesting viewpoint comes from experts—members of professional associations or universities, consultants, or even employees of suppliers or distributors. Their opinion is useful in forming a more precise idea of future market tendencies or the probability of a technological breakthrough.

Three methods can be used to obtain expert advice. The first is a discussion group, which brings together several experts who aim to arrive at a common idea. The second is a synthesis of individual opinions that are collected from each expert and combined by an organizer.

The third is the Delphi method, in which every expert sends his or her recommendation and, after receiving the synthesis of opinions from the other experts, is invited to explain himself verbally. The process can be repeated several times in order to bring forth a group opinion.

Calling in experts is always questionable. A marketing director for a large computer company cunningly noted that if you ask a group of experts today if UNIX will become the standard operating system for all computers in the future, 50% of the experts will answer "yes," and 50% of them will answer "no."

3.2.3   Sampling groups and test markets

Sampling means the choosing of a limited number of units that have the same characteristics as the total population of customers, consumers, or businesses that marketers want to study in order to determine their assumptions about the future as well as their buying behavior. Sample groups can also be used to test new products, after the development stage. The group members try the new product in its proper environment (at work, at home) and give their opinion on the same criteria as those that were measured during concept and prototype tests.

To determine the composition of the sample, marketers use different methods.

- In random sampling, all the units of the studied population have an equal chance of being selected.

- In stratified sampling, the studied population is divided into subgroups with a common characteristic and then each group is determined by probability.

- In quota sampling, the units are defined by two or three main characteristics and selected by the interviewers as representative, as, for instance, in the survey illustrated in Table 3.1, where only the 500 largest firms in Europe were surveyed to evaluate their spending on information systems; accordingly, those samples are not a probability sample, and sampling errors cannot be calculated statistically.

Usually, the last step before launching the new product involves its evaluation on a test market (for a consumer good) or on a trade show (for an industrial product). Companies often market a product directly because they want to put a product on the market very quickly and want to protect the innovative secret against competitors who can copy the innovation and misappropriate it. These companies will observe the product's impact on the customers and make possible modifications after marketing the product. Japanese companies act in this way, whereas American and European companies often prefer to surround themselves with a maximum of caution before launching a new product—their

Table 3.1

Top Investors in Information Technologies Among the 500 European Large Accounts (1997). (*Source: Informatique Magazine*, Spike Cavell, 1997.)

Firm	Industry	Yearly Investment ($ million)	I.T. Investment/ Turnover (%)
Siemens	Industrial goods	2,160	3.6
Royal Dutsch/Shell	Oil	1,580	1.4
Barclays	Banking	1,425	6.2
Daimler-Benz	Car	1,103	1.5
ICI	Chemicals	981	6.0
Deutsche Telekom	Telecommunication	973	2.6
ABN Amro	Banking	948	3.5
BT	Telecommunication	907	4.1
Volkswagen	Car	868	1.4
Electricite de France	Energy	850	2.4
Deutsche Bank	Banking	804	2.4
Credit Agricole	Banking	763	2.6
National Westminster Bank	Banking	760	3.2
Credit Lyonnais	Banking	714	2.6

product will often arrive too late. Samples or test markets facilitate the receipt of data directly from the customers, which is called "primary data," as opposed to "secondary data" collected through reports, publications, databanks, and other indirect sources. Those data can be obtained by using different survey methods, which are mail, telephone, and face-to-face interviews.

Each method has its pros and cons, as listed in Table 3.2.

3.2.4 Using a quantitative analysis

Once a product has been shown to the sales force and the distributors prior to the actual marketing, the marketing manager can also adjust the sales forecast, as prepared by the sales force, or key channel partners, by correcting their traditional bias (underestimating demand for quota

Table 3.2

The Different Ways of Collecting Primary Data

	Pros	Cons
Mail surveys	Lowest cost per interview No interviewer bias (anonymous questionnaires)	Return rate is often low (less than 25% in consumer surveys and 1% in business surveys) Lack of flexibility in the questionnaire (which must be short and easy to answer)
Phone surveys	Less expensive than face-to-face interviews Flexible because interviewers can probe or stimulate correspondents to answer Relative anonymity	No observation Sample limited to people listed with phone number Interviewer bias Engaged line and no answer can be significant
Face-to-face interviews	Very flexible: respondents can be shown visual materials and helped to answer questionnaires Refusals may be lowered by a positive attitude from interviewers Observation provides more quality data	Interviewer bias Expensive

calculations, lack of long-term views). These forecasts can supply the marketing manager with interesting information.

One of the characteristics of high-tech-product marketing is the lack of historical data due to the product's short life and innovative quality. Also, a quantitative analysis often involves working with product data that are going to be replaced (classic televisions by HDTVs, cassette recorders by compact disc players, and telephones by videotex computers). Scenarios should be made according to the hypothesis regarding the replacement of these products and on the expansion possibilities for other uses.

Quantitative analysis techniques and related models, frequently used for consumer goods, must always be dealt with carefully. Actually, even for consumer goods, such as microcomputers and HDTVs, the market changes so quickly that the obtained information is rarely reliable.

It is also very important to keep in mind another market limitation in high-tech business: customers must be able to employ the product, which will limit the ultimate market potential. As an example, consider the original small size of the videotex market, which depended on people who had a PC at home. On the French market, France Telecom, the videotex manufacturer, tried to solve this problem by giving away millions of Minitel terminals. Although this move helped to create the market for videotex, it did so at a significant cost for France Telecom. The demand for transponders in Europe was likewise limited until more transmitting and receiving dishes were installed. Similarly, there is a strong correlation between the development of the online services market and the PC equipment rate by households. For instance, it does not come as a surprise that the countries that have the biggest number of Internet users, namely, Finland, Norway, and the United States, also have the biggest number of households equipped with PCs.

The biggest danger for the marketing manager is to perform quantitative extrapolations based upon limited qualitative information, which can lead to a generalization of hastily acquired, limited results from a small sample.

Agencies that are specialized in the market analysis of the computer industry have a tendency to overestimate the level of demand and the rate at which demand will develop. This was the case for the evaluation of the PC home-consumer market as well as for the system integration business-to-business market. Conversely, AT&T and other telecommunication operators underestimated the market for cellular phones and none expected the World Wide Web to explode like it has. Those two markets are growing at such a rate that the number of subscribers will equal the number of fixed phone subscribers at the beginning of the next century (see Figure 3.5).

In fact, these forecasting methods are merely tools that can help reach the final decision. These methods contribute to the clarification of the company's choices, but they cannot guarantee results. In many cases, the ultimate decision (for example, launching a product) depends upon the attitudes of the company's managers toward a double risk: losing a market if the company expects too much or making a mistake by going too fast.

Such is the case, for instance, in the biotechnology business. One of the leading biotech companies, Synergen, lost more than 90% of its market value when it appeared that its major drug, Antril, had no real potency. Ultimately, Synergen was acquired by one of its main competitors, Amgen.

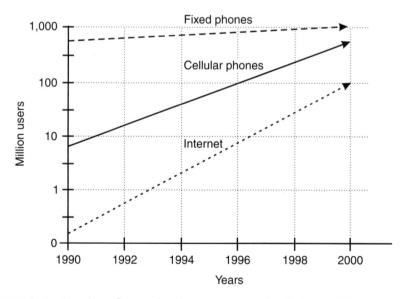

Figure 3.5 Number of users for the Internet and cellular and fixed phones, according to various sources. (*Source*: International Telecom Union, Network Wizards, Salomon Brothers, compiled by Eric Viardot, 1997.)

Besides, one must note that very often incumbent companies fall short of realizing the potential effect of a new radical technology in their industry and consider visions of it as "overhyped." Since the potential customers for this technology are usually not well identified, market research may infer that the potential for revenue is small and that the development of such a market will be too expensive. For instance, when early xerography technology was presented to IBM, senior management declined the offer because their analysis concluded that demand for copiers was too low. In the 1980s, DEC made the same error in dismissing the potential of PCs as a growing computer solution for firms preferring to stick with their policy of offering more traditional minicomputers.

Conversely, one leading American PC manufacturer underestimated demand for two of its best selling products and lost around $300 million in potential sales. Eventually, when it had its manufacturing capacity in line with the demand, the market for these products had already vanished!

At this point, common business sense appears at the same time as a business vision. According to the definition given by economist Schumpeter, isn't the entrepreneur the one who knows exactly what the market is waiting for, and doesn't the entrepreneur know it even better than the market itself?

3.3 Chapter summary

First of all, a marketing manager must know the purchasing behavior of his or her customers in order to know the needs of the market. The manager can then develop ideas for new products or approve sales applications of a new technology.

When dealing with high-tech consumer products, purchasing factors can be divided into four large categories: sociocultural factors, psychosocial factors, personal factors, and psychological factors. For industrial goods, these factors are grouped into three classes: environmental factors, organizational factors at the purchasing company, and personal factors for each buyer. Finally, there are two specific purchasing factors for high-tech products: the customers' attitudes toward innovation and risk. The marketing manager must identify, among all these factors, those that may influence the purchasing of products so that these factors can be taken into account when defining the marketing strategy.

Estimating the overall demand of a high-tech product is not easy because high-tech marketing deals with markets that are in a constant state of flux. Nevertheless, the manager can rely on several tools such as concept tests and prototype tests, expert opinions, sample groups, test markets, and sales forecasts. The manager must, however, keep a critical eye on these methods due to the unreliability of certain data. He or she should also never make the mistake of extrapolating the outcome of qualitative studies on a large scale.

References

[1]   Rogers, E. M., *Diffusion of Innovations*, New York: The Free Press, 1983.

[2]   Easingwood, C., and C. Beard, "High Technology Launch Strategies in the UK," *Industrial Marketing Management*, Vol. 18, 1989, pp. 125–138.

[3]   Rosen, B. N., "The Standard Setter's Dilemma," *Industrial Marketing Management*, Vol. 23, No. 3, July 1994.

[4]   Sculley, J., *Odissey*, New York: Harper & Row, 1988.

[5]   Bennet, P. D. (ed.), *The Dictionary of Marketing Terms*, Chicago, IL: American Marketing Organization, 1988.

[6]   European Society for Opinion and Marketing Research, Annual Market Study, Amsterdam, The Netherlands, July 1989.

[7]   Churchill, G. A., Jr., *Marketing Research—Methodological Foundations*, 5th ed., Fort Worth, TX: The Dryden Press, HBJ, 1991.

[8]   "Attitude Research, Conjoint Analysis Guided Ma Bell's Entry into Data Terminal Market," *Marketing News*, May 13, 1983, p. 12.

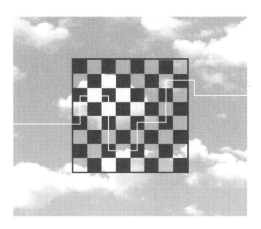

4

Understanding Competitors

The high-tech area is located at the heart of a modern economic battlefield and deals with a war of position. The winners often use new "weapons" that are actually technological innovations. For example, integrated software has driven away spreadsheets, workstations have swept away minicomputers, and robots have pushed away digital control machines.

Positions are constantly changing, as illustrated by the market development of the photoresist material, a chemical material used in manufacturing semiconductors. In 1975, four companies whose leaders were Toyo Ohka Kogyo and Shipley mastered the sophisticated photoresist material technology. Profitability was high. Then other companies developed similar technology and entered the market; the number of competitors grew to 20 in 1988.

Overinvestments in manufacturing capacities coupled with cutthroat competition drove down prices and profitability, putting many players out of the photoresist market in the early 1990s. Many sold their businesses to the remaining companies: Dynachem was bought by Hoechst, Kodak was acquired by KTI, and T&T was picked up by Olin. Today fewer than 10 companies are significant players in this market.

The marketing manager cannot ignore competitors who are also struggling to better satisfy and acquire (new) customers. The marketing manager must identify and analyze these competitors and understand their strategy while incorporating their technological dimension (because this dimension is very characteristic of the high-tech sector). Finally, the marketing manager must participate in the development of a systematic monitoring strategy for competitive information.

4.1 Identifying competitors

Arrogance and the underestimation of competitors can lead to a quick death in high-technology industries. One should always remember the haughtiness of mainframe computer makers toward the PC when it came out twenty years ago. They considered it a hacker's toy that did not interest business firms nor threaten their supremacy. Surprisingly enough, minicomputer makers—like DEC, HP, or Data General—had an identical opinion, though they had defeated the mainframe the same way desktop computers were going to defeat them.

When one considers the competition, one cannot only consider direct competitors but must look also at all the competitive forces on the supply side of firms that serve much the same markets within a given industry (or sector) and that may have an impact on the long-term industry average profitability.

4.1.1 Identification by market and by product

A competitive analysis must first analyze all the existing competitors who meet the same needs that the company currently meets or plans to meet. For example, a new resin based on polybutarene that can be used in the manufacturing of fire-resistant material does not only have similar resins as a competitor but also other fire-resistant components, such as asbestos and ceramics. What the customer buys is not a resin but a "resistance to fire" that will be integrated into his or her own product.

The marketing manager must identify his or her main competitors on the basis of market/product combinations by trying to identify possible future uses of these products by customers in different markets. Figure 4.1 uses this method to provide an example of an analysis for the computer industry.

Sun Microsystems started out manufacturing workstations for university researchers. However, a workstation is really a large local computation capacity for the user who is connected to a standard operating system such as UNIX. This system corresponds exactly to the needs of banks for their trading rooms. Sun Microsystems was able to respond to the banks' demands and became one of the leading suppliers of this industry. Silicon Graphics (SG) has a similar story. The vendor of the most powerful workstation, SG made its fame first as the favorite tool for computer-aided design in the manufacturing industry before successfully entering the financial market as well as the governmental organization. Building on its technicality and power, SG offered a more powerful computer and entered the mainframe market, namely, worldwide Fortune 500 companies, major universities, and big government agencies. Ultimately, SG bought Cray, the scientific supercomputer vendor, and secured almost half of the market. Its biggest competitor is now Compaq, which bought Tandem Computer to complete its offer in the mainframe business. Compaq originally began in the PC business. It started as an IBM PC clone vendor, the smartest in its category. Then in 1989, it introduced its first server, the system Pro, which could run up to five different operating systems, before launching in 1992 the successful Prosignia server, a low-price, high-performance solution, and then, in 1993, the Proliant 1000, an easy-to-install, easy-to-use server. Ultimately, Compaq bought Tandem, the leading fault-tolerant minicomputer vendor, and DEC, which gave Compaq access to the mainframe customers, mostly in banks, education, and government offices.

Dell is on the same track as Compaq. It started as a PC vendor, only through direct marketing, first to consumers, then to small business, and finally to larger organizations. Then Dell managed to move successfully upscale by offering to its corporate customers first workstations and then servers. Gateway is less advanced on the experience curve. It started providing PCs to consumers before expanding its customer base to small businesses and then big firms.

Market segment

Product offering	Corporate (+)	Education	Government	Small business/ Home office	Healthcare	Personal
Mainframe	Compaq Silicon Graphics IBM	Compaq Silicon Graphics	Compaq Silicon Graphics IBM		Compaq Silicon Graphics	
Minis (servers)	IBM Compaq HP Silicon Graphics Sun Unisys Dell	IBM Compaq HP Silicon Graphics Sun Unisys Dell	IBM Compaq HP Silicon Graphics Sun Unisys Dell	IBM Compaq HP Dell Gateway	IBM Compaq HP Dell Gateway	
Workstation	IBM Compaq Silicon Graphics Sun Dell	IBM Compaq Silicon Graphics Sun Dell	IBM Compaq Silicon Graphics Sun Dell	IBM Compaq Dell	IBM Compaq Dell	IBM Compaq Dell
PCs (portable and desktop)	IBM Compaq HP Silicon Graphics* Sun* Unisys Dell Gateway	IBM Compaq HP Silicon Graphics* Sun* Unisys Dell Apple	IBM Compaq HP Silicon Graphics* Sun* Unisys Dell Gateway	IBM Compaq HP Dell Apple Gateway	IBM Compaq HP Dell	IBM Compaq HP Dell Apple Gateway

(+) Corporate includes: Manufacturing, insurance, and financial sectors
* Manufactures only desktop PCs

Figure 4.1 Product/market segments in the computer industry (manufacturers with largest market share).

IBM is still the leading mainframe vendor for financial and nonscientific applications. It also has the biggest relative market share with its AS400 minicomputer family, which is a winner with all kinds of organizations—big and small, private or governmental. The RISC work station family is also giving IBM a strong position in all those market. In the PC business, IBM covers all the market segments with its different PC brands but is the second vendor behind Compaq but before HP, the minicomputer specialist whose solutions are appreciated by various types of business customers and governmental organizations.

These various examples clearly indicate that competitors may migrate from one market segment to another. Consequently, a firm that wants to match its competitors' capabilities must be ready to extend its technology base.

A similar analysis can be done for the electronic commerce industry, which encompasses all of the firms that are trading information, goods, services, and payments by electronic means. This industry has two chief markets, businesses and consumers, and offers three broad types of solutions, online information services; messaging, including electronic data interchange (EDI) for business customers; and market transactions.

If for the same product, several brands can compete with each other on similar or different price levels, it is also important to identify close-substitute products that can take a product's place. For a long time, the ultrasound market consisted of only two-dimensional ultrasound echographs, but they are now beginning to be replaced by three-dimensional ultrasound echographs.

4.1.2 Identification of the competitive forces at the industry level

After positioning the competitor's offer to meet the market's needs, the marketing manager must analyze the competitor's situation in the industry (or sector) in which his or her own company operates. M. Porter has presented a useful framework for diagnosing industry structure that is built around five competitive forces [1]: the rivalry among existing competitors (as discussed previously), the threat of both substitute products and new entrants, and the bargaining power of both suppliers and buyers.

4.1.2.1   Threat of substitute products

Because of the highly innovative nature of high-tech products, it is important to understand the threat from substitute products driven by indirectly competitive technologies. Substitute products can put an end to an existing technology by making it useless. To understand risks imposed by new technologies, these risks should be evaluated by application (by type of needs being met) rather than by product.

Consider how an integrated software (spreadsheet + text + graphics) such as Microsoft Works competes directly with word-processing software, for example, Microsoft Word. These software programs could be endangered by pen-recognition software used on personal digital assistants such as Newton message pad and Change by Palm III. So far pen-recognition software packages have flopped because they had limited abilities and capacities and were not really helpful to nonspecialized users. One day, however, new software like that from Papyrus Limited, a small European software company highly specialized in pen-recognition software, may succeed where Apple Computer and EO, a former subsidiary of AT&T, have failed so far. This will make the integrated software programs in their current form obsolete and unusable. In any case, the customer's need and, therefore, the market stay the same: the ability to easily and quickly write documents that are easy to read and to understand.

Similarly, data and voice transmission via the Internet is increasingly competing with the proprietary solutions offered by telephone companies. In data communication hardware, router and switch vendors like Cisco, Bay Networks, or Alcatel are facing the Asynchronous Transfer Mode (ATM) technology, which could make all their equipment obsolete.

In the online services industry, companies offering solutions on PC-based information networks are facing new competitors who try to set up an audiovisual gateway through televisions and set-top boxes. European companies like BskyB, British Telecom, Sagem Canal Plus, and others are competing to develop such a gateway, which requires the joining of access devices, file servers, and distribution networks. Meanwhile, software suppliers like Oracle, Microsoft, and others are struggling to design the standard for the operating system software that will run the access devices and files servers, looking for the same supremacy that MS-DOS gave Microsoft in the PC market.

4.1.2.2 Threat of new entrants

New entrants are companies that are attracted by the high profit level in a sector and wish to establish themselves in that sector, usually with the help of both new products and technologies. Their access depends on the level of entry barriers. In the high-technology sector, entry barriers can be high if there are strong capital requirements (it cost Intel $1 billion for its latest state-of-the-art components factory), if significant economies of scale and learning effects are present (an absolute necessity in the computer memory industry), if a high number of governmental licenses are necessary (as in the biotechnology industry), if gaining distribution is particularly difficult, if a strong corporate or brand image exists already (as in the case of home electronics products), and if there is a significant product differentiation that leads to strong customer loyalty.

In the high-tech sector, as in many other sectors, the entry barriers are lower at the early stage of the technology or product life cycle. For instance, in the PC business, the big Japanese consumer-electronics companies like Matsushita and Sony have the marketing abilities and the distribution channels sufficient to enter the game and to become direct competitors of IBM, Compaq, or Apple in the United States and European markets. Matsushita already sells the "Woody," an all-in-one TV/PC/CD player, in Japan under its Panasonic brand, and in 1993 Sony sold nearly $1 billion in CD-ROM drives, monitors, and other PC parts in the United States through its components and computer peripheral division.

Similarly, over the past decade in Europe, some of the leading multimedia companies are new entrants. In Sweden, Nethold, through its film net subsidiary, dominates the pay-TV industry, while the German company Kirch owns one of the most successful television stations. In the United Kingdom, BskyB towers above the satellite television market, while across Europe, Astra, belonging to Luxembourg-based SES, is the leading distributor of satellite TV. In France, Canal Plus now leads the pay television market, while Lyonnaise des Eaux and Générale des Eaux—originally water utilities—are running much of the country's cable infrastructure.

4.1.2.3 The bargaining strength of suppliers

The power of suppliers is an additional major determinant of industry competition, and its impact can be significant, especially if there is a limited number of suppliers. It is exercised largely through an increased price, which may lower the margin of the suppliers' customers if the customers cannot pass the increase to their own customers. The power of suppliers is even more important if the switching cost and the prices of substitutes are high. Such is the case for almost all the PC manufacturers that must rely on Intel for microprocessors and on Microsoft for operating system software.

4.1.2.4 The bargaining strength of buyers

In their efforts to get reduced prices, added services, or better product quality, among other concessions, buyers play individual suppliers against one another. The extent to which they succeed depends upon the extent of buyers' concentration (the more limited the number of buyers that account for a large portion of industry, the more clout); the switching costs; the product's importance to the performance of the buyer's product (the greater the importance, the lower their bargaining power); the buyer profitability (the more a product is an important part of the cost, the more aggressive the bargaining); and the threat of backward integration, which may soften the need for the supplier.

In 1994, Carrefour, the biggest French retailer, started to sell a new Pentium-based PC under its own private label. Given the steady growth that the private label has enjoyed in an increasing number of nonfood categories, this may be the beginning of a vast shake-out of the PC market in France and probably in the rest of Europe. Already private labels represent a significant part of the sales of TVs, cameras, and VCRs.

In conclusion, the size of the sector and the number of players should always be carefully analyzed. The higher the number of participants, the more difficult it will be to establish prices. It is also necessary to differentiate product performance and quality of service in order to achieve competitive advantages on a market segment. Because of their highly technical specialization, high-tech companies that operate worldwide deal with a limited number of customers, which requires them to have an international strategy. On the other hand, the limited size of the target market and the amount of investment required to succeed in the high-technology sector often limit the number of competitors. Therefore, the difficulty is to locate these competitors and, more importantly, to analyze their game.

4.2 Analyzing a competitor's strategy

Before performing a detailed study of individual direct competitors, it is a useful practice to identify and group different types of competitors.

4.2.1 Strategic groupings of companies

Generally speaking, in a particular market, the more companies are alike, the more they will have a tendency to compete against each other. This observation leads to the definition of strategic groups—a collection of companies that have performed similar strategic choices.

For example, in the database software market, there is a clear division between very general-application, easy-to-use database software products and highly specialized, mission-critical packages.

In the former category, companies like Microsoft, with its Access product, and Borland, with its Paradox, have carved niches with fairly inexpensive, graphical users interface (GUI) database packages for inexperienced database users.

In the latter category, companies like Oracle, with Oracle 8, and Sybase, with SQL, have developed a market for advanced, relational database products. These databases run networks and handle unstructured text, images, audio, and video information in addition to traditional structured alphanumeric data in familiar database tables and rows (see Figure 4.2).

The boundaries of strategic groups are open and susceptible to change, especially in a sector where markets are formed and disbanded very quickly. For example, the great generalists are more often challenged by computer manufacturers such as IBM and Digital Equipment that hope to expand into the software sector. Certain developers of specific microcomputer products compete today with the superspecialized group by adapting their products to more powerful machines, such as minicomputers and workstations.

The number and size of strategic groups as well as the "strategic distance" that separates them should be correctly identified. Groups that are larger, more significant, and more recent will experience more fierce competition.

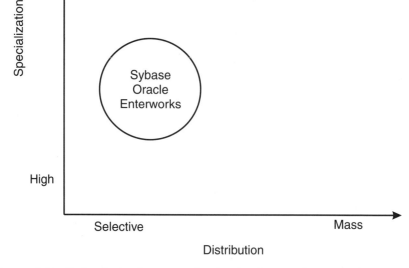

Figure 4.2 Main strategic groups in the database software industry.

4.2.2 Competitive analysis

When the marketing manager performs an analysis of strategic groups, he or she must collect and evaluate a certain amount of data about the company's competitors that will enable him or her to identify their strengths and weaknesses simultaneously (so as to exploit their weaknesses better). For each competitor, sales, financial, industrial, and political information should be analyzed.

Sales data essentially concerns sales figures, market share, the type of sales, the level of competition in the selected sales channels, brand awareness and product availability, and the level of after-sales service.

Financial data includes profit margins, analysis of costs (which appear on the income statement), profitability, asset turnover (which measures the efficient use of resources), long-term debt ratio, and the short-term cash flow. For companies listed on the stock exchange, the price/earnings ratio (PER) reflects their position on the stock market and their credit in the opinion of investors.

The information used to provide financial data should not be underestimated. Bain and Company, a large American consulting firm, earned admiration and respect from one of its clients when it predicted that the client's main competitor would soon be forced to increase its prices, not because of the market, but because of a considerable rise in the dividend paid to stockholders. Increasing the amount of dividends paid forced this competitor to adjust its margins and, as a result, increase prices. Rising prices for the competitor's main products could, therefore, be anticipated and actually took place about two months later.

The most important industrial data concerns investment programs and manufacturing capacities. The opening or closing of a factory is an important sign of success or failure for a product. This type of information also often leads to short- or long-term price changes because of resulting volume fluctuations. Many high-technology firms are inclined to overinvest in manufacturing facilities because they believe, incorrectly, that they will secure superior product quality and lower costs as well as dissuade potential entrants. For instance, in 1995, Sony and Sanyo announced investments in lithium ion battery cell manufacturing facilities of $30 million and $40 million, respectively, in a market worth only $400 million. Consequently, such massive investments increase a firm's tendency to persist in businesses long after they have ceased to be profitable. Technology changes in the manufacturing process will also allow a competitor to earn a productivity gain that can then be reflected in the sales price.

Political data concerns, for example, the relationship between a parent company and a subsidiary and the subsidiary's degree of autonomy in making strategic choices. When the subsidiary of a competitor is not very independent and merely executes the parent company's policies, understanding its strategy will be easier than for a more autonomous company.

In the computer industry, NCR was recognized as a worldwide, rather centralized company whereas IBM subsidiaries used to enjoy, each in their own country, a fairly large degree of decision-making autonomy when selecting the markets and products they preferred (but this has

definitely changed with the new more centralized organization introduced by the new CEO Lou Gesteener in 1994).

Governmental relations in the high-technology industry should also
be analyzed due to the influence of governments in this sector, either on
the demand level (government markets, military markets) or on the supply level (Plan Calcul in France, SDI program in the United States, and
Jessi and Eureka programs in Europe).

Interacting with governments is a very important feature of the competitive game in high-technology sectors. For example, Apple was barred
by the French government from entering the French education market to
the benefit of Thomson, the French government-owned electronic company, and its TO5 computer; on the world market, Arianespace struggles
against the dumping prices of Chinese and Soviet rocket-launching companies that are completely financed by their governments.

Finally, governmental constraints can especially be felt by the importance of standards in international contracts. For example, the European
Union's taxation on the broadcasting of television programs by the
D2 Mac satellite killed the market of D-Mac decoders. This decision
caused problems for companies such as Thomson and Philips because
they had to stop production (more than 60,000 per month) of D-Mac
decoders, but this same decision benefited a Finnish company, Nokia,
which was already very advanced in the development of D2 Mac
decoders.

The competitor's culture should also be taken into account. For
example, many American companies are obsessed by their quarterly
earnings. These figures determine their stock's value (a decrease can
considerably increase the cost of financing) or can lead to a collapse
of the value. This happened to some American biotechnology companies, the best known of which is Genentech. After being the stars of
Wall Street, these biotechnology companies saw their stock value collapse due to their inability to quickly come up with profitable products.
Some of these companies still find it difficult to finance and maintain their
daily business activities.

In comparison, Japanese companies, whose presence is continuously
becoming more important, value capturing markets even if it reduces
earnings and is time consuming. These companies are not playing poker

but the Oriental game of go, and they faithfully practice "surrounding." Once these Japanese companies master a new technology, they file applications for a vast number of patents, even on spin-off products. Then these companies inundate the market with continuously improved products that aim to provide a product "tailor-made" for the customer's needs. These companies will lead a fierce struggle to increase their market share by offering lower prices.

The manager's personality is also an element to be taken into account. Certain companies cannot advance when their founder (usually the person who came up with an innovation of genius) refuses to understand that his or her technology is outdated and that others must be developed.

Finally, a competitor's management style and organization must also be studied. For example, a large electronics company analyzed in detail the average time period spent by executives in the industry on certain jobs so that it could determine if it was moving its own managers at the same rate as the majority of companies in the industry.

All these analyses as well as the evaluation of technology form a competitor's profile by identifying strengths (to be avoided) and weaknesses (of which to take advantage). This will help companies identify their various competitive advantages. For instance, competitors like satellite providers and cable operators can use distinct competitive advantages. Satellite providers offer a low-cost solution, especially to cover rural and thinly populated areas, that is able to bypass local content limitations. Cable operators offer an interactive solution through services like PPV or video-on-demand (VOD), a high-speed Internet access with better broadband capacity and picture quality than satellite, without the need for satellite dishes. However, the significance of the analysis depends in large part on the quality and the reliability of the information sources.

4.3 Finding information about competitors

Table 4.1 lists the most important available information sources that are used to evaluate a competitor. More than 20 sources are listed. Without going into detail, let us examine them by distinguishing between a company's external and internal sources.

Table 4.1
Information Sources Used for Competitive Purposes

Information Source	Type of Information				
	Sales	Finance	Industry	Politics	Technology
Customers	•		•		•
Competitors	•	•	•	•	•
Benchmarking			•		•
Patents			•		•
Licenses	•	•	•	•	•
Trade shows	•			•	•
International conventions and conferences	•				•
Partnerships		•	•		•
Standardization committees			•	•	•
Study trips			•	•	•
Consulting firms	•	•	•		
Governmental competitive intelligence organizations	•	•	•	•	•
Data banks	•	•	•	•	•
Specialized press books, other media types	•	•	•	•	•
Suppliers/subcontractors	•	•	•	•	•
Distributors	•	•	•	•	•
Sales force	•	•			
Maintenance service					•
Employees who used to work for the competition	•	•	•	•	•
Employment applicants	•	•			•
Former employees	•	•	•	•	•
Alumni networks	•	•	•	•	•

4.3.1 External sources

Clients, of course, are the sources of privileged information. This is particularly true for industrial goods and services, where customers are usually few in number and always ready to talk if the right questions are asked. Every good marketing manager should regularly visit customers to determine their needs; this visit is the perfect opportunity to learn more about recent offers or propositions from competitors.

Competitors also furnish a great deal of information. If analyzed sufficiently, their annual reports are a good source of financial information. The information sent to stockholders and speeches given by their executives also provide good ideas regarding the company's strategy and key success factors.

Their advertising literature, especially catalogues and descriptive product information, supply useful information for technical specialists who are familiar with decoding these types of documents. Company newsletters and press releases also mention new product launchings and sales data that have yet to become public knowledge.

Becoming a supplier for a competitor is another way to obtain practical information. Supplying supplementary products to its product line, necessary components for the manufacturing of certain products, or spare parts for after-sales service is a good way to become familiar with a company. Fujitsu, a Japanese company, was a long-term supplier to British ICL before finally buying out the company in 1990.

Understanding a competitor's products is obviously an essential step. It can be realized through reverse engineering, which means tearing down the machines of a competitor and then trying to rebuild them, or benchmarking, which means comparing the performance of a business component with others. In the early 1980s Xerox used benchmarking to obtain cost-reduction ideas. It targeted organizations in other industries that were particularly efficient in functional areas similar to those at Xerox. Hence, Toyota and Komatsu became models for quality control, American Express for invoicing, American Hospital Supply for inventory management, AT&T and Hewlett-Packard for research and development, Ford Motor and Cummings Engine for factories layout, Procter & Gamble for marketing, Deere and Company for information technologies management, Texas Instrument for strategy implementation, and L.L. Bean for warehouse operations. In the logistic and distribution area, the benchmark study of L.L. Bean, the outdoor sportswear organization and mail-order house, along with five other warehouse benchmark studies, helped Xerox improve its annual productivity gains from 3 to 5% to around 10% [2].

Patents are a useful source of information about a competitors' technological know-how, as in the case that concerned the IBM Personal Computer. In the mid-1980s, various companies, including Compaq Computer and AMD Computer, succeeded in designing a piece of firmware, the Read Only Memory Basic Input/Output System (ROM-BIOS), which coupled the PC hardware to its operating system software. It was similar to IBM's but did not violate the IBM proprietary microcode.

Consequently, such companies were able to make and sell IBM-compatible PCs, the so-called clones, without paying any royalty fees to IBM. For this reason, in some industries, it may be better not to patent a component or a process but to rely on secrecy. Coca-Cola or Michelin have used this rule for years to keep their technological know-how out of reach of their competitors.

Trade shows also present opportunities to examine competitors' products on display, especially new products. The Japanese have specialized in obtaining this type of information, using video cameras that are capable of capturing 90% of a product's interesting elements in less than five minutes.

Conferences and conventions also present the opportunity to meet competitors and to take advantage of information, often first-hand and very recent, presented at meetings. These types of events often facilitate the building of strong relations. Competitors become colleagues, and these contacts can become useful at a later date.

Partnerships with other companies for important projects are also a way to create privileged relations. In the partnership, information circulates more quickly and more easily. Sometimes this is the only reason to participate in an important project. For example, it is widely suspected that IBM wanted to stay involved in the European Union–funded JESSI project so that it could share the work of major European manufacturers.

Standardization committees, very common in the high-tech industry, often shed light on many topics. When competitors present propositions for standards, the competitors often use their own standards. On the contrary, a competitor's refusal to accept a product's standardization often reveals a company's technological, industrial, or political position.

Study trips, if well prepared, are a good source of sales and industrial information. These trips allow one to locate products that have not yet appeared on the local market or discover unknown manufacturing methods.

These trips have a very high cost. To make them worthwhile, they must be planned and focused around a set of information-seeking objectives. The tasks should be divided in order to facilitate collecting information in a thorough manner but without duplication. In addition, the newly acquired information should be outlined in reports that can be distributed to interested parties.

Specialized consulting companies that follow a certain industry on a regular basis also supply sales, financial, or technological information. In the computer industry, companies such as Dataquest, the Gartner Group, the Meta Group, or Ovum send market information to their subscribers on a regular basis and provide forecasts and consulting specialists to obtain additional information.

All these companies, and some even more specialized companies, can do ad hoc studies of a certain field, a selected market segment, or a particular competitor. These studies are completed with the help of interviews with specialists, clients, distributors, or even competitors. The results are then analyzed and synthesized.

For consumer high-technology goods, panels are becoming a viable information source. These high-tech panels are based upon panels for more traditional goods such as detergents, soft drinks, and industrial goods. Consumer or distributor panels can very quickly follow changes in demand and a competitor's position. Panels provide a realistic picture of a competitive situation at a given moment, but the specific characteristics of high technology limit their usefulness. Particularly, a panel's predictive value is weak due to the fast evolution of products and the difficulty in understanding innovation.

Specialized administrative agencies assist technological development and can furnish useful information.

Public or private data banks furnish exhaustive information on nearly all subjects. Their main shortcoming is that they can furnish a limited piece of information immediately (often the size of one or two computer screens per subject) but require a long waiting period (one month or even more) in order to obtain any additional documents.

The specialized press inundates its readers with information. The news that the press brings is readily available and relatively inexpensive but also often late and rarely confidential. The number of journals and magazines continues to grow exponentially.

For true operational efficiency, it is necessary to read useful periodicals, not only those for one's own profession but also periodicals in the competitor's field. Previewing information in magazines can be achieved by distributing magazines among members of the marketing department.

Periodicals can be used to acquire technical, marketing, financial, and industrial data on competitors in a useful and operational way. For example, small employment ads can often reveal a great deal to those who read between the lines. The same principles apply to the study of books and other media such as television (commentaries), films (for public relation purposes), or radio (interviews with managers).

A supplier, or a subcontractor, who works with several competitors, often has valuable information regarding his or her customers' strategies. In the computer industry, 50% of all disk drives come from the same supplier, who must have an overall view of the market.

However, a talkative supplier chats with his or her own clients as well; one cannot keep hidden forever. The high-tech world is small and everybody knows everybody. Nevertheless, it is not the manufacturing secret that counts but rather how quickly a product is put on the market.

Distributors can provide information on the business policy and technological experience of competitors. These distributors are also centrally "located" so as to evaluate the general policy of different actors in the market. Not all distributors are able to do this, but time is never wasted in discussions with well-informed distributors.

4.3.2   Internal sources

The sales force, of course, is a source of privileged information about competitors—through contacts with a customer's or a prospect's intermediary. Actually, such is the case for all employees who have contact with the outside buyers (who can use the same suppliers as competitors), maintenance services people, or delivery people (who often frequent customers).

High-technology companies (especially in exploding markets) are often characterized by a high rate of turnover, but this can be an advantage. Employees who used to work for the competition—from executives to interns—are obviously good informers, even more so if they recently left their previous employer.

The same is valid for employment applicants who have had interviews with competitors; an interview offers a good opportunity from which to proceed to a competitive evaluation. Obviously, competitors can carry out the same maneuvers.

Finally, it is always useful to keep in contact with former employees, especially if the firm is a startup company that could become a competitor in the same industry. Alumni meetings and networks supply contacts that can be extremely profitable. Alumni networks can also lead to opportunities and additional information.

4.4 Organizing competitive analysis

Certain companies have instituted permanent "monitoring" systems, while others have less formal structures. This leads to two questions: "Who is responsible for competitive analysis?" and "How should competitive analysis be performed?"

4.4.1 Who performs the competitive analysis?

Modeled after Japanese companies, monitoring departments in charge of examining a company's long-term environment have been established in Europe and the United States. This department is responsible for competitive studies. From the marketing department it receives sales and financial information. From the research and development department(s) it obtains technological evaluations; manufacturing provides industrial elements. The finance department also makes contributions.

However, the majority of companies do not have a separate structure devoted to this type of exercise. When asked about monitoring competitors, marketing managers are among the first to admit that monitoring is often insufficient or inadequately performed due to a lack of financial resources and available methods.

In our opinion, in the absence of clearly defined responsibilities, the marketing manager must carry out the competitive analysis, for two reasons. The first reason is of a theoretical nature: the purpose of marketing is to serve the customer's needs, although competitors can unfortunately prevent the achievement of this goal. The most attractive marketing strategy with the best combination of possible resources can be reduced to nothing if the marketing manager does not timely identify, for example, the competitors' new solutions, their exact market introduction, their new advantages for the customer, and their price. The competitive analysis must be included in the marketing strategy because it is one of the elements necessary for its success.

The second reason is a practical reason: scale economics. Essential information about the competition is obtained from the same sources as those necessary to understand the market and its needs (see Chapter 3). Consequently, all the data can be obtained at the same time (for instance, in a questionnaire or a sales call) at a lower unit cost. This is quite significant because every piece of information about competition comes at a cost. Accordingly, the marketing manager must weigh cost by the value that it represents, and in the high-technology industry this necessary procedure is even more important than in other areas because information can become outdated much faster.

4.4.2   Performing the competitive analysis

Experience shows that when performing the competitive analysis, the marketing manager must have a basic assumption to be efficient: better keep it simple instead of thinking big. Because the marketing manager's task is to pass on competitive information that he or she has at his or her disposal to areas where it can be the most useful within the company, his or her first challenge is to define the information needs. To do so, the marketing manager can perform an internal market study of the different departments of the company with the help of a questionnaire to determine their needs.

The second challenge is the organization and collection of information. As an executive of the Boston Consulting Group indicates: "Too often, in high-tech companies, the monitoring of competitors is not taken seriously. For example, reverse engineering is practically never carried out." The responsibility of the marketing department is to identify the different necessary sources of information and to set up methods for the systematic disbursement of information to appropriate departments. Without asking for long reports from each sales person, it is obvious that "walking the hallways" will not lead to a precise understanding of the competition in the market. These methods can be adapted to every company, but the marketing department must assure its implementation.

Finally, coordination between research and development, manufacturing, and after-sales service departments is a necessity (as we will see in Chapter 10). As stressed by numerous marketing managers, the information is usually available, but the analysis is not performed correctly. More particularly, putting sales and technological data in perspective is important when performing a competitive analysis.

Only departments with technological expertise can carry out an evaluation and a serious monitoring of the competitors' possibilities. The marketing manager must then be able to compare these evaluations and monitoring activities to his or her own sales, financial, and industrial data. Is a company with a new revolutionary manufacturing process really a dangerous competitor? Are its distributors or its customers not satisfied with the current product's poor performance and ready to switch to another company? Is the company on the edge of bankruptcy? If so, which other competitor has sufficient cash flow and strategic interest to buy out this company?

In fact, the monitoring of competitors is everyone's responsibility. Analyses performed by a company's headquarters (usually by employees who are often far removed from the company's day-to-day activities) must be enriched by viewpoints from all members of the company who can add useful information.

Marketing has to combine these energies in such a way that the monitoring of competitors becomes "an obsession, even if in this field much can be improved," according to the marketing director of a major European software company.

4.5 Chapter summary

The high-technology-product world is extremely competitive. Positions are gained and lost much more quickly than in other markets. Therefore, the marketing manager must know his or her competitors in order to set up a strategy.

First, the competitors must be identified. Competitors are companies who respond to customers' expectations with similar products or with different substitutes for the actual products. Furthermore, a product's technology cannot only be challenged by a direct technology but also by an indirect technology that can completely take over.

Next, strategies of competitors (including strengths and weaknesses) must be analyzed. In order to do so, a synthesis of sales, financial, industrial, political, and technological data must be performed.

This information can be obtained from many different sources from outside (competitors, trade shows, conferences) or inside the company.

When a monitoring department (a "watch dog") exists for the monitoring of a company's long-term environment, it is usually in charge of evaluating competitors. If no specially assigned department exists, the marketing department is usually in charge of this activity. Actually, responsible for the market, the marketing department will be the first to feel the impact of a competitor's actions and must anticipate these actions. In addition, competitive information sources are similar to those needed to understand the market.

For a good evaluation, the informational needs of the entire company should be well defined and efficiently coordinated with the technical departments. Information must be complied in an organized and systematic manner but with the realization that monitoring the competition is everybody's, not just the specialist's, responsibility.

References

[1] Porter, M. E., *Competitive Strategy: Techniques for Analyzing Industries and Competitors*, New York: The Free Press, 1980.

[2] Tucker, F. G., S. M. Zivan, and R. Camp, "How To Measure Yourself Again the Best," *Harvard Business Review*, January–February 1987.

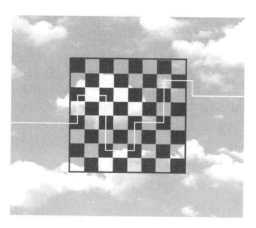

5

Selecting Markets

B ecause the role of marketing is to ensure that a company's products correspond well to customer wants and expectations, it is necessary to know these customers well and to determine the most important customers.

Actually, few companies target all consumers or all companies. Even when this is possible, customers' needs are so varied that these customers must be offered different products. The time when one product sufficed to satisfy demand is over. Consumers have become more demanding and more informed, and competition drives companies to differentiate themselves and individualize their markets.

There is no longer one Coca-Cola; there is Coke Classic, new Coke, Diet Coke, and Coca-Cola in a bottle and in a can. Ford stopped only producing its "Model T" when it was surpassed by General Motors; today Ford produces more than 20 different models of cars. In the services industry, airline companies fight to prove that they offer different products than their competitors by offering a "bonus" to frequent flyers, more leg room in their business class, classier meals, friendlier airline attendants, or simply more practical schedules.

This situation can also be found in the world of high technology: the same chemical molecule can be sold under two different names and with a different price depending on whether it is used as an adhesive or an insulator; the same software will be sold as a basic version—without an instruction booklet or a set of installation guidelines—to universities with limited funds by many software specialists, while a more comprehensive version that will include installation, instruction, and maintenance will be sold to companies at a higher price.

Because not everyone can be satisfied with the same product, groups of customers with similar needs must be identified. This process is called "market segmentation." A "market segment" groups customers who have the same demands, buying behavior, or some other significant characteristic.

One should note that segmentation always concerns customers and markets, never products. This fact is important in avoiding any misinterpretation, especially for high-technology companies that sometimes have a tendency to see the world more through the beauty of their products than through their customers' needs.

Once they have segmented their markets, high-technology companies need to target one or many of those markets in order to respond better to their customers and to optimize the use of their resources. Their strongly innovative side requires that these companies group the most innovation-receptive customers who then will be able to convince other customers. Furthermore, the short product life cycle and the urge to develop products quickly require a very precise determination of the needs of a limited number of customers, taking into account the necessary resources to respond to their demands while keeping an eye on the development of new technologies. This is one of the reasons why markets for high-tech products are often very specialized niche markets. Once a segment has been targeted, the ultimate step is to define the positioning of the solution that the firm wants to offer so that it will have a unique image and position vis-à-vis the competitors in the mind of the selected customer group.

By following this three-step strategic marketing process, namely:

- Segmentation;
- Targeting;
- Positioning;

the marketer will be able to design an effective operational marketing mix for a solution, namely, the definition of the product, the choice of the distribution channels, the type of promotion and communication, as well as the pricing policy.

5.1   Two market segmentation methods for high-tech products and services

When marketing successfully high-tech solutions, two approaches exist: market-driven marketing for products that customers are awaiting and product-driven marketing for technically revolutionary products. The first approach is based upon market demand, whereas the second approach is based upon the views of the technical creator (see Figure 5.1).

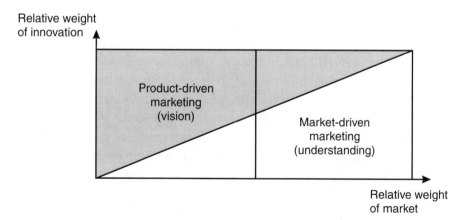

Figure 5.1   Selecting target markets from vision to understanding. Shaded areas represent technological breakthrough in product; nonshaded areas represent technological improvement in product.

On one side, a large number of high-tech products are launched by customer demand in response to an expressed or latent need. Many of these products only show variations of an original product with simply some improvements that were requested by the customers. Microcomputers are becoming more and more compact, portable, and powerful; but, apart from the introduction of PDAs, they have not really changed since 1981. The same applies to laser-technology consumer goods: since the introduction of laser video discs, no other revolutionary products have been introduced.

For these market-driven products, segmentation methods that are developed and frequently used in marketing can generally be used. These segmentation methods rely on a good market understanding in order to keep a close watch on the market's expectations.

However, on the other side, how can a market for a new technology (coming from a research laboratory or a creative genius) be evaluated? Who were the customers for the first Philips buffered terminal video recorder, the first Vivitar reusable photocamera, or for the new chip card for an innovation automobile? Sony's founder, Akio Morita, has always contended that "the public does not know what is possible, but we do..." [1].

To determine the potential customers to whom these new technologies are directed, the needs that these technologies satisfy as well as the products that will materialize them must be anticipated and understood. Each in his own way, Steve Jobs (Apple Computer), Ken Olsen (DEC), and John Watson (IBM) saw the incredible potential of the computer industry. Anticipating the changes that a new technology will bring to the market requires foresight [2], and the traditional methods that are used to identify particular market segments must be adjusted.

The dichotomy between market-driven marketing and product-driven marketing leads to two different segmentation methods, depending on the situation. Market demand divides the market into different segments, the needs of which are analyzed before defining a product. This is called segmentation by breakdown. The market's vision, from an already existing product, can identify a certain number of customers who will serve as a basis, by extrapolating, for the definition of segments. This is called segmentation by grouping.

In reality, these two approaches sometimes end up concurring; an extremely innovative high-tech product sometimes becomes a successful product very quickly; the more popular it is, the more market-driven. The marketing manager must therefore adjust his or her segmentation methods. He or she must change from segmentation by grouping to segmentation by breakdown.

The last specific feature of segmentation for high-tech products involves time, a fundamental dimension that shapes the market's outer edges and forces them to change very rapidly.

5.1.1 Product-driven market segmentation: the customer-grouping approach

Big ideas, great revolutionary inventions of new technical procedures, are at the start of a new product. More than 80% of all researchers of all time are still alive and working today, so it is not surprising to see the number of discoveries accelerate. Nevertheless, the intrinsic value of an invention does not necessary lead to a business success; the invention must be marketed adequately toward the right customers.

So, to efficiently assure the launching of products derived from a new technology, there is a five-step process that we have labeled "customer grouping." The first step is to estimate the product's value for the potential customers; the second step is to identify market segments by grouping easily identifiable customers; the third step is to evaluate those segments; the fourth step is to select the most profitable segments; the final step is to choose the positioning of the product within each selected segment before defining the marketing means that are implemented. Let us now review in detail those steps.

5.1.1.1 Internal evaluation of a product's marketing value

Marketing managers of high-tech products all agree that one of the essential qualities in their field is the ability to translate a new technology into a tangible response to a customer's need. This is the only way that a new technology can be sold on the market.

Every new technology must therefore be "transformed" into a product that corresponds to a need in order to determine the value in use and the utility value. For example, the electrochemical control of superconductivity—which is a technology—can have potential value for a customer because it responds to the need to measure magnetic fields or the need to detect magnetic aberrations using products such as the infrared adjustable detector.

In the same way, the use of barium ferrite for the magnetic recording of data instead of metal oxide—another technology—responds to the increasing need for information storage by users of microcomputers by incorporating this technology in the manufacturing of a new generation of diskettes. A final example is a new system of carbon atoms that was discovered in the United States in 1985 and has been dubbed the "carbon of the third kind," whose performance is such that researchers foresee a multitude of applications in the manufacturing of lubricants, batteries, or cancerous tumor treatments. If a new technology and its applications can be linked together to satisfy a need, marketers can start considering all potential customers.

Brainstorming and creativity techniques are often useful during this phase because a new technology can respond to different needs for various customers. For example, an underwater robot with an intelligent camera can be used for offshore oil drilling as well as for the maintenance of cooling systems in nuclear power plants. After a lot of thinking, ceramic fibers used by Bronzavia, a major European company, in the manufacturing of thermoprotected shields for the future European space shuttle Hermes have been adapted for the automotive industry to insulate turbo engines and catalytic pipes.

Another example is that of Casidiam, which is a new material that is harder than sapphire but nevertheless very pliable; it is an excellent thermal insulator but also a good conductor of heat. Casidiam is also impervious to hydrogen and chemically inert. All of these properties lead to Casidiam's various uses in electronics, mechanics, and the biomedical field.

5.1.1.2   Study of potential segments

Once a certain number of customers have been identified, they are grouped into categories of homogeneous needs to form different market segments.

The aforementioned robotics firm can distinguish between three large categories of customers: oil companies, nuclear engineering companies, and national power companies. The segments are defined by all the customers in the same category. For example, the "nuclear" segment groups EDF (the French electricity utility), CEA (a major laboratory specializing in R&D in the nuclear field, and Framatome (a major nuclear engineering firm).

For the first microcomputers, the first video recorders, or the first HDTVs, the high introductory price (due to the need to optimize R&D costs and to the lack of an economy of scale at the beginning of the manufacturing process) immediately determines segments of consumers with a high purchasing power because only a limited number of consumers can afford a product, whether it is innovative or not, whose price ranges from $6,000 to $10,000.

In those last cases, the marketing manager may complete the segmentation by selecting potential consumers according to sociocultural, psychosocial, personal, and psychological criteria, as seen in Chapter 3. For example, potential customers for an HDTV can be defined as TV addicts and showoffs, over 40, or people who watch TV at least four hours per day, like innovation in video, already own a video recorder and camcorder, are financially able to purchase an expensive product, and like to show it off.

It is not always easy to precisely identify these potential customers even though in the industrial market the number of actors is much more limited. The identification process often requires a long and complicated analysis of several files. However, when making a first estimation of potential segments, one possible short cut is to stick with the consumers who are currently using products that will most likely be replaced. Actually, HDTV replaces television, the computer ousts the calculator, and the compact disc player substitutes for the traditional turntable.

When these groupings and crosscheckings have been carried out, the marketing department will select key potential customers who are interested in the new innovation and are ready to test it. The process in which the product is subjected to extensive acceptance testing by a set of preferred customers is usually called "Beta testing," as opposed to "Alpha testing," which proves concepts in the protected environment of the company.

5.1.1.3 Selection of test customers

Beta testing is heavily used in many high-technology industries, like computers, software, telecommunications, or materials. Beta tests are run under nondisclosure agreements. Prototypes are installed at customer locations for a given period, usually for free or at bargain price, in order to measure users' reactions to the new product as well as possible product shortcomings.

The beauty of Beta tests is that they sometimes identify radically unexpected needs that the company had never previously considered. For instance, in the case of the underwater robot, the need for the maintenance of cooling systems in nuclear power plants was discovered during a test at a major electricity utility; the prototype was originally proposed for the inspection and the maintenance of white-water power dams.

In some firms, Beta tests are run exclusively by the R&D personnel, usually when the prototype comes from the R&D department under the assumption that the prototype needs only technical refinements to become a product. However, the ultimate goal of a Beta test is to evaluate the fit of the prototype with the needs of the customers. Too often R&D people will focus only on technical difficulties and possibly refuse to develop a new version of the prototype, even at the customers' request, because it is too simple (rarely, because it is too complicated, because researchers love tackling technical problems) or "not interesting."

Accordingly, it is essential that the marketing department be included in running the test so that the marketers can understand which solution the customers desire. Furthermore, by working closely with test customers, the marketers may gain not only a better knowledge of their needs but also hints about the price the market will be ready to accept, as well as ideas about the most efficient way to advertise and distribute the future product.

5.1.2   Market-driven market segmentation: the market-breakdown approach

Identifying market segments according to methods currently used for traditional products are valid for all high-technology products if the customer is the driving force. The products are improvements of products already on the market, so the market's boundaries have already been roughly identified. For instance, marketing managers of a company that is considering launching a new generation of personal computers or a new industrial welding robot usually have data about actual or potential users of personal computers or welding robots at their disposal.

On the basis of this information, these managers will also segment markets to determine which markets should be targeted first. This market breakdown approach is based on a very thorough understanding of the market and is also a five-step process. First, the marketer must select the segmentation criteria to break down the total market; second, he or she has to define each segment; the third step is to evaluate the business value of each segment; the fourth step is to select a certain number of segments; and in the final step the marketer has to choose the positioning and the marketing mix of each product in each segment.

5.1.2.1   Selecting segmentation criteria

The segmentation criteria that need to be considered are different when breaking down consumer markets and industrial markets.

For consumer markets, two large categories of segmentation criteria exist: criteria related to consumer characteristics and criteria related to their response to need (see Table 5.1).

Table 5.1

Major Segmentation Variables for Consumer Markets. (*Source*: [3].)

Characteristics			
Personal	**Psychographic**	**Sociocultural**	**Geographic**
Age	Social class	Religion	Region
Sex	Lifestyle	Race	City size
Family life cycle	Personality	Nationality	Density
Annual income			
Education			
Behaviors			
Benefits	**User status**	**Usage rate**	**Attitude Toward Product**
Economy	Nonuser	Light user	Loyal to brand
Convenience	Ex-user	Medium user	Enthusiastic
Prestige	Potential user	Heavy user	Positive
	First-time user		Indifferent
	Regular user		Negative
			Hostile

Because consumer characteristics have been discussed at length in Chapter 3, we only comment about consumers' behavior because segmentation by response seeks to divide homogeneous consumer groups by product knowledge and attitudes.

For instance, when considering the laser video disc market, it is interesting to know and to classify customers according to the advantages they seek in this product: performance (sound quality), prestige of new and expensive products, or use (laser discs take up less space than videocassettes). Consumers can then be classified according to the use of the laser video disc: Are they nonusers, potential users, current users, or ex-users? Users can be differentiated by their user rate (low, medium, high) and their degree of brand loyalty (Sony, Thomson, Philips). Attitudes of nonusers to this new product should be known: Are they aware of its existence? Are they interested? Do they plan on purchasing the product soon?

For industrial customers, segmentation criteria can also be regrouped in the categories of characteristics and behaviors, but some of the criteria to be considered are different from those used to segment consumer markets (see Table 5.2).

For instance, the size of a firm is very often an efficient basis for discrimination because the needs of small firms differ dramatically from those of large companies. Similarly, the geography of a firm is a key driver: in many aspects, one cannot compare the needs of a medium-sized company working only on its national market, whatever its size, with the needs of a medium-sized company doing business with 150 countries worldwide through 10 subsidiaries, 50 foreign distributors, and four manufacturing facilities located on four different continents.

Business or economic characteristics are also very useful in determining various groups of business customers. The nature of the industry, the size of customers, the kind of production and technology used, and the type of solutions offered create various needs in business firms.

Finally, the business needs of a firm are closely related to its organization, which can be heavily centralized or decentralized; the profile of the decision makers; and the purchasing policy.

Regarding the behavior criteria, they are quite similar to those used to segment consumer markets because they focus on the personalities of the identified buyers. However, in business-to-business marketing, contrary

Table 5.2
Major Segmentation Variables for Business Markets

Characteristics			
Dimensional	**Geographic**	**Economical**	**Organizational**
Number of employees	National or multinational	Turnover	Centralized or decentralized
Number of factories	Location of the headquarters	Main activity	Buying procedures
	Localization of subsidiaries	Type and size of customers	Profiles of decision makers
		Type of production process	
Behaviors			
Benefits	**Application**	**Attitude**	**Preferred Buying Behavior**
Economy	Type of application	Technical or nontechnical	Direct
Performance	User status (non-user, first-time user, regular user)	Attitude toward innovation (positive, negative, indifferent)	Through sales people
Prestige	Type of use (light, medium, heavy)	Brand loyalty	Through distributors
Reliability			Through OEM
Convenience			

to a product bought by consumers, a solution is bought for a specific application identified within the various processes of a firm, be it manufacturing, research, marketing, or administration. Furthermore, firms appear to have preferred ways of acquiring the solutions they need to perform their business; consequently, understanding their favorite channels is sometimes an interesting way to analyze a business market.

Many high-tech firms offer solutions to both consumers and business. Various examples are IBM and Compaq in the computer business,

Hughes and Thomson in electronics, and AT&T and British Telecom in the telecommunication business. All these firms have discovered that the needs and the buying behaviors of consumers and businesses are radically different even if sometimes the solutions they require are similar from a technological standpoint.

5.1.2.2   Defining segments

After selecting some key segmentation criteria, the next step is to define the content of segments by identifying the characteristics and behavior of customers. In consumer markets, segment contents are defined via market studies that consist of questionnaires filled out by population samples. These questionnaires often also measure the recognition and awareness of existing brands or the customer's opinion of product features for products already on the market. The processing of data (by factorial analysis or conjoint analysis) can classify and arrange all answers by regrouping them in different segments that are as homogeneous as possible.

In industrial markets, the limited number of customers can more easily lead to interviews with company representatives. Generally speaking, if a company's activities are more technical, then its customers are more identifiable. The potential users of space shuttle-launching services or of triaxial gyrolasers currently total only a few dozen in the entire world. For larger markets, using databases can lead to interesting selection procedures for segment identification purposes. One long-distance phone company identified a price-sensitive segment by mining its database for customers who placed their phone calls 15 minutes before rates increased in the morning and just after they decreased in the evening. Face-to-face and telephone interviews can fine tune the approach and redefine the narrowest segments characterized by a market profile.

5.2   Evaluating and selecting segments

Not all segments are of interest. Determining the most significant segments requires the evaluation of their potential—in terms of attainable volume and profit, their accessibility to the company's resources, their strategic significance for the company's mission, the position of competitors, and the level entry barriers. (See Figure 5.2.)

Marketers must perform these evaluations together with R&D and manufacturing departments, most specifically to check the technological possibilities. Actually, although a segment, such as consumers who wish to have multimedia functions on their computers, can prove to be attractive, it may be impossible to satisfy due to the current state of the company's technical abilities.

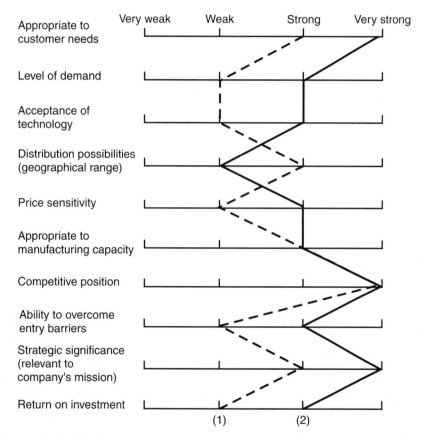

Figure 5.2 Evaluating two segments: an example. Segment 2 will be selected but distribution should be improved. (This could be the case for a company that is only present in the European market and not yet in the U.S. market.) Segment 1 is characteristic of an industry or a niche that is not yet ready to accept a new technology and its applications.

Outside the prospects of volume and profit by segment, industrial markets need to think more about their possibility of entry. Besides analyzing the position of competitors, all entry barriers of a segment—in particular, administrative and governmental stumbling blocks—must be evaluated. Actually, many markets are protected in the high-technology industry.

For example, the majority of U.S. military markets remain off-limits for non-U.S. companies. Hence, successfully penetrating these markets takes time and significant resource, but it is not an impossible task: the Department of Defense (DoD) selected ADA, a software developed in France, as the standard application development language and chose Thomson's telecommunication equipment for its troops out in the field.

Within the selected segments, marketers define the most significant customers who will be targeted first. They have two choices: either making a concentrated marketing or making a differentiated marketing.

Concentrated marketing selects only a few segments. Smaller companies often prefer having a smaller number of niches rather than having a small market share of a large market. For example, Cray, the U.S. manufacturer of the most powerful computers in the world, which now belongs to Silicon Graphics, only targets organizations with enormous calculation needs and large information system budgets (such as meteorological organizations and research centers). Sagem, a major French electronics firm, has taken this niche strategy to heart: in markets as diverse as guidance systems for airplanes and missile; decoders for TV cable channels such as Canal Plus; and small telephone, telex, and railroad signaling systems, Sagem always has sizable market shares and has increased its sales figures significantly due to this niche strategy.

Differentiated marketing selects several segments with marketing methods adapted to each segment. For example, IBM addresses a large, diverse group of computer users in different sectors (banking, insurance, industrial) with varied financial resources, ranging from small companies to large multinationals. Each segment has its own type of product, price, place, and promotion that require, of course, the involvement of more resources.

Marketing that is concentrated on a segment is less expensive but riskier than marketing that is divided over several segments.

The choice also depends upon technical possibilities and the company's capacity to quickly put a quality product with a truly competitive advantage on the market. The choice depends as well upon the company's overall strategy. Certain companies wish to postpone entering a market segment until the pioneers have shown their existence. When IBM estimated that the segment of personal computer users was sufficiently attractive, it only needed a few months to perfect the IBM PC, which then took the market by storm and nearly reduced all other producers to nothing.

Because many opinions must be taken into account, the segment choice must integrate not only the marketing department but R&D, manufacturing, service, and financial services as well in order to confirm all technological, sales, and financial evaluations. The final decision is usually made by management.

5.3   The positioning of the solution

The last step is to choose a "positioning" of the new product in order to ensure that it is well perceived, identified, and recognized by the customers of the key selected segments. Positioning is the creation of a product's perceived image in customers' minds. The customer's perception of the product rather than the product's use is now considered. Positioning is the ultimate step in differentiating between existing and would-be competitors.

However, positioning is difficult in the high-tech world—first, because customers have difficulties distinguishing between the best and the rest within the large number of frequent new product announcements. In addition, customers often have difficulties understanding how a new technological feature can be an improvement, especially as long as they have not experienced the product nor figured out how the product or service will meet their need.

So, for the marketer, the results of interviews with customers of a particular segment as well as the reactions of prototype users are fundamental in identifying the distinct advantage offered by the new technology. As emphasized by Michael Porter [4], the competitive advantage of a solution is proportional to its value to the customer. In the case of innovative high-technology products, this solution either provides a very high value due to its newness (differentiation) or a value equal to more traditional solutions but at lower cost (cost advantage).

For example, in the offshore oil-drilling business, the mining of deep-sea deposits pushes technology to its limits. One technology distinctly stands out—that of risers. Risers are vertical pipes that connect underwater wells to floating platforms. This technology can develop a floating oil field in 12 to 18 months instead of four to five years for permanent platforms, at an almost identical cost.

In the CAD-CAM business, Parametric Technology (PTC) is a good example of a successful competitive strategy based on a cost advantage. Its main competitors' systems, namely, Computervision and Dassault, were selling sophisticated three-dimensional software to major companies like Airbus, Boeing, or General Motors at a very high price. In 1988, PTC entered the market selling a down-sized software with fewer features to smaller companies in mechanics and electronics and even independent professionals like architects, but at less than one-tenth of the price of the solutions available on the market. Nine years later, with revenues of over $600 million, PTC stands as the new leader in the CAD-CAM market with more than 80,000 customers for its Pro/Engineer software; in November 1997, PTC acquired Computervision, the firm that invented the CAD-CAM business but concentrated too much on the single large account markets with customers like Rolls Royce, Airbus, or PSA, the French car manufacturer. Like some of its early competitors of the 1980s, namely, Apollo and Wang, Computervision did not believe in the future of adapting its software solutions on personal computers or small workstations. Consequently, it faced increasing competition from established companies, such as HP, IBM, and Sun Microsystems, as well as new entrants like PTC and had more and more difficulties with continuing to invest in the development of new solutions in a business where companies spend between 30 and 40% of their yearly turnover on research and development.

Similarly, in the computer industry, Silicon Graphics has successfully challenged the leadership of Cray Computer in the scientific calculation market. While Cray was offering the most powerful computer in the world at a cost of between $1 to $6 million to a limited number of big firms and administrations, Silicon Graphics entered the market with

slightly less powerful computers at a price range between $100,000 and
$1 million. In 1996, Silicon Graphics bought Cray Computer.

Regarding the cost advantage, NCR provided a good example with
the introduction of its 3600 supercomputer based on a new parallel
machine architecture technology. Actually, as its main selling point, outside of the machine's extreme power, NCR focused on the fact that the
3600 was 10 times less expensive than its direct competitor, IBM's
ES 9000, with equal performance.

Actually, this competitive advantage should be emphasized in order
to distinguish the product from today's existing solutions and to position
it according to the segment's customers.

To be effective, a positioning statement must be:

- Simple to understand and to express. As a rule, it should not exceed
  more than two phrases (see some examples that follow).

- Relevant to a given customer need. In any case, a positioning statement must be phrased only in terms of product features. It must
  convey at least one key benefit that must be in line with the need of
  the market segment.

- Credible. Since positioning deals with customer perception, one
  has to be careful about the possible perceived gap between the positioning statement and the reality of the product. For instance,
  "the most powerful computer in the world" is credible for a
  Cray/Silicon Graphics computer, but it would be almost laughable
  in reference to a PC, even a powerful one.

- Fresh, meaning that it must be different from the positioning of
  competitors. The difficulty rests in being unique while meeting
  customer needs. For instance, in the PC markets positioning based
  on offering a different, easier-to-use keyboard has repeatedly
  failed because customers are not really interested. On the other
  hand, Nokia touched the right chord with customers when it very
  successfully managed to position its portable phones as fashion
  objects, with a special look and various flashy colors, when all
  its competitors were emphasizing power, price, small size, or
  performance.

Marketing-savvy firms emphasize their positioning when communicating with their customers. For instance, the same product, a handheld computer, will be positioned differently by various vendors. Philips will position it as the best quality product, while LG, a Korean manufacturer, will emphasize the timesaving value it provides to customers ("When you can fit your office in your pocket, why spend so much time in your office?"). Hardbody has a different and original positioning with "The first handheld PC that's tough enough for any occupation."

Ericsson positioned its new portable phone for consumers as "Made for business. Good for life," while to corporate customers its GSM phone gives "The mobile business advantage."

In business-to-business, IBM has positioned its family of solutions as "It's just better business." While Arthur Andersen is "helping improve your business performance," SAP, the leading German software firm, is offering "a better return on information," and Siemens Nixdorf introduces its "user centered computing." Microway, an OEM, is selling "Technology You Can Count On."

For example, Figure 5.3 identifies the options of the marketing manager of a computer company that targets the segment of the engineers using computer-aided manufacturing (CAM) in companies with more than 500 employees. The two main features are the output quality (graphic on-screen quality) and the waiting period at the screen (data-processing speed). Reviewing customers' expectations, an original positioning seems interesting: proposing a fast system with a high on-screen quality. The final choice depends upon the particular advantage that the company can offer, such as a new, faster processor or specific knowledge regarding the manufacturing of graphic high-resolution screens.

Then the marketing department communicates the product's constraints to R&D, which develops the first prototypes, before they are tested by a sample of the target group, which validates (or invalidates) the positioning. If the positioning can be supported, then its strong specific advantage must be reflected in the other components of the marketing mix:

- The price of a fast workstation with a high graphic on-screen quality could be higher than that of an average product because of its higher performance.

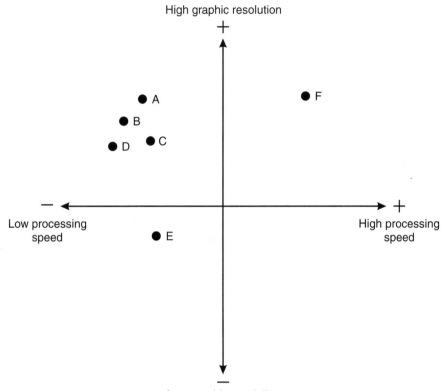

Figure 5.3 Rating of major CAD systems by design engineers in French companies. (For confidentiality reasons, brand names have been omitted.)

- Its distribution will rely on a network of specialized dealers.

- Its promotion can improve new performance or will increasingly aid the user in his or her work.

5.4 Segmentation and time

One of the most significant characteristics of high-technology products is the rate of change. This means that segmentation criteria also change very quickly. For instance, when Sun Microsystems successfully introduced workstations using standard UNIX software, its compatibility with UNIX became an important segmentation criterion that was used to analyze the market for workstations. Traditional manufacturers had previously segmented the market according to performance and application criteria.

However, with the entry of Sun Microsystems, these manufacturers had to differentiate between customers who wanted UNIX and those who were indifferent to UNIX. Since customers with a preference for UNIX represented a larger segment, the manufacturers had to react and adapt their supply of workstations and market products under the UNIX brand name, even though these products were usually manufactured by a different company.

Every marketing manager should therefore regularly reevaluate his or her segmentation criteria while continuously examining the markets. On the other hand, developing segments is costly and time consuming. This development requires, for instance, analysis tools, lengthy and frequent interviews, and several meetings with a company's departments. This process must be adapted to the particular situation.

Certain high-technology products are launched on a very long-term basis. In the chemical industry, out of 15 synthesized molecules by R&D, only one will be put on the market. Taking into account investment costs (on average, $40 million for R&D alone) as well as administrative approval costs, this molecule will not be profitable for 10 or 15 years. A thorough segmentation is both necessary and possible for the evaluation of the market in this time frame.

In another industry, Arianespace must know its market ten years in advance in order to prepare for rocket launchers. It defines its segments on the basis of technical needs, economic resources, and the political ambition of different customers. All these criteria are measured and projected into the future to estimate the type of the market that is needed when performing technical studies.

Other sectors move along very short time frames. The computer industry is a good example. In this sector, the boundaries between mainframes and super minicomputers, between super mini-computers and minicomputers, between minicomputers and workstations, between workstations and microcomputers, between professional microcomputers and personal microcomputers continue to change according to new product announcements for even better performing products.

In this sector, even without access to perfect information, a delay in the market introduction of a product can be very costly. In less than three years, Wang computers, which specialized in office automation, was swept away because Wang did not know how to change fast enough to satisfy its markets, so its niche was invaded by microcomputers with word-processing capabilities.

However, working hastily is never the answer, as a product should not be launched if it does not respond to customer needs. So monitoring customers on a permanent basis (using consumer panels, distributors, and vendors) and reevaluating the segmentation criteria on a regular basis are both necessary in continuously updating the market's expectations.

This ever-changing market demand can never be final. The marketing manager must always complement this market demand with his or her own foresight of the market. He or she must also be willing to take certain risks when proposing the launch of a new product and a corresponding marketing strategy.

5.5 Chapter summary

High-technology companies must segment their markets in order to optimize their resources and to correctly respond to customer needs. A segment regroups customers who have the same demands and the same buying habits or other significant characteristic.

Two segmentation methods exist in the marketing of high-technology products. The first method concerns technologically innovative products. The business value of the new product should be determined for some key customers using test prototype. If this step is successful, that is, if the new product fulfills a need, then all the potential customers are clustered in various segments. Then the product has to be positioned in the minds of the target customers on each segment.

The second, more traditional approach defines the segmentation criteria to divide the market according to homogeneous categories. Then market surveys and research define the segments that need to be evaluated and selected. The choice of the segment that needs to be reached depends upon the potential and the accessibility of each segment as well as the company's technical possibilities and overall strategy. For each segment, the marketing manager defines a product proposal with its positioning and all the components of the marketing mix.

Finally, since the high-technology field is in constant movement, marketers must reevaluate their segmentation criteria on a regular basis and continuously examine the markets. In addition, marketers must also know how to adjust the demand analysis according to the appropriate time frame.

References

[1]   Rosenbloom, R. S., and M. A. Cusumano, "Technological Pioneering and Competitive Advantage: The Birth of the VCR Industry," *California Management Review*, Summer 1987.

[2]   Hamel, G., and C. K. Prahalad, "Competing for the Future," *Harvard Business Review*, Vol. 72, No. 4, July–August 1994.

[3]   Kotler, P., *Marketing Management: Analysis, Planning Implementation and Control*, 6th ed., Englewood Cliffs, NJ: Prentice Hall, 1988.

[4]   Porter, M. E., *Competitive Strategy: Techniques for Analyzing Industries and Competitors*, New York: The Free Press, 1980.

6

Product Strategy

Because the purpose of marketing is to ensure that high-technology products truly meet the needs and wants of the market, three basic product levels should be distinguished.

The essence of a product corresponds to its satisfaction for the customer and is the reason for the product's legitimacy. A marketer must communicate this legitimacy that justifies its existence. A computer is a "faster calculating machine" or an "intelligent machine"; a robot is a machine that "makes assembly more reliable" or "manufactures higher quality"; a rocket "opens the door to the universe."

The product's physical attributes such as its characteristics, style, brand, and quality wrap up its basic essence. It is important to note that the physical attributes apply also to high-technology service: software has certain characteristics (spreadsheet, database); a style (access menu, icon-driven commands, window applications); a brand name (1–2–3, Windows); and a quality (evaluated by users through surveys).

The product's shell includes all the additional services offered with the product for customization. Since high-tech products have a high-technological content, change rapidly, and often have relatively high prices, these services are essential. Services include delivery, installation operation, instruction, maintenance, after-sales support, warranty, and credit terms.

However, a company rarely sells only one product, and any product is usually part of a product range that fits into the company's overall offer. Furthermore, all products change over time. The decisions to be made for an innovative product in its market introduction phase are different than those for a product that is already "established" in a market segment. Consequently, for each product the marketing organization, usually the product manager,[1] must manage each of its three components as well as its place in the product range and its product life cycle.

6.1 Managing the three product components

6.1.1 Managing a product's essence

For the marketer, the product's essence is obviously the first important aspect to be identified. On one hand, this essence corresponds to customer needs and has been measured or evaluated, so it can be used as a basis for defining market segments. On the other hand, the product's communication and sales presentations are based upon this essence because the customer buys these product advantages. For example, the essence of Lotus Notes, a network software product, is to empower groups of people to work together and share knowledge efficiently while in various locations.

---

1. Regarding the organization, one must note that usually the management of the three dimensions of a product, a product line, or several distinct products is the responsibility of a product manager. Some companies, mostly in consumer goods and services, have brand managers who are responsible for a single brand. Besides the product manager and the brand manager, the marketing manager is in charge of managing the marketing activities that serve a particular group of customers; for instance, a company that serves the industrial market and consumer market may have one marketing manager for each of these two markets.

If a product's essence cannot be changed, the product manager should always investigate if another type of need that the high-tech product can satisfy exists because this other customer need can lead to a change in the product's physical attributes and shell. Let us consider the example of computers.

Computers were first used for polling purposes, then to perform scientific calculations, before performing accounting services and facilitating a company's communication process. Nowadays, computers are used by household consumers to play games, do homework, or keep a family budget. Computers have been successful through continuously improving performance, miniaturization, user friendliness, and maintenance, attributes which all satisfy various needs and different customers. Likewise, the use of smart cards (plastic cards including a microchip for their identification) has evolved enormously from its origin, which was to make payments as credit cards. Today, smart cards are used:

- In telecommunications, either as low-cost payphone cards or as storage facilities for mobile phones;

- In health care, where they act as portable electronic files to be used by doctors and insurance companies;

- In transportation, as a complete turnkey solution in ticketing for ski lift access or urban parking lots.

Similarly, the initial concept for the video camera recorder was that of a capital good for use by television stations to record and store their video shows. However, Japanese firms like Sony and Matsushita quickly found out that the VCR could be of interest for consumers if it came with different characteristics such as a bigger storage capacity and a smaller size. The marketing success of the VCR is a triumph of both vision and engineering talent.

Interestingly enough, Japanese firms are repeating the same process with solar battery cells. As with the video cassette recorder, they continue investing when American and European companies have given up. Japanese firms are making hundreds of improvements in design and manufacturing, so they will be able to offer a low-cost solar cell for the mass market in the near future.

Rethinking a product's basic quality is in a way redefining a company's offer such as when Intel redefined its 80286 microprocessor. From the beginning, Intel defined and sold this product as a computer and not as a simple semiconductor, as it previously did similarly to its competitors. By offering a "computer on a chip," Intel created a new category of products and a dominating market position for itself.

6.1.2   Managing a product's physical attributes

6.1.2.1   Product characteristics

Beyond its essence, a product or a service is materialized in a given set of physical features or operations. For instance, a numeric camera like the Kodak DC50 includes within its box a CDD captor, a motorized zoom, operating software, and PCMCIA cards to store pictures.

We have seen that the physical characteristics of a high-technology product are first determined during the development of prototypes but that these characteristics change rapidly in order to better satisfy customers and, because they can be mixed into various options, to speed up the product's life.

In the PC business, the development time for a new product is roughly the same regardless of the firm, that is, about 10 months. However, while some vendors need to freeze their product design five months before market launch, the most successful companies, like Compaq or HP, manage to refine products until five weeks before launching. Consequently, they can include the most recent changes in technology and customer requirements in the development process and deliver a superior solution to the market on time.

However, features that are not valued by the customer should not be added to the product because customers might find these features useless or too expensive. In high technology, adding useless gadgets to products just to please inventors or designers is a frequent temptation, but customers are rebelling more and more often against these useless details. As a result, every addition or deletion of a feature must first be tested on customers by the marketing department [1].

So, in consumer goods, the new remote control for a Sony television only contains nine buttons instead of almost 100 previously. The latest JVC VCR is operated using a menu with four on-screen instructions instead of the nine buttons and twenty adjustable minibuttons that appeared on the first VCRs. Xerox now offers a simple photocopy system that uses an on-screen touch-driven menu, which replaces older systems that had the complexity of cockpits and could not be used by the poor soul who wanted to make one single photocopy. Similarly, the best manufacturers of portable PCs focus their engineering creativity on designing features, such as readable screen and friendly keyboards, that are very important for customers. A modification of 1 cm to the width of a laptop display screen can make a big difference in readability, for which some customers will be ready to pay.

Another trend in the design of consumer high-tech products is miniaturization, which makes them easier to store for customers, thanks to microchips: EchoStar in the United States and Sagem in France are developing satellite dishes no larger than a dish plate; Ericsson, the giant Swedish telecommunication firm, is selling portable phones smaller than a cigarette pack; while the Elp camera by Canon is smaller than a pair of glasses.

On the other hand, high-tech industrial products (directed at smaller markets) tend to be individualized in order to closely correspond to customer needs. The Arianespace launching rocket is modular and "intelligent," so its performance can be adapted according to the number or weight of a satellite that a customer wishes to launch. For its antitank systems, Aerospatiale developed a large number of options, such as interference resistance, tandem shelling, and accessories designed for night use, to meet customer needs.

6.1.2.2 Product style

The style or design of a product is also very important and crucial for consumer high-tech products. Style or design is often an important criterion in the purchase of a compact disc player, a cellular phone, or an HDTV.

Similarly, to find success on the Internet, firms must present attractive interactive applications to digital customers; they cannot simply adapt content from traditional media because doing so often falls short of creating effective interaction. Actually, developing content for interactive applications requires a specific know-how, as shown by the rise of specialized agencies such as Agency.com, Redesign, Doubleclick, I.traffic, and many others.

For industrial products, ergonomics (arranging equipment or machines for higher efficiency) often determines a product's style. For example, computer screens are designed to give good visibility, and software menus guide inexperienced users step by step through a program's functions. Experience shows that a good design gives a product personality, helps differentiate it from competing products, and justifies a higher price. Typical examples in the software field are the user-friendly Macintosh icons from Apple that were unmatched for almost ten years before Microsoft launched Windows. In its consumer electronics division, Bang and Olufsen adheres to this strategy: the sophisticated aesthetic look and quality of its products support its upscale, high-priced product strategy.

6.1.2.3   Product brand name

A brand is a name, a set of words, a sign, a symbol, a design, or a combination that identifies a seller's goods or services. In the high-tech world, a brand is a basic necessity. One of the criteria that determines a customer's choice is confidence in a company and its products. As the purchase of a high-tech product often represents a leap into the unknown, an individual or industrial buyer needs to be reassured by a well-known and familiar brand.

A brand facilitates product identification while attaching a quality image and a personality that establish customer loyalty and justify a price difference. A product's registered trademark can protect against clones, which is at least as important as protecting technology with patents. DEC's VAX symbolized a scientific computer; IBM is a reference model for management use; while Intel, through the "Intel inside" ad campaign and the "Pentium" public relations campaign, has provided brand consciousness for computer chips buried inside products of different manufacturers.

For these various reasons, building a strong brand creates a real value addition to customers, which translates into brand equity for the vendor. The value of a brand is measured by the degree of awareness in customers' minds. Typically, a powerful brand will go through various stages:

- From zero awareness;

- To assisted recognition, when it is mentioned in a list of brands submitted to respondents;

■ To unaided recall, meaning that the respondent associates the brand name directly with a given product or communication message;

■ To "top of mind," when the brand is mentioned first without any assistance.

A strong branding strategy is based on three key principles: dominance, exclusivity, and singularity.

Usually, in a consumer's sequence of thought, first the product or service is identified, then the brand comes to mind. Consequently, a dominant brand is the one that comes first in customers' minds before competitors. A research program developed by the U.S. Strategic Planning Institute (SPI) in the late 1970s indicates that such dominant brands have greater returns than their competitors. On average, the "top of mind" brand has a return on investment of 34%, while the second competitor has 21%, and the third 16%.

An exclusive brand is a must because experience and research show that two brands cannot both occupy one position at the same time. Even worse, any major communication investment by the second brand usually reinforces the leader's position with customers by making the association more salient. For instance, in France, when the new French telecom operator, Bouygues Telecom, made an advertising campaign announcing a new offer for portable phones, many people instead asked for more information from the sales representative of France Telecom, its main competitor and the leader in the mobile phone business.

Finally, a brand cannot occupy two distinct positions at the same time in customers' minds. When one position increases, the other must decrease. This is the main reason why it is very difficult to sell the same brand to both businesses and consumers. For instance, IBM or Oracle have a strong image in business that does not translate well in consumers' minds. Conversely, Microsoft had to invest heavily to promote Windows NT as a "serious" operating system for the business environment because Windows is perceived much more as a consumer product for individual users.

Respecting the three conditions of dominance, exclusivity, and singularity is achieved through a good segmentation process and the right choice of positioning. For a given segment, if a brand cannot be first in a product category or own a particular association, it must be positioned on a new dimension that either opens a new category or divides the existing one. Such is the strategy of Psion, the leading vendor of handheld PCs (HPC), which has deliberately differentiated its product from the PC and laptop categories by inventing the concept of the "organizer," an easy-to-use, easy-to-store digital assistant. Psion is currently under assault by major computer vendors like Compaq and HP, who are trying to position their offerings as a "third computer," fully compatible with notebooks and desktop computers, like the PC companion from Compaq.

However, a strong brand recognition also means a significant amount of money invested up front to promote the brand. The human mind does not build up favorable impressions slowly over time (see Figure 6.1). Usually, once a customer's mind is made up, it rarely changes, and a perception that exists in the mind is often interpreted as truth. Consequently, a strong branding strategy for a new product or technology requires a "big bang" to establish an initial position in customers' minds; only then can subsequent input strengthen and sustain this first impression.

When a company markets its products or services under its own brand name, it can decide to organize brand names by product (Lisa and Macintosh for Apple's microcomputers) and by product range (T and

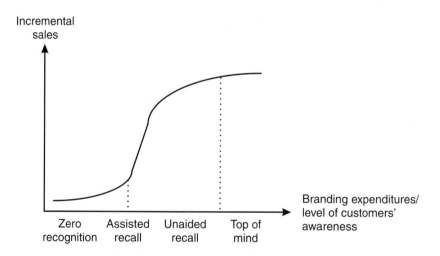

Figure 6.1   The S model of customer response to brand awareness.

EOS for Canon's cameras) or adopt the company's own name combined with a number identifying the product or product range (for example, IBM 4381, Intel 486, Ariane 5, Boeing 767).

One of the benefits of branding by product is that the company's corporate image is not associated with its products. This can be beneficial in the case of a failure: Macintosh did not suffer from the Lisa disaster. On the other hand, brand policy by product range is justified if the products are very different. DEC calls its 16-bit computers PDP, its 32-bit computers VAX, and its 64-bit computers Alpha AXP. Finally, using a company's name with a product or product range number individualizes these products while protecting them by using the company's name.

As a matter of fact, large companies often use several of these strategies. IBM has its IBM 3090 and 4381 series but also its product range S390 and AS 400 as well as the Thinkpad PC family and system software OS/2. Aerospatiale, in its helicopter division, uses names for products (such as Dauphin, Ecureuil, Superpuma, Tigre); however, in its aircraft division, the company uses names for product ranges (ATR 42, Airbus 320).

In the high-tech business, experience indicates that, for market-driven products, a company is well advised to associate its name with a product; while, for technologically innovative products, it should choose one brand name for each product that then emphasizes the particular innovation.

A brand name is not chosen hastily or haphazardly but has to be tested on future customers of the selected segment. A brand name must evoke a product's features (like in Mecasoft or Laserdyne); be easily memorized, recognized, and pronounced; stand out; and suggest the product's advantages (like in Spacesystem). Unfortunately, this is not often the case: few brand names of high-tech products bring to mind the product's essence, and most high-tech products hide behind a number or an abbreviation that is usually incomprehensible to a novice. Product managers should take this theory into consideration. In this respect, the brand strategy of European firm Matra is a good example (see Figure 6.2). Matra has always cared about its visual identity. Its name is a true brand symbol of quality and high performance. The changing logo is significant of its communication strategy:

- 1945: A cogwheel and a diamond shape, Matra's first logo reflects the image of a mechanical engineering company and its original activity.

| 1945 | 1962 | 1967 | 1977 | 1989 |

Figure 6.2   Brand importance in high technology using the example of Matra.

- 1962: The new, more high-tech logo represents Matra's new activities. The cogwheel has been replaced by a circle. The words "Engins Matra" explain that Matra is not only a company but also a brand name. The arrow symbolizes innovation in defense and space industries.

- 1967: The arrow is turned to the opposite side to stress the dynamic effect. The words "Engins Matra" have been removed to beneath the circle to improve overall readability.

- 1977: When Matra's computer division was created, the arrow moved inside the circle. The circle's 9 white optical lines convey high technology.

- 1989: Matra is now a highly diversified company, with a widely exported technology, especially into the United States. For this reason, Matra's brand name has been moved to the forefront. The visual identity renders the three elements of the logo—Matra's name, type of business, and emblem—inseparable.

6.1.2.4   Product quality

Quality is a basic characteristic of a high-tech product because the purchase of a high-tech product is justified by performance expectations that will be disappointed if the product does not function well or at all. Furthermore, a low-quality product betrays the confidence that a customer has placed in a company.

So, it does not come as a surprise that a better quality product leads to higher profits, as researchers from the SPI have clearly established this correlation in a study among a large number of firms. This survey covers all product types, but its results can be extrapolated to high-tech products.

Let us make clear that a product's quality is what the buyer expects and not what can be manufactured in a factory. Consequently, marketers must measure the target customer's expectation level as well as the perceived quality during prototype testing.

Once this has been determined, the members of the marketing department should work in conjunction with all the other departments to assure this level of quality continuously. Quality obviously concerns the manufacturing department but also the research and development department, which can integrate the quality issue at the product's design, and the maintenance services, which are in charge of repairs of defective products.

This search for quality is not always easy in the high-tech-product world. The rate at which opportunities appear and disappear in a market or a segment and the need to act quickly when launching products sometimes leads managers to sacrifice a product's quality. For some technologies in which the process has not yet been finalized, it is tempting to launch a product without completely mastering all of the aspects.

This is a risky and often dangerous speculation because a product with performance that is below customer expectation almost always has negative consequences on its own image, even on the company itself.

In the minicomputer industry, Hewlett-Packard had some difficulties getting back on its feet after its Spectrum series experienced some technical problems. In 1994, Intel faced similar problems when it appeared that the first Pentium chips had a bug. Though the flaw was quite small and concerned one customer out of 100,000, the rumor spread on the Internet that Intel had blundered with its new Pentium, forcing the company to stop production, revise the design of the microprocessor, and exchange the bugged chip with a new one for free. In the aeronautics industry, Lauda Air's crash of a Boeing 767 in Thailand during May 1991 put jet engine control computers in the hot seat because these computers were also used in Pratt & Whitney's PW 4000 and Airbus A320's CFM 56. Even if their responsibilities have not been clearly established, for some potential customers the doubt will exist forever.

NASA experienced some difficulties getting back on its feet after the Challenger disaster, which happened because of a rocket booster problem. Its competitors are in the same boat. Confronted with a risk of failure with its new cryogenic engine HM7, designed by SEP (European

Propulsion Company), Arianespace preferred to delay a launch; a failure would have had a negative effect on its European customers during trade negotiations concerning the continuation of the European space program (for the space shuttles Hermès and Colombus).

Finally, continuous quality improvement is very important before launching a product but also during a product's entire life. The product manager must organize and follow surveys that treat this subject as well as associated services (for example, installation and repair). He or she must also participate in setting up "quality circles" or their equivalents in the company to encourage any and all improvements that can increase customer satisfaction.

6.1.3 Managing a product's shell

Theodore Levitt, one of the leading marketing specialists, observes that "the more technologically sophisticated the generic product (for example, cars and computers), the more dependent are its sales on the quality and availability of its accompanying customer service" [2]. How many marvelous technologies have remained unused or underutilized because of insufficient maintenance service or information that disappointed or annoyed their users?

That service is often a key to market success was the case for the Video Timesharing Service (VTS) developed by Hughes Communications. When Hughes Communications started business in 1983 they had to sell whole satellite channels called transponders. The prices ranged from $8 million to $15 million, and only leading cable TV companies like HBO, ESPN, and Turner Broadcasting could afford to be customers. This left the company with an inventory of about 12 unsold transponders. Hughes Communications repackaged those transponders for use in the occasional video markets by customers who needed capacity for special events like football and baseball games and news stories around the United States. The traffic volume grew as the company added customers who previously could not afford the high cost of entry. The service, now offered by Pan Am Sat, supports anywhere between 12 and 24 transponders at a given time. The key to success was providing a responsive service at market price.

Similarly, convinced that extended services like speed and reliability were the keys for successfully marketing its PCs, Dell Computer offers a telephone diagnosis and order system as well as 24-hour repair service and the installation of various software on request. To speed up its operation in Europe, Dell is working with shipping companies that deliver and install its systems and with media firms that call customers to assess satisfaction. Such quality in associated services helps to improve customer loyalty, thus explaining the performance of Dell in the PC industry.

Product marketing must include a marketing of the entire product that is being offered to the customer. For instance, like many high-tech solutions designed for consumers or businesses, the aforementioned numeric camera Kodak DC50 also includes two notebooks translated into five languages and as a one-year warranty. The product's physical characteristics are of concern to the R&D and manufacturing departments, and services associated with a product are essentially the responsibility of the finance department (for credit terms) and the installation and maintenance departments. Accordingly, the product manager must work in close collaboration with these departments to efficiently respond to customer expectations. He or she must be actively involved in the assurance of impeccable service quality for the company's products.

On one hand, financial engineering is a key service for high-priced high-tech products, in an absolute or relative value. IBM's success with mainframes can be attributed to its computer quality as well as to its flexible and innovative financial solutions. In France, the compact disc player owes its success to the development of new consumer credit solutions such as the "Carrefour" credit card (offered by Carrefour, the biggest French distributor) and the Cofinoga credit card (a specific credit card offered by the banks for financing purchases at retail stores).

On the other hand, the creation of after-sales service presents a delicate problem. Who performs this service: the manufacturer, the distributors, or a third party? The answer depends upon the market needs and the company's abilities.

Maintenance service is often a very lucrative business because the customers are captive. It is very clear for an industrial product but holds true for consumer products as well. For instance, General Electric provides a free telephone number (for example, 800 numbers in the United States and a "green number" in France) that allows technically qualified customers to obtain advice on how to fix their own appliances 24 hours a day.

However, there is always a tradeoff between efficiency and cost. If the number of customers increases too much, it is advisable to reduce this effort by relying on a network of distributors to respond efficiently to these after-sales needs. The main inconvenience lies in the distributor training time because these distributors risk being fully operational only when the product is already obsolete, as has been the case for software too often.

The best way to control the quality of the after-sales service operation is to simplify its conditions at the product development stage. In electronics, for example, more profitable and easier-to-repair models are built using a modular design; an electronic circuit can no longer be repaired, so only the board on which it is installed is changed, which can be performed in a few seconds by a low-skilled operator. The integration of self-diagnosing systems that can anticipate trouble and notify maintenance and repair service has also lead to more profitable and easier-to-repair electronics equipment.

6.2   Managing a product range

A successful product often has different product versions that can adapt to customer needs from top-of-the-line products (high-quality attributes and shell) to bottom-of-the-line products (low-quality attributes and shell).

A product line consists of all the existing variations of a given product. Therefore, the product manager of a high-tech product must often decide whether to extend or to reduce a product line. He or she has to find the right balance: a product range that is too small risks foregoing market share, but a product range that is too large risks burdening profitability with high debt because of the costs associated with, for example, the production, storage, packaging, promotion, distribution, and billing of too many products.

To extend a product line, the product manager must first ascertain that the line meets customer needs and that the extension is technically feasible. In the majority of cases, high-tech companies start out with upscale products and then step down to products of lower quality.

In the beginning, the need to optimize very high R&D costs in a short time period forces the company to target industrial or individual customers with a high purchasing power. Then, when the upscale product market slows down, due to market saturation or the arrival of competitors, it is tempting to target more price-sensitive markets by introducing low- and average-quality product versions. Using this approach, the company can take advantage of its high-quality image.

The risks of this choice should be carefully evaluated because this type of decision implies modifications of production (Can production keep up if volume increases?) and distribution (Will distributors accept less classy customers?) and because it can encourage existing competitors in the low-quality range to counterattack with higher quality products.

During the 1980s, IBM experienced a serious failure with the PC Junior (derived from the IBM PC) on the consumer market. IBM failed to adapt to this new market and had overestimated its size. By attacking Apple, the leader in this niche at that time, IBM caused Apple to react. Apple upscaled its Macintosh line to attack the business market, which had been IBM's favorite. Another risk of an extensive product range is reducing the company's focus on the more successful products or those needing special attention.

Extending upward into a realm of higher quality products is justified if a company wants to conquer a more profitable market where competitive positions are likely to change.

However, this is a difficult undertaking as the company must have all the abilities (technical, sales, and financial) necessary to assure a new positioning on its new market segments. In addition, it might already suffer from a low image because it is primarily known as a supplier of low-quality products, which is one of the reasons why Philips or Wang never really succeeded in microcomputers. Success stories do exist: before positioning the Macintosh as a workstation, Apple successfully entered the business-to-business market with professional versions of Macintosh by focusing on the narrow segment of desktop-publishing users who prepare company newsletters, reports, and presentations.

A product line can be extended in two directions. The advantages and inconveniences of the two aforementioned (and analyzed) movements can accumulate. Compaq has followed this strategy since 1983 when it announced the first industry-standard portable PC. From then, it entered the desktop PC business in 1986, introduced its first laptop computer in 1988, announced its first minicomputer/server in 1989, launched the Presario PC for consumers in 1993, and introduced powerful standards-based workstations in 1996. In 1997, Compaq put on the market its first handheld PC, the PC companion, and expanded its offer to fault-tolerant mission-critical mainframes when it bought Tandem Computer.

Each time, this two-way product range extension allowed new products to capitalize on Compaq's strong image of providing low-cost/high-performance computers with industry-standard technology and components. (See Figure 6.3.)

In every extension case (upward, downward, or in both directions), the "cannibalization" risk of existing products is high. Cannibalization is the possibility that the new product in line "devours" its fellow product line members. This event happens frequently in the high-tech

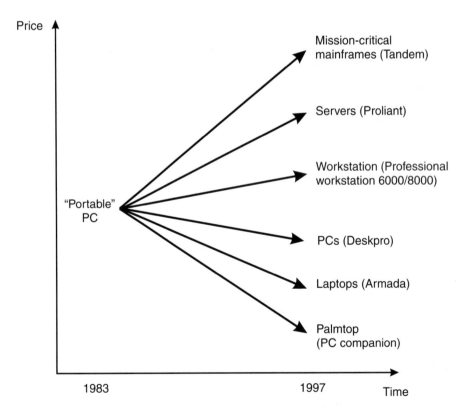

Figure 6.3 The evolution of Compaq's product range (not including Digital's product range). (*Source:* Compaq.)

sector because the rate of technological change is such that the most recent product is more appealing and offers a better price-performance ratio than its product line members.

Experience shows that, in this field, companies who favor this dynamic cannibalization of their own products are also highly profitable. Rather than recreating different product lines every time, cannibalization is a way to remain dynamic by strengthening the durability of the line's name. Cannibalization can build up a basis of trust that is required to reassure buyers of high-tech products.

The opposite of extension, the reducing of a high-tech product line, is a necessary decision when part of the line is no longer profitable. This decision can be linked to a structural insufficiency of demand, to overly optimistic predictions that overestimated the number of customers in a segment, or to difficulties in reaching these customers, especially for products that have no predecessor. This is also often the case for older products that are no longer in demand. Consequently, managing a range of products has to closely take into account the products' life cycles.

6.3 Managing a high-tech product according to its product life cycle

The importance of the product life cycle must be examined via the changes in markets and technology because a high-tech product exists not only because it meets a market need but because it is closely related to a technology.

We saw in Chapter 1 that the product life cycle is the mirror image of the changing needs that the product satisfies and reflects the customer diffusion of innovation curve (see Figure 6.4). At its introduction, the product must convince the innovators and the forerunners because as soon as they buy the product and make it popular, a larger majority will be interested in the product. Sales will increase until the late majority has adopted the product and its level of sales stabilizes. Finally, the eventual decline will be accelerated by the arrival of a new technology.

Furthermore, fast-changing technologies and the customer's failure to understand a technique encourage fads for a given product. As many product managers know, in the consumer and industrial high-tech world,

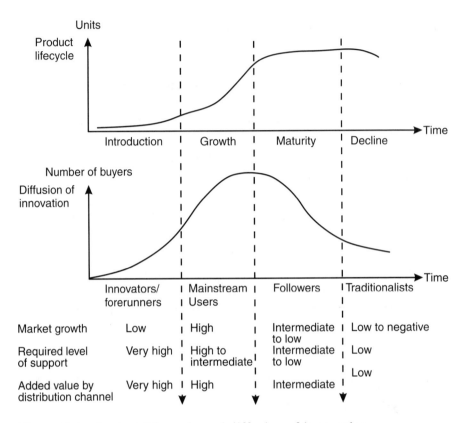

Figure 6.4   Product life cycle and diffusion of innovation.

the product life cycle is quite similar to that of "faddish" products: both have a quick growth stage and a sharp decline.

For example, over the last 10 years, the average life cycle of the PC has decreased from four years to nine months. At a given time, 70% of the products in the portfolio of a typical PC vendor have been introduced in the last six months. Consequently, manufacturers must juggle powerful suppliers' demanding lead times as high as four months (like for disk drives) and distributors unwilling to carry large inventories. Other industries such as mobiles phones, consumer electronics, and publishing, as well as fashion and sporting goods, face many of the same problems.

The product life cycle theory is sometimes criticized for two reasons. On one hand, it is very difficult to identify stages because they are led by sales that can be influenced by marketing activities. On the other hand, no method exists that is capable of identifying when stages actually change, particularly to identify signs of maturity or decline.

Nevertheless, in the high-tech-product world this model appears to be very useful to the product manager, not so much for making market predictions, but rather for planning and preparing strategic product-management decisions. Every stage of a life cycle requires different actions, as we will now examine in detail.

6.3.1 Introduction stage

A high-tech product actually exists long before its market introduction. Whether it is demanded by the market (market-driven) or encouraged by a technical innovation (product-driven), the product is always part of a pro-totyping phase that verifies the response rate of the needs of a test market in a certain segment. So this pre-introduction stage is also the time to fully check the readiness of all technical manufacturing details and details of associated services (for example, documentation and training).

Theoretically, a low level of sales at the introduction stage is not explained by logistic problems but only by two main factors: the low number of buyers ready to be innovative and the product's initial high cost as a result of the need to break even with research and development costs.

Accordingly, the main challenge of a market introduction is to reduce a new product's risk—a risk that is higher because the product is innovative, for the company as well as for the customer—while increasing its diffusion. The analysis of successful product introductions shows that several strategies are possible and can be executed at one time.

- Aiming at innovators who are tempted to buy the product immediately is a top priority. For instance, in the scientific computer industry, research laboratories and universities are ideal candidates for new products because their researchers want to benefit from maximum performances of these machines, computers, or peripherals. Sun Microsystems has built an image and a reputation with its successful workstations by aiming first at these research laboratories and universities. Once firmly recognized as a first-rate workstation supplier, Sun Microsystems then used this customer basis to expand into other industrial and banking markets.

Some new products experience difficulties identifying these innovators who have certain psychological differential characteristics. Innovators among consumers are often people with certain levels of education who read certain publications and earn a certain income, while industrial customers are companies that are very performance-oriented, with a strong market power, and that practice state-of-the-art technology.

- Educating a part of the target market to whom the advantages of the new technology are explained is also a good technique. It establishes credibility because informing potential customers centers on technology whereas traditional promotion centered on the product. In the beginning of the 1970s, when the potential of microprocessors was not yet completely understood, Intel developed a large program of seminars and brochures that described and explained the infinite variety of possible applications. Oracle, a manufacturer for specialized software, based its success on this practice of seminars and dedicates 90% of its promotion budget to seminars (see also Chapter 8).

- Targeting users of similar products also pays off because experience shows that these users are often forerunners. The forerunners of personal computers also appeared to be owners of sophisticated recording equipment and video game machines. Pharmaceutical companies aim their new products at hospital-based medical specialists who are advisors in their special field; if these specialists adopt the new drug, then it is the appropriate time to approach general practitioners.

- The approach can be more direct by aiming, whenever possible, at users of the current technology like Thomas Alva Edison, when he offered his electric lighting system by voluntarily duplicating all of the existing forms of gas lighting. However, in doing so there is always a risk: confusion should not be created within the already existing customer base, of which few are innovators but most belong to the early or late majority. These users can become frustrated with the existing product, of which the shortcomings are presented, without having any inclination to buy the new product. The key here is to make the transition between technologies as smooth as possible. For instance, keeping the QWERTY keyboard as a common feature of manual, then electric, and now computer-based typing systems have clearly blocked the adoption of new technology by typists. Similarly, the addition of a mouse to computers has facilitated the adoption of computers by users who had no previous typing experience and were relying only on pen technology to write letters and other documents.

■ Spreading a successful product image is a good approach because success attracts success and more quickly convinces customers who only ask to be reassured. A costly promotion campaign is necessary to establish a strong image. In 1984, the Macintosh launching campaign was prize-winning not only because of its originality but also due to the most expensive microcomputer introduction campaign at $15 million. Apple sold $7.5 million worth only a few hours after its introduction and its first 50,000 Macintoshes within 74 days instead of the forecasted 100 days; as a reference, Apple sold its first 50,000 Apple II computers in 2.5 years, and IBM set aside more than seven months to sell its first 50,000 IBM PCs. However, the ultimate launching of a product to date is that made by Microsoft for Windows 95. After a media blitz, Microsoft managed to sell one million copies of its new version of its operating software in less than four days, 10 times less than what it took to sell the same number of copies of its previous MS-DOS version!

■ Publicly announcing references and recommendations of well-known organizations and companies that have already tried and adopted the product will present a credibility that will convince hesitant consumers. In order for this method to succeed, prestigious customers must first agree to participate in a "beta test," which they will rarely refuse if the innovation is of interest to them. This is how the research and development departments of Microsoft, Renault, and Thomson, to name a few [3], continuously test new high-tech products before deciding whether to place one on the market.

■ Among other possible market introduction strategies are actions toward opinion leaders, such as journalists; free trial uses (Uniroyal installed its "High Torque Drive Belt" system in customer factories for a free trial and without any obligations for 90 days); sharing technology with other suppliers (Philips worked with Sony, Hitachi, Akai, and Panasonic on a universal video laser disc, and Sony negotiated an agreement with Aiwa, Sanyo, and others to sell its 8-mm camcorder); and leasing possibilities.

All those actions share the objective of achieving the acceptance of a new high-tech product and launching this product as quickly as possible to more risk-averse, less-innovative customers who form a large part of the market. It is their acceptance of the new product that will make it a success from business and financial standpoints. The failure of the Digital Compact Cartridge (DCC) launching by Philips NV illustrates the point. Philips wanted the DCC technology to replace the analog (cassette) tape technology, just as CD players replaced analog record players. To ease the transition for customers, it designed the DCC tape-decks to play both analog and new digital tapes.

However, Philips performed poorly when trying to sell the benefit of digital recording technology because it never mentioned the compatibility of the two technologies. At the same time, its main competitor, Sony, was introducing its minidisc system, another incompatible digital recording technology. As a consequence of this confusion, few consumers switched from analog cassette tapes to the DCC system or to the minidisc system. Furthermore, Philips had priced the DCC tape player quite high, between $900 and $1200 per unit, which did not help its market entry.

Overall, the failure of the launch prevented Philips from originating increasing returns, and the DCC technology ended up locked out of the market.

6.3.2   Sales growth stage

During this stage, the number of customers and sales increases. The company benefits from the experience effect, which lowers its unit costs and allows it to recover its research and development costs. Prices tend to decrease fairly quickly, which increases demand while raising entry barriers for competitors who may be unable to show a profit on a long-term basis at this low price.

This happened, for example, in the market for microwave ovens, and Figure 6.5 shows the development of sales during the 1980s on the

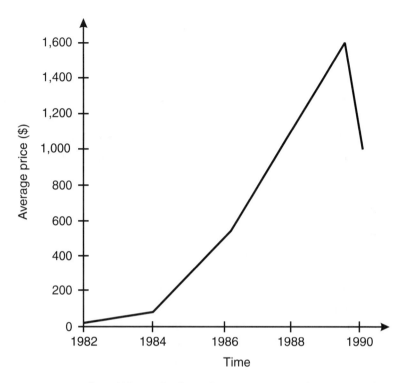

Figure 6.5 Product life cycle for microwave ovens in France. (*Source:* Market analysis by Eric Viardot.)

French market. At the beginning of the decade prices of microwave ovens were very high, between $1,200 and $1,600, because at that time microwave ovens were considered luxury goods and were directed at innovative customers. Then, in 1984, a major French retail company, Intermarché, offered a microwave oven for sale at a bargain price of $239. The market responded immediately, and the product was a big hit. The forerunners adopted this new high-tech product that revolutionized food preparation. At that point, Korean and Japanese manufacturers then entered the market; prices came down to less than $400, and sales of microwave ovens reached their highest point in 1988.

Usually, high-tech products experience steep sales growth phases. For example, from 1989 to 1995, the market for battery components increased by more than 11% of revenues. Likewise, from 1990 to 1995, the compound annual market growth rate was 15% for the semiconductors, 18% for PCs, and 32% for flat panel displays!

To sustain the growth phase, marketers must stimulate increasing returns by expanding the installed base of customers and looking for new market segments. Accordingly, they must understand the key drivers that will help them create a reinforcing feedback loop to get more customers, as illustrated in Figure 6.6 by the typical example of Microsoft's Windows.

Today, the vast majority of customers buy Windows because of the application programs that run on it. The quality and quantity of those programs is constantly increasing because software developers are always designing new programs that run on Windows; its installed base allows them to aim at more than 100 million potential customers. Likewise, the availability of new applications and the number of existing Windows users motivate new customers to buy, further expanding the installed base.

To keep such a growth cycle going requires the erection of high genuine or perceived switching costs to competitors for business partners and final customers. Thus, in the product growth phase, a company will have to increase its distribution channels as well as its communication.

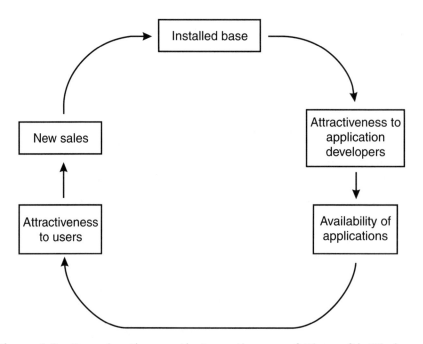

Figure 6.6   Managing the growth stage: the case of Microsoft's Windows.

However, these actions have high costs, and the company must decide between market share and profitability within the limits of the technological possibilities.

6.3.3   Maturity and decline stages

A company called CLTO, a branch of Cables de Lyons, a major French industrial firm, that specializes in fiber optics used the life-cycle concept strategically to manage its businesses (CLTO held 85% in the French market in 1990). Its sales executive affirms that every time a product is standardized, the firm withdraws from the market because it is not sufficiently equipped for mass production. To meet customers' needs, CLTO developed a reflectometer that measures a fiber's strength and flexibility. This technique standardized very quickly and was taken up by American and Japanese companies that specialized in manufacturing measuring instruments. This structure did not allow CLTO to manufacture a reflectometer at a competitive price. Because the firm knows the sector well, it was able to make the decision to abandon the product quickly.

When facing flat sales of a product, the product manager must analyze the reasons for this dullness. If this reason involves a simple sales problem that is related to a problem regarding price cuts, sales promotions, remotivation of the sales force, or the restructuring of distribution, an adjustment will suffice to boost growth. For short-term planning purposes, in the maturity stage, the product manager must also research whether he or she can try to modify certain product features (physical characteristics or the entire product) or enter new market segments.

Often this sales flattening develops into a decrease in sales, which only translates the arrival of a higher performing product or technology that takes some time to spread throughout the market, as is shown in Figure 6.6. Two other possible reasons are changes in customer needs and the impossibility of following competitors in a price war. In any of these three cases, the company is better off if they anticipate these changes and are in a position to launch a new generation of products, for the high-tech world is filled with failed companies who could not or did not know how to adapt fast enough.

This decrease in sales then causes manufacturing overcapacity and sinking profits. A decision has to be made, though canceling a product is never easy. Besides a company's sentimental relationship with a product, certain customers might want the product to be continued because it perfectly corresponds to their needs and because they use it regularly. For instance, history shows that customers forced DEC to continue producing its PDP past the 1970s because these customers had developed many different types of software for this particular machine.

However, continuing to sell a declining product is costly. The company must produce special series, maintain a parts inventory, and keep technical and sales specialists. An interesting solution would be to sell a line of declining products to a company that wishes to continue these products for a certain market, like when Thomson sold its medical electronics activity to General Electric or DEC sold its database to Oracle.

However, there are not always buyers, especially for lame-duck products. So, once the decision to phase out a product has been made, it is the marketing's department responsibility to plan, in close cooperation with other involved services, the exact date for the last sale of a product so that sufficient time exists during which to convince customers to change their current product for a new, higher performance product by using attractive sales terms to facilitate their decision.

6.4   Controlling complementary products

As seen in Chapter 2, the expansion of a new technology often relies on the availability of complementary products. Accordingly, those products must be managed synchronously with the main solution, either directly, if they are provided by the same vendor, or in close cooperation with the marketing departments of external suppliers.

For instance, Apple Computer secured the success of the Macintosh computer in the desktop publishing arena by simultaneously bringing to market some crucial desktop publishing software applications, supplied by Adobe and Aldus, as well as its own laser jet printer.

Complementary solutions may end up being as or even more profitable than the main solutions, as in the case of CD audio players. Following the successful introduction of CD technology, there was a strong demand for disc pressing services, which directly benefited Philips and Sony, the main vendors, who had also invested in disc facilities to feed the new CD audio players.

6.5 Chapter summary

A product can be broken down into three elements: its essence or basis for legitimacy; its physical attributes (characteristics, brand, level of quality); and the complete shell, including the related services. Every dimension must be handled by the product manager in the scope of the marketing mix development.

The product manager must find a need that his or her product can satisfy. He or she must develop the product's characteristics while improving the product according to customer expectations and perceptions of the product. The product's quality should be given extra attention because a defect could damage the reassuring image of the company. The product manager must also ensure the quality of all services for the product, particularly installation, after-sales, and financial services.

A product usually fits in a product range that must be studied continuously so that it can be extended or reduced appropriately. In high technology, very dynamic companies do not hesitate to manufacture products that replace existing products, but dynamism is not free from financial and sales risks.

Marketing decisions vary with the product's position in the product life cycle. Launching a new product requires a precise action plan that leads target customers to adopt a product. These customers can then urge the rest of the market to buy the product. The sales growth stage forces the company to anticipate competitors' moves and to adjust prices, promotion, and distribution of the product accordingly. High-tech marketing is a marketing of growth and is less interested in a product's maturity and decline stages. However, during these stages, the market introduction of a product's successor can be prepared.

References

[1] March, A., "Usability: The New Dimension of Product Design," *Harvard Business Review*, Vol. 72, No. 5, 1994.

[2] Levitt, T., "Production Line Approach to Services," *Harvard Business Review*, October 1972.

[3] Voss, C. A., "Determinants of Success in the Applications Software," *J. Product Innovation Management*, Vol. 2, 1985, pp. 113–121.

7

Pricing High-Tech Products

Prices of high-technology products are much higher than average prices of standard products: the price per kilogram of a satellite is 20,000 times higher than a kilogram of building material and 2,000 times higher than a kilogram of an automobile (see Figure 7.1).

Therefore, price is an important part of the marketing strategy, first because a price strengthens a product's positioning in a market segment, that is, high-quality products usually call for high prices; second because price is a basic element in the exchange between a company and its customers, even if it is not the only decision factor in the purchase of a high-technology product; and finally because the impact of price is felt not only in sales volume and market share but also financially as price determines a company's profitability.

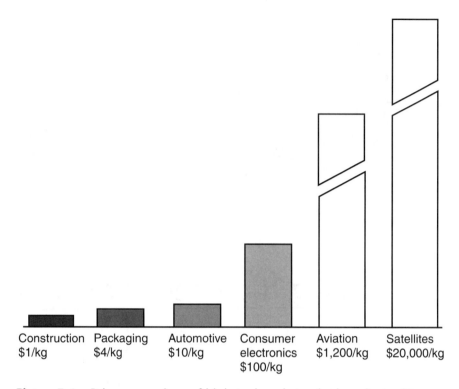

Construction	Packaging	Automotive	Consumer	Aviation	Satellites
$1/kg	$4/kg	$10/kg	electronics	$1,200/kg	$20,000/kg
			$100/kg		

Figure 7.1   Price comparison of high-tech and standard products. (*Source:* French Ministry of Industry.)

Consequently, price decisions are rarely made by just the marketing department but usually in close collaboration with the finance department. According to a study performed in French high-tech firms, the final price decision in 50% of the cases is made by the chief executives, in 40% of the cases by a sales manager, in 30% of the cases by a multifunctional committee, and only in 20% of the cases by a marketing director [1].

In a world where products and competitive positions change very quickly, a marketing manager must know how to continuously adapt his or her offered price. The marketing manager must first determine the general framework of his or her price policy, and then he or she must select a pricing method according to the type of products he or she wants to market as well as other determinants.

7.1 Determining price limits

The price of a product always changes between two points: the price ceiling and the bottom price. The price ceiling is set by the market segment that is being addressed; no customer will buy above this level, and this price ceiling will be translated into a zero market share. The bottom price is established by the cost structure of a product; below this price the company loses money on every product sold, which leads to a negative return (see Figure 7.2).

With the specifications of high-tech products, a marketing manager must evaluate these two limits by analyzing the price elasticity of demand of the targeted market segments and by estimating the costs learning curve.

7.1.1 Evaluating the price elasticity of demand

The price elasticity of demand in relation to price measures the variation of customer purchases according to an increase or decrease in price: if elasticity is high, demand for a product is influenced by its price. Understanding demand elasticity for a product allows firms to

Price pointers	Actions	Pricing techniques
Market segment acceptance	Evaluation of demand elasticity to price	Comparison with substitute products Pricing to value
Competitor's pricing strategy	Competitor's price checks	Market price Bidding price
Product cost structure	Measure of the learning curve	Break-even point Cost + profit margin

Figure 7.2 From bottom price to ceiling price.

determine which products drive market penetration and thus require a low penetration price and which solutions can be priced at a premium, like in the case of subscription TV or online services like VOD.

Usually, innovative high-tech products have low elasticity. This means that high variation in price, an increase as well as a decrease, does not significantly modify demand. These high-tech products have few substitutes, and competitors and buyers are less sensitive to price than to additional performance. Furthermore, the high price of these products is often perceived as a sign of quality and reinforces a customer's confidence in the company.

The price elasticity of demand increases for market-driven or less innovative high-tech products. The entry of competitors with similar but less expensive products or new products with a better price-performance ratio makes the buyer more sensitive to price. Ultimately, the product becomes standardized and its high price loses a part of its reassuring value. In this case, a significant decrease in price would lead to a large increase in demand as can be seen now in the home electronics and personal computer markets.

A foolproof method does not exist for determining the elasticity of a product. In the case of high-tech products, the task becomes even more difficult because of the short product life and fast rate at which these products change. In addition, it is impossible to use statistics of past demand usually because these numbers do not exist. Finally, test markets are very costly and quickly outdated, so a high-tech company often must rely on surveys of customers who used the prototypes or tested the new products in the hope that these customers are representative of the overall segment. This is not always the case, and experience shows that innovators and early adopters are less price-sensitive than other consumer categories.

Often chances must be taken and an analysis must be performed in order to hypothesize the buying behavior of target customers while referring to available data for products that the new product will replace.

Eventually, a high-tech product's elasticity can usually be measured by noticing shifts in price through sales figures. For instance, when the major U.S. chemical company DuPont, soon after introducing a new fiber called Kevlar, had to revise its price upward, customers protested but in the end accepted the increase. In another case, when a large French chemical company increased prices of all its molecules (mostly elastomers) by more than 30%, it managed to keep almost all its customers; only one segment changed suppliers.

Similarly, in the mainframe computer industry, whose customers are big private firms or governmental agencies, the recent trend of decrease in price has led to a volume extension (see Figure 7.3). A new CMOS technology as well as the use of more standard components have allowed vendors like IBM, Amdahl, or Hitachi to decrease their price since 1992. On average, a 25% decrease in unit price has translated into an increase of 10% in volume.

In a totally different case, consumer video equipment such as camcorders and VCRs proved to be products with a high elasticity. In 1990, under pressure from Asian competitors, prices of camcorders fell 8% and the market's volume grew 40%, which shows that although one cannot predict elasticity, one can certainly observe it.

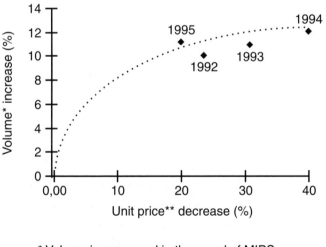

* Volume is measured in thousand of MIPS
(million instructions per second) capacity memory
** Unit price is MIPS price in $

Figure 7.3 Price elasticity of mainframe computers. (*Source*: IDC, Gartner Group; compiled by Eric Viardot.)

7.1.2   Estimating the costs learning curve

To show a profit that allows future investments, a company must at least cover its variable costs that are linked to production volume and its fixed costs (salaries, rent, administration, R&D) that are necessary to manufacture its product. Identifying and controlling these costs can lead a company to measure its learning curve.

This learning curve effect corresponds to the company's improved know-how as its production increases during the growth stage of the life cycle: purchasing optimization, design simplification for manufacturing purposes, output increase for production facilities, improvement of sales force, selection of distributors, and increased performance of sales promotion campaigns. All these gains in productivity lead to a decrease in the average unit cost. This decrease in cost could be passed on to the price in order to react to a competitor's actions or to increase price-sensitive demand.

This strategy is characteristic of the electronics industry. Intel and Texas Instruments use this strategy for pricing their memories and semi-conductors; microcomputer and workstation manufacturers have also chosen this strategy. In the pager business, Motorola, the world leader, applies the same strategy in the face of Japanese competition, relying on industrial robots made by Seiko of Japan to drive its manufacturing costs down.

As a matter of fact, the average annual decline in price for purchased parts in computers and communications is roughly 10% per year; such an abrupt curve is unique to the electronics industry.

The learning curve is valid for high-tech products because of the high level of R&D costs that these products require. Because the product life cycles are fairly short, these expenses must be written off very quickly (for example, in one year for computers, and in two years for robotics) and these R&D costs inflate the average unit cost at the beginning of the product's life, before decreasing very quickly. This unit cost variation is reflected in the changing unit price (see Figure 7.4).

Every marketing manager must continuously follow the changes in the average unit cost and its position on the price experience curve according to the trend of the market price. A company that notices its costs decreasing much faster than market prices knows that it is benefiting from its experience and is gaining by profit margin and market share.

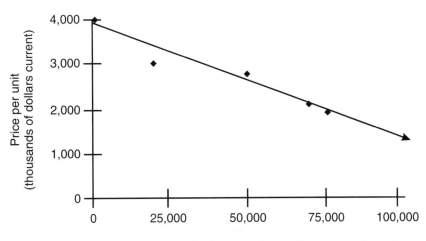

Figure 7.4 Price learning curve in the personal computer industry. (*Source:* Bain & Co., IDC.)

On the contrary, a company with costs that are increasing faster than the industry average will see its margins fade away. This company is losing its maneuvering autonomy as well as its market share. Usually, at this point, the company will complain of "dumping," "unfair competition," or "companies that are undercutting prices," without realizing that its inability to be more successful (attaining a higher performance) is leading to its own failure.

Actually it is to be noted that the learning curve analysis is adapted to products that can be mass produced rather than to very customized manufacturing systems, even if R&D costs need to be written off in both situations.

7.1.3 Taking competitors into account

In the high-tech world more than in any other industry, the first company on the market sets the market price, particularly for a very innovative product. For a company that does not take the pole position, competitors will set the standards and this company must position itself according to them, as seen in Chapter 9.

For example, in the phone business, new entrants are pricing their solutions to maximize the number of users switching from the incumbent. In Europe, like in the United States, most new entrants have begun with a 15 to 20% discount, as did Cegetel and Bouygues Telecom in France, or Sprint and MCI in the American market. Experience shows that those discounts decrease to an almost nil point over time once the average market price reaches a level where the relative market shares of the major players are stabilized. It happened in the United States, and it is currently occurring in Europe in the mobile phone business where competitive struggles are still a reality in France, Spain, Germany, and Italy. It will probably happen in the fixed phone European markets in 1998 when the deregulation imposed by the European Union will free those markets to competition.

Price contributes to the competitive positioning of a product on a given market segment and may be a competitive weapon by changing customers' perceptions of the competitors' products. Accordingly when facing a particular competitor, a company can set a higher price if its customers feel that its product provides a higher level of performance and if they have a better image of the product. In the photocamera business, Cortax, a Japanese firm, has always chosen a high-quality position for its products that are manufactured in Germany. Cortax systematically and successfully practiced a policy of high prices in comparison with Nikon or Canon, for example.

The marketing manager must know and understand competitor prices; he or she can inquire about price reports with distributors, obtain competitor rates, ask the sales force to catch up with competitor prices, and seek customer input.

7.2   Various pricing techniques

Only after estimating demand, evaluating costs, and identifying competitor prices can the marketing manager set the price of his or her product. Several methods of determining prices of high-tech products are possible. Asked about setting prices, marketing managers of high-tech products usually give priority to pricing based upon the company's offer using cost + profit margin or break-even point methods (see Figure 7.5).

If necessary, these marketing managers take into account competitors (using market price method), particularly in the case of a bidding process,

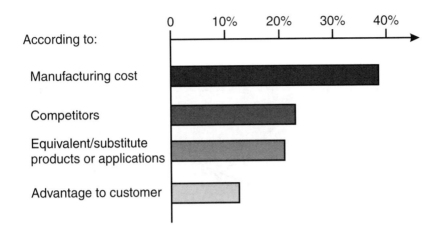

Figure 7.5 Different pricing tactics. Tabulation of responses to the question "How do you determine the price of a new product?" (*Source:* Interviews by Eric Viardot.)

which is very common in military or government markets (using the bidding price method). Few of these marketing managers establish a pricing method based upon customer demand (with the perceived value or comparison with substitute products methods). All the six different pricing techniques will now be detailed.

7.2.1 Cost + profit margin

This simple method, which is frequently used in the high-tech field, consists of adding a profit margin percentage to a total cost. This method is simple—almost simplistic—and is usually justified by the fact that it is easier to estimate changing costs than a changing customer demand of a particular segment. However, because it is completely independent from the market, this technique will never lead to an optimal profit.

7.2.2 Rate of return and break-even point

This financial price approach seeks to determine the price that can earn a sufficient middle- to long-term return on the investment. The unit price is calculated as follows: $p = $ unit cost $+$ (rate of return $\times$ investment)/quantity sold, and the break-even point is the level at which sales figures cover related fixed and variable costs. For example, as shown in Figure 7.6, a company invests $200,000 in new product and expects a 15% profit. If the unit

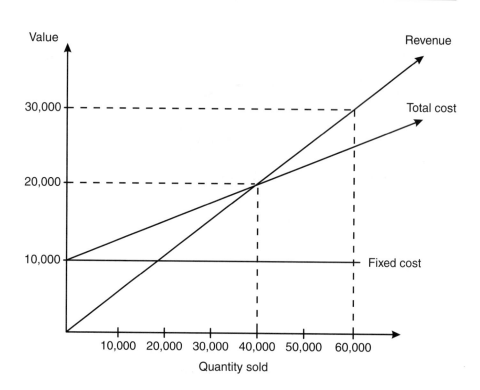

Figure 7.6   Profitability, price, and break-even point.

cost is $45,000 and the sales objective for year one equals 6,000 units, then the unit price will be 45,000 + (15% × $200,000)/6 = $50,000. Furthermore, if fixed costs total $100,000 and variable costs (per unit) are $25,000, then the break-even point equals 4,000 units. Should the break-even point not be reached, a new price would have to be calculated with a lower level of sales.

Again, this method does not take into account customer demand or reactions. For instance, a high price may lead to a low break-even point, but it is possible that no products will be purchased at such a price level.

7.2.3   Market price

When competing products already exist on the market, they must be taken into account. Setting a price according to prices of a main competitor is a better approximation of the market than the preceding techniques because this price reflects demand. Furthermore, a price can be used to reinforce the product's positioning in relation to its competition.

It is fairly easy to measure competitor prices for standard and not very differentiated products, but this method cannot be easily applied to highly innovative products or to very specific, customized systems. The only way is to conduct customer interviews or to rely on the sales force or any other source of information detailed in Chapter 9.

7.2.4 Bidding price

Bidding processes are traditionally used for military and government contracts but also for some private industry contracts. In a bidding process, competition is open and usually the supplier with the lowest price for the contract is selected. The bidding price is set according to the available information about competitor bids and the customer's opinion of the product's advantages.

Because a higher profit but fewer possibilities to achieve this profit are directly associated with a higher price, an expected profit graph can be drawn according to the bidding price. However, when the marketing manager is given a "must win" direction from management, he or she may have to ignore cost and profit: in such a case the concern is to be lower than the lowest competitor. (For more details on bidding price, see [2].)

7.2.5 Comparison with substitute products

When an innovative product appears on the market and does not yet have a competitor, this product should be evaluated in relation to the products for which it could substitute. For instance, when launching a new biotechnology product, a pharmaceutical laboratory positioned its product's price according to the price of a traditional cancer treatment because, for patients, the new product was an improvement over long and costly classical treatments.

7.2.6 Value perceived by customers

This last pricing technique is based on a simple assumption: when a product responds to customer needs, these customers know the product's value, taking into account the different advantages; consequently, they know the price that they are prepared to pay for it.

Customers can directly communicate the price of the product according to the value it represents to them. Overall economic gains of the new product (saving time, manufacturing, labor, maintenance costs, and usability) can be estimated, and the potential value of these economic gains to a targeted segment of customers can be assessed.

ICL launched a colza-controlling product with a 10% increase in the performance of colza harvest that could be easily measured by customers. ICL set the price of this product, taking into account the cost-benefit analysis of the solution offered to customers in different segments of selected markets. Likewise, in the beginning of the 1990s, a company had to decide whether it should enter the computer systems facility management business, dominated by companies like American EDS or European Cap Sogeti. To many large industrial customers, the value of such a service is straightforward: it is the amount of savings they can make by externalizing the operation of their data centers.

The company compared the costs of operating various corporate data centers with its own operating costs and thus estimated what its pricing could be for such a service. It then successfully entered the market, aiming at firms that had data centers operating at above-average costs.

Customers can also be asked to voice their opinion on the value of product features by comparing them with those of other products. The product's perceived value can then be calculated and its price can be established accordingly. Table 7.1 is an example that involves three

Table 7.1
Sample Product Characteristics Comparison

Characteristic	1	2	3	% of Importance
Product performance	30	25	45	45%
Product quality	32	28	40	25%
Enhancement capacity	41	25	34	13%
Ease of use	18	49	33	11%
Ease of maintenance	24	23	53	6%
Weighted value	30.2	28.3	53	

products. For each characteristic the buyer can give a total of 100 points divided among the three products, weighing each characteristic.

At the same prices, the company can increase its price compared to the market average. It can also decide to lower the price to reach new customers (with the difference between the perceived value and the actual value) and to increase its market share as a result.

7.2.7   Pricing below costs

In some cases, pricing below current costs can make sense for a company that anticipates significant cost reduction from scale economies and experience effects, once enough volume has been made. To do so, it must meet two prerequisites. The first is to carry important short-run losses whose amount must be compared with the drawback of not having the technology as a standard. The second is to have a manufacturing capacity strong enough to satisfy demand so that supply shortages will not drive the market price back up again. The short-run loss must be balanced against the potential gains.

This is precisely what Matsushita did when launching the VHS recorder. Similarly, in the software area, Netscape gave away its browser to various firms and organizations in order to achieve maximum market penetration. Profit should come later in the form of fees that Netscape could collect for every transaction executed using its browser once it has become a de facto standard.

In the same way, Dolby licensed its high-fidelity sound technology to numerous firms with a very low licensing fee. Though it reaped only a few cents for every audio player that included its technology, Dolby has built such a large volume that it manages to make a satisfactory profit while preventing any push by competitors to develop a superior technology with so little unit margin.

On the down side, consumer electronics firms like Toshiba and Matsushita made this bet on the nascent digital videodisk market in 1997 and failed to achieve the sales they anticipated. It seems that the entrenched VHS tape and larger laser disk users segment cannot be easily breached and will require time and money to surrender.

7.3   Adapting a price policy to different types of high-tech products

When asked about determining prices for high-technology products, marketing managers emphasized the difficulty encountered in making decisions vis-à-vis customers; instead, they prefer to refer to their company's offer. Their answers also showed the underutilization of price as a key marketing variable. A price, when determined according to the expectations and needs of customers in a segment, reinforces positioning and allows a company to earn more substantial profits by remaining closer to the market.

In reality, four types of situations can be distinguished depending upon whether high-tech products are standardized or differentiated and whether these products are pushed by the company's offer (product-driven) or pulled by the market's demand (market-driven). Each situation calls for a different approach, as is represented in Table 7.2.

1. Whether basic or differentiated, when products are pushed by a firm because they are innovative, we recommend pricing them according to the value they bring to customers. As a matter of fact, being the first on the market gives room and flexibility to set up the price and extract the maximum premium from customers. This was the strategy of Cray when it introduced its first scientific supercomputers. The test markets showed that the value of such powerful computers was enormous to clients like military forces, weather forecasting agencies, or research laboratories because

Table 7.2
Price Policies and Product Types

Type of Product/ Marketing	Standard Product	Differentiated Product
Supply	1. Customers value	1. Customers value
Demand	2. Competitors/costs	3. Competitors/ customers value

they could perform calculations that were previously either impossible or too long and complex to make. Intel pursued a similar strategy when introducing its first 286 microprocessor family.

2. However, as soon as standard products achieve success and are pulled by demand, new competitors enter the market. Pricing must therefore be adjusted to competitors while maintained above costs. This is the current situation in the microprocessor business, where Intel is under pressure from cheaper competitors like Cyrix, AMD, or IBM. The key to achieving success is to constantly lower the product unit cost through scale economics by aggressively managing the production volume. This is the current strategy of Intel, which has built up a strong manufacturing capacity in order to drive the price of its chips down so as to counter its competitors.

3. When demand "pulls" the sales of differentiated products, the company must obviously adapt its prices to the market. For this reason, all large IBM, DEC, or Unisys computers are subjected to quotations adapted to every customer, even if the market represents several thousand companies. A standard list price does not really exist for an IBM or a DEC top-of-the-line computer; prices depend upon the complexity of the product demanded by the customer as well as the supplier and competition's aggressiveness in sales. Similarly, major integrators like EDS or Cap Sogeti offer customized software to customers who demand complex programs that are perfectly adapted to their needs. They determine the price of these products depending upon the customer's financial abilities and the cost of available resources to assure the best possible performance within the scope of the customer's budget.

Overall, high-tech companies still have room for improvement when setting prices based upon the value for their customers; this is part of learning about marketing. These companies can benefit considerably from the experience of companies that market more traditional products.

7.4   Integrating the other determinants of price

Every price decision about a product must take into account the prices within the product range, when applicable, as well as the overall price policy of the company and the reactions of other market participants.

7.4.1   Pricing according to the product range

The high rate of new high-tech product releases often leads to large product ranges that are frequently updated. So, for every new product belonging to a range, a correct understanding and forecasting of customers' perceptions is a necessity, as far as pricing is concerned, to balance two risks.

On one hand, if a new product is introduced at a price that is too high compared to the product range, the risk exists that sales will not take off because customers continue to prefer an older model with a more attractive price-performance ratio. On the other hand, a new product that is introduced with a very low price compared to the rest of the products in a range can "ruin" these other products, leaving large quantities of unsold goods, or can generate a demand that the company might not be able to satisfy immediately.

Price is the determining element in curbing or accelerating cannibalization of a product. Furthermore, a decrease in price for an already existing product can accelerate its phase out and prepare its replacement. In high technology where dynamics are a requirement for survival, this type of price policy is often necessary but not always without difficulties. For instance, in 1991, Apple had to lay off 1,500 employees, who fell victim to the success of lower priced Macintosh computers that cannibalized a part of higher priced Macs. As a result, an 85% increase in the quantity of Macintosh sold translated into only a 13% increase in sales figures and a stagnant profit for the first quarter of 1991; at that time, Apple had to decrease its number of employees in order to remain profitable.

7.4.2   Pricing according to the company's pricing strategy

The price of a new product must fit into a company's usual practice because of its psychological importance and the need for high-technology companies to continuously reassure and secure their customers.

When IBM chose to attack the family computer business (with lower priced products compared to its existing range), it priced its microcomputers at a higher level than the average market price because, on its industrial markets, IBM usually sets its prices higher compared to the rest of the computer industry.

When Apple chose to attack the business computing market, its high-quality Macintosh was relatively low in price compared to competitors in the same segment; this was symbolic for a company that started off with a mission to make computers available to everyone.

7.4.3 Pricing according to the reactions from other competitive forces in the market

Sales force, distributors, and dealers should be consulted prior to taking final decisions on the pricing of a high-tech product because they can react negatively when facing a product that they consider too expensive.

Finally, a government can have a restricting role on pricing, for example, when setting up monopoly regulation and antitrust policies and, furthermore, through price controls as is the case in most countries for the biochemical industry where every new drug requires government approval not only for its content but also for its price quotation.

7.5 Chapter summary

Price is an essential component of the marketing strategy. For high technology products, prices are on the average much higher than prices of standard products, and high technology products often succeed each other at a higher rate than standard products.

To determine a product's price, a marketing manager must know the ceiling price above which customers will no longer buy and the floor price below which his or her company will lose money. Besides these two limits, the marketing manager must also observe competitor prices.

The marketing manager has at his or her disposal different pricing techniques that depend upon the company's offer (cost + profit margin and break-even point), the competitor's offer (market price and bidding price), and customer demand (comparison with substitute products or perceived value by the customer). Logically speaking, prices should be set according to customer demand, but marketing managers still overemphasize the company's offer.

Pricing techniques must also be adapted to the particular type of high-technology products; standard or differentiated, product-driven or market-driven.

Finally, each price decision must take into account prices within the product range as well as the company's usual price policy and government regulation.

References

[1] Boss, J.-F., and L. Tuvée, *Le Marketing des Entreprises de Haute Technologie*, Rapport au Ministère de l'Industrie, Adetem, April 1990.

[2] Helgeson, D., *Engineers and Managers Guide to Winning Proposals*, Norwood, MA: Artech House, 1994.

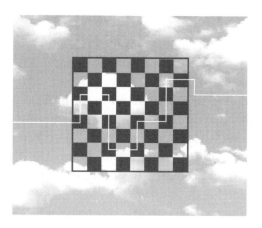

8

Communication Strategy for High-Tech Products

A ny company in the high-technology business must communicate to make its products known to targeted customers and to strengthen its solutions positioning. However, the specificity of high-tech firms imposes a certain number of characteristics, from the development of a communication budget to the planning of communication campaigns, including the use of different media, the particular importance of public relations, and corporate advertising.

8.1 Communication for high-tech products

The three main characteristics of a high-technology product (technology, rate of change, innovation) have an important impact on the communication strategy for the selected market segments.

First, the product's high-technological content requires the interpretation of the advantages that the product offers the customer in response to his or her needs and wants. Second, the product's rate of change leads to an announcement to customers about the product's availability. Third, the innovation intrinsic in each product requires an explanation of the new technology and the added value for the customer.

Furthermore, because the customer's main purchasing criteria for high-technology products, besides price, are confidence in the selling company, the product's performance, and quality (see Figure 3.4), these criteria determine a very specific communication style. As a general rule, the communication of high-technology products must above all be reassuring and instructive instead of captivating and attractive, as is the case for more traditional products.

Finally, the targets of any communication campaign for a high-tech solution are heterogeneous; not only should the person (user) who defines the need be reached, but also the person who recommends a solution or a brand (advisor) and, last but not least, the person who signs the check (decision maker). These specifics for high-technology products can be found when setting and then allocating the communication budget.

8.2 Setting a communication budget

The recommended method for developing a communication budget is the so-called objective-and-task method, where marketers first define their specific objectives, then determine the tasks that must be performed to achieve these goals, and finally estimate the costs of the necessary resources to perform these tasks. This method has the advantage of spelling out assumptions about the relationship between dollars spent, exposure levels, and sales.

Unfortunately, in the high-technology business, this method is not of much use because most related data are not easily defined. The make-up of the target market (consisting of innovators and early adopters) makes it difficult to assess the exposure cost of a message and even more difficult to assess the number of exposures to the message that are needed before a part of the target market decides to try the product.

Consequently, advertising budgets are very often determined pragmatically as a percentage of sales figures or sales forecasting or advertising budgets of previous years for similar products, if available.

The key point is to be able to react quickly and with flexibility to any major change in the market while taking into account any move from the competition such as when Apple spent $15 million to launch Macintosh and established a new threshold considerably raising the market's entry barrier for advertising. Similarly, in the United Kingdom, Orange, a new entrant into the phone business, launched its first cellular mobile network in 1994 with a $15 million advertising campaign; only four years earlier, advertising expenses for the entire industry totaled only $2.5 million. In France, France Telecom spent more than double the advertising budgets of its two competitors combined, or $6 million, when launching Tatoo, a mass-market paging system.

The amount of advertising varies significantly depending upon the type of business. Figure 8.1 indicates the importance of advertising budgets in the computer and telecommunications industries.

8.3 Allocating the advertising budget

Experience shows that the selection of communication tools varies significantly according to a company's push marketing strategy (which pushes the product to the customer using distributors) or its pull marketing strategy (which attracts customers with advertising). This selection also depends upon whether the company sells its products or services to businesses or to individual consumers.

Nevertheless, besides these differences, high-technology companies similarly prefer a certain number of media types. Figure 8.2, which was compiled after surveying 164 companies, represents their choices.

Sales and sales management usually appear at the top of the market's preferred communication tools. Implications of this method will be explained in the following chapter.

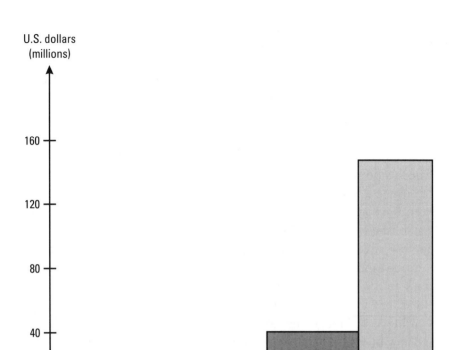

Figure 8.1   Media advertising budgets for high-technology industries in France in 1990. (*Source:* CAM, 1990.)

Trade magazines that specialize in and target a specific audience are a preferred medium when presenting an innovation or developing the advantages of a new product or a new technology. These magazines have a strong educational role. The most simple way to provide them with information is the news release, usually a typewritten copy of less than 400 words with the firm's name, address, and phone number as well as the contact person. There are also feature articles, which are longer manuscripts that are written by a member of an association, a distinguished researcher, or an executive for a specific magazine. Articles are always preferred over interviews, which are more difficult to control from the interviewee's side.

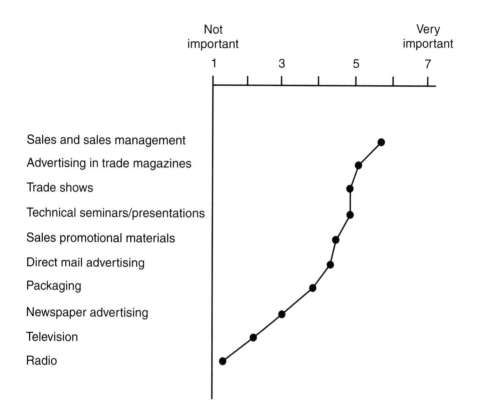

Figure 8.2 Importance of promotional tools used by high-tech firms. (*After:* [1].)

In addition, advertising can take advantage of the high level of credibility of these professional publications; readers use these magazines as tools, and this reinforces the efficiency of ad campaigns. Furthermore, communication campaigns for products can be developed using a technical angle while minimizing the risk of being misunderstood, because the readers of these publications are familiar with technology.

Every industry has its specialized publications that often have a worldwide coverage like *Flight International, Défense, European Polymer News, Computerworld,* and *Via Satellite*; and nearly 50 publications are in circulation just for the computer industry.

However, with the exception of the main publications, the readers of these periodicals are usually difficult to evaluate. This difficulty hinders the task of calculating the profitability of a company's media investment as it is usually measured by its expanse of readers.

Other communication publications are sponsored magazines, like *IBM Think* or *AT&T Technology, Telesis, and Uplink,* and newsletters. They are distributed to customers and interested parties at no cost. They contain some useful articles and can gain respectability even though they are clearly partisan.

Trade shows are frequently used because a product's technical features as well as its advantages to the customer can be shown more easily. Furthermore, attending customers have made the effort to come and are often more receptive to any innovation presented.

Trade shows are usually specialized by industry. Some are more prestigious than others, and every large manufacturer must be present in order to maintain the company's image, even if participating in the trade show yields very little. Trade shows are also large "get-togethers" where, at regular intervals, all market participants can be found and competitors and their activities can be observed. Often new-product announcements are made at these trade shows to take advantage of the presence of journalists and the public. Examples of trade shows are Comdex for microcomputers in Los Angeles, Kunstoff for the plastics industry in Düsseldorf, and the Paris Air Show for aeronautics.

The main problem of trade shows lies in the large number of attending participants and the presence of competitors who can negatively affect the messages that a company wants to communicate to its customers. A new tendency is that of individual trade shows organized by only one company and where business partners and third-party product makers also exhibit. DEC's "DECWorld" and Apple's "Apple Expo" are the most famous. At this type of trade show all of a company's proposed products can be presented in one large area instead of in a small booth. These trade shows, which are always very impressive, can assure that customers have faith in the organizing company (which is a very important element of choice in high technology).

These individual trade shows also offer the opportunity to organize a gigantic public relations event for customers, distributors, and journalists while ensuring that its impact will not benefit competitors. However, this type of trade show does require sizable financial resources.

A more economical solution consists of making company visits. All large high-technology companies, from Intel, Aerospatiale, and Rhone-Poulenc to IBM, but many small- to medium-sized high-technology companies as well, organize trips so that their existing and prospective customers can visit R&D facilities, under a nondisclosure agreement.

These visits are also part of a purchasing activity by allowing customers to test new prototypes, to find out about a potential supplier's long-term plans, and to ask questions about a new technology.

Scientific conventions are communication tools reserved for companies who sell to manufacturers of chemicals, aeronautics, or nuclear technology, for example. At conventions, researchers have the opportunity to meet and communicate their latest technological innovations. For this reason, conventions as well as trade shows provide excellent opportunities to observe the competition.

Seminars are educational marketing tools particularly adapted for high-technology products. Oracle, one of the leading U.S. software companies, has set the standard for this mode of advertising. Every year it organizes more than 600 seminars for 75,000 existing and prospective customers.

During a seminar, a new technology can be thoroughly explained and customers can familiarize themselves with this technology before adopting it. A seminar explains what a technology is all about and will show that this technology functions well. A seminar is always focused on customers and not on products. Because the objective is to break a customer's natural resistance to innovation and to supply all necessary explanations, seminars are usually led by coordinators who have both technical experience and communication talents. The same type of profile can be found in speakers who appear at conventions.

Some seminars are also addressed to distributors. The messages are nearly identical; distributors must also be experts who can advise their customers accordingly by offering, from among all the available products, those that truly correspond to customer needs.

For sales communication materials, the largest part of budgets and efforts is dedicated to catalogs and product literature. Product literature presents technical characteristics of each solution, emphasizing the idea that a picture can say a thousand words.

Furthermore, the importance of the performance factor in the purchase of a high-technology product requires the availability of a large amount of technical data in order to allow for precise evaluations. In certain sectors, such as the computer industry, aeronautics, or nuclear technology, brochures that describe a single product can exceed ten pages. Finally, experience shows that the greater part of early majority buyers thrive on perusing technical catalogs that stimulate their desire to purchase a new product.

Video cassettes and CDs also tend to become additional communication tools. Due to their format, they lend themselves less to detail than brochures and are therefore often used for corporate communication purposes. In January 1989, Thomson, Compagnie Française de Promotion, and Société Française de Promotion created a demonstration and user method for the European HDTV, titled *International HD*, which in one year led to more than 30 short films with European standards.

Direct marketing, which consists of mailings or telemarketing, is more often used for products with a low unit cost and can efficiently replace a sales force with its lower cost. Dell Computer was the first company to sell PCs by mail only; today, for large computer manufacturers such as IBM, DEC, and Machine Bull, income generated by mail order represents up to 20% of total sales revenue.

Furthermore, direct marketing relies on more sophisticated database processing techniques. Direct marketing better targets the messages for particular market segments by personalizing the relationship with the consumer. Apple relied extensively upon and successfully executed this direct marketing strategy when it launched the portable Macintosh in 1991 by mailing various differentiated messages to different target markets.

A marketing tool of the 1990s, direct marketing is destined to develop itself in high-technology companies as well, especially in companies that sell to the public. Sales representatives for microcomputer software or camcorders, for example, can more and more often resort to direct marketing due to the availability of toll-free numbers, which provide a direct link to the customer.

Packaging plays an important role when communicating a product's advantages and positioning to customers. For consumer goods, packaging is a very important product dimension and, as we showed in Chapter 6 for high-technology products, a tendency toward simplification and streamlining exists in conjunction with eliminating overly sophisticated and useless accessories. This trend can also be found in industrial markets. Companies must invest more and more in packaging to make their products look more attractive for decision makers or users without either technology obsessions or even mere technical backgrounds.

General news publications that can be used to communicate high-technology products are generally news magazines (*Time*, *Newsweek*, *The Economist*). Their readers fit an "executive" profile and are sensitive to the innovation and prestige of a technology. These periodicals can reach users such as technical and financial decision makers. Daily newspapers that are geared toward the same type of readers can also be used.

Nevertheless, the style of news magazines makes technical advertising for a product inefficient. In these magazines, pictorial advertising for corporate advertising campaigns is more appropriate. The same holds true for the general economic press (for example, *BusinessWeek* and *The Financial Express*), which targets senior executives. On the other hand, the business press (for example, *Forbes* and *Fortune*), which is more concentrated on management, allows certain product-advertising campaigns, provided they are speaking the customer's language and not imposing a technical view.

A particular segmentation and positioning can lead to the selection of specific publications. For instance, Xerox places advertising inserts in women's magazines because it assumes that doing so is a means of reaching secretaries; secretaries are often influential decision makers in purchases of sophisticated office equipment (such as color monitor microcomputers, laser printers, or intelligent photocopiers).

Television is not frequently used because of its cost in absolute value; it is usually reserved for very large companies that target sizable market segments. In 1990, IBM spent 60% of its media budget on television, mainly on the promotion of its microcomputers. Compaq, its most important competitor in this market, has also made television its preferred form of media.

Besides its coverage of an enormous target market at a reasonable cost per thousand contacts, television's other advantage is its ability to rapidly create a high rate of awareness. This led Compaq to use television in France—when the company arrived in France, it was practically unknown to executives of French companies, who are the principal purchasing decision makers for microcomputers for professional use.

Television allowed Compaq to quickly pull itself up to the level of its competitors in terms of awareness.

This same reason led the Société Nationale des Poudres et Explosifs (SNPE), a national French company that develops products for space and defense markets (explosives and rocket fuel), to use television in order to quickly increase its awareness and establish an identity that nowadays no longer corresponds to what its name suggests (that is, the manufacturing of gunpowder and explosives).

Radio is a secondary form of media; it has a low cost but is very limited in format because in three minutes it is impossible to explain a product or a technology without actually physically showing the audience. Therefore, radio is more useful for increasing awareness and especially for stressing specific activities such as the announcing of a trade show.

As far as online advertising is concerned, with only $324.5 million invested in the United States in 1996 (and less in Europe and the rest of the world), it is not yet a heavily used media. Today, the majority of firms using online advertising are computer, software, and telecommunication vendors; according to a recent survey by Cowles/Simba, 17 sites represented 55% of total advertising spending on the web. However, online advertising should get more and more significant as new firms try online advertising, mostly on the Internet, targeting not only businesses but increasingly mass consumers (see Figure 8.3).

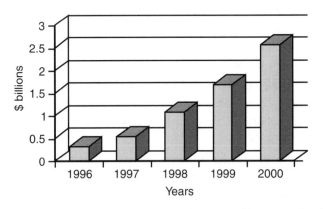

Figure 8.3 Online advertising expenditures. (*Source:* Cowles/Simba Information, 1997.)

As a conclusion regarding the allocation of the communication budget, let us reiterate that a very cost-effective way of getting general (and specialized) free media coverage is to announce major events at press conferences where media personnel are invited and supplied with written materials, photographs, and video materials.

Once the advertising campaign is implemented, marketers should always try to evaluate the effectiveness of the campaign. There are various ways according to the schedule of the advertising campaign.

- Pretests are made before the campaign starts to evaluate the effectiveness of one message, usually through focus groups.

- Post-tests are performed after the campaign to measure the changes in customers compared to the initial communication objectives, which are awareness, understanding of the product, appreciation, and purchase decision of the product.

Because it is not easy to assess the direct effects of advertising on sales, post-tests are based on memory, assuming that customers are more inclined to buy a solution if they can remember an advertisement about it than if they cannot. In the recognition test, respondents are shown the actual advertisement and asked whether they know it or not. In recall tests, respondents are only asked about what they have seen or heard recently. Recall tests can be aided or unaided. In the former, respondents are shown a list of products or brand or company names to refresh their memories, while in the latter they are not given any clues.

Quite recently, Texas Instruments launched an advertising campaign to demonstrate the advantages of its new Digital Light Processing, a new video projection technology. Post-test surveys clearly indicated that this campaign increased the brand awareness and purchase intent among potential users as illustrated in Table 8.1.

Although we do recommend using tests to evaluate the efficiency of an advertising campaign, marketers should be aware that advertising agencies and the published media they sell may use those surveys to serve their own interests. To eliminate any bias, the best solution is to have those tests performed by an independent third party and not directly by the advertising agency.

Table 8.1

An Example of the Value of Post-Test Surveys: The Measurement of the Impact of an Advertising Campaign. (*Source:* Texas Instruments.)

Attribute	Before Ads	After Ads	% Change
Unaided brand awareness	0.7	4.3	514
Aided ad awareness	21.3	39.6	86
Purchase intent	9.2	18.4	100

8.4   Corporate advertising and public relations

Different marketing studies prove that in the buying process of any product, the company's reputation is of a comparatively greater importance when the products are more complex, the business risk is higher, and the buyers are less knowledgeable. This situation perfectly corresponds to cases of high-technology products where one of the three main purchasing criteria states that buyers must have confidence in the selling organization. This need to reassure potential customers and buyers leads to a particular emphasis on corporate advertising and public relations.

Corporate advertising publicizes a company as a whole, with its subsidiaries, its people, its range of products, and its vision of the future. Corporate advertising tries to create a visual identity that can be recognized easily through all the company's permanent media (such as logos, brochures, business cards, signs, stationery, building, and uniforms) and all the other media (such as TVs, newspapers, and radio) with specific advertising campaigns.

Corporate advertising affects a company as a brand name affects a product. The goal of corporate advertising is to establish a long-term image in the minds of buyers; its messages deal with a company and its objectives. In the computer industry, IBM shows that it stands for security; DEC shows that it offers customized and standard products; and Compaq shows that, as a leader, it is the first company to offer the best solution.

Corporate advertising is interested in projecting an everlasting image with buyers. Buyers remember a permanent reference point that will not be disrupted when new technological announcements are made. A company must, of course, keep its promises for its products because, if it does not do so, it will fail. However, its corporate advertising will build the trust for customers in targeted segments.

Public relations seeks to establish and reinforce goodwill between an organization and all its publics (customers, employees, suppliers, shareholders, financial publics, mass media, consumers' associations, government officials, and the general public). The major tools in public relations are news (from creating news stories to getting them accepted by the press or a given public); speeches; events; public service activities; written materials (such as annual reports, brochures, articles, company newsletter, and magazines); audiovisual materials; and telephone information services.

Compared with advertising, public relations provides a higher degree of credibility and better efficiency when overcoming resistance to change; actually, these messages are perceived as if they were not directly sent by the company and are therefore more readily accepted. Credibility and overcoming resistance to change are two key elements of success in marketing a high-technology product or a new technology.

Emphasis on trade shows, conventions, and seminars as well as editorials in professional journals shows how high-technology companies are aware that communication is not limited to single advertising actions, even for consumer markets. Usually, companies provide their own development and coordination of public relations strategies, although some companies use special consulting firms, particularly when launching a new product, to maximize the impact of the event.

8.5 Managing promotional tools

Not all communication tools have the same purpose with regard to a purchasing decision. In the online services business, the main objective of a promotion campaign is to inform customers of the benefits of a little-known solution. Conversely, in the mobile phone business, the goal is to proclaim a company's value proposition as compared to the competitors' because the problem is not product awareness but inducing customers to switch from the competition. Some communication tools are appropriate for establishing awareness; others are excellent for communicating a better understanding of products and technology; even others strengthen product appreciation or finalize the purchase (see Table 8.2). Accordingly, these tools must therefore be used at different points in time.

Let us consider the case of the launching of a new product. First of all, a marketing manager must plan advertising and direct marketing campaigns in order to establish product awareness. These campaigns are followed by invitations to seminars and the publishing of papers in professional journals as well as participation in trade shows to explain a new technology and its benefits. The sales force and distributors will be invited to reinforce customer beliefs by organizing product demonstrations where they will be allowed to test, touch, and see the new product.

Trade shows, seminars, literature that can be read and reread at leisure, and packaging help to familiarize the customer with a product. These tools pave the way of the sales force and distributor by helping the customer make a choice that best corresponds to his or her needs. If

Table 8.2
Efficiency of Different Promotional Tools Used in the Purchasing of High-Technology Products

	Awareness	Understanding	Appreciation	Purchase Decision
Sales and sales management	+	+	+	+++
Professional journals	+	+++	+	+
Trade shows	+	+	+	+
Seminars and conventions	+	+++	+	+
Sales promotional materials	+	+	+	+
Direct marketing	++	++	++	++
Packaging	+	+	+	+
Newspaper advertising	+++	+	+	+
Television advertising	+++	+	+	+
Radio advertising	+	+	+	+

necessary, actions to stimulate awareness can be planned, particularly if demand takes longer to emerge than estimated.

However, in reality, because new product announcements in the high-technology industry follow each other rapidly (even if not all products are revolutionary), a marketing manager must concentrate on the preparation of communication activities for product launches and slightly neglect the rest.

A good communication campaign will reinforce the key success factors for product launches and should be addressed first to "innovators," explaining a new product's advantages, conveying a successful product image, or publicly announcing credible references. On the other hand, an inferior communication campaign could destroy a product.

Often, product launches are at the heart of the game! A failed product launch very often means a delay in sales and can give a competitor opportunities to take advantage of this lapse of time and jump into the market. A new product should be announced at the right time, neither too early nor too late. Managing communication activities is truly an art [2]. In the computer industry, IBM and Microsoft are masters of timing; they are examples for many other high-technology companies.

8.6 Chapter summary

Advertising for high-technology products must be able to clearly translate the advantages that a customer will derive from a new technique or a new product. This type of advertising focuses on announcements of new or unprecedented products and must reassure customers.

Traditional budget-setting techniques cannot always be applied to high-technology products. When determining a budget, flexibility and pragmatism are important.

Professional journals and public relations are highly adapted to high-technology products because they provide an additional credibility for a company and are influential when overcoming resistance to change.

Communication tools must be adapted to selected objectives. Some communication tools are used to establish awareness or reinforce support while others can explain a product or will help finalize a purchase.

References

[1] Traynor, K., and S. C. Traynor, "Marketing Approaches Used by High-Tech Firms," *Industrial Marketing Management*, Vol. 18, 1989, pp. 281–287.

[2] Rabino, S., and T. E. Moore, "Managing New-Product Announcements in the Computer Industry," *Industrial Marketing Management*, Vol. 18, 1989, pp. 35–43.

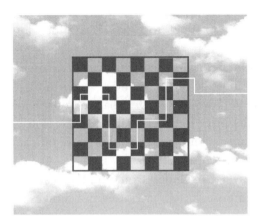

9

Distributing and Selling High-Tech Products

Selecting a selling channel is a deciding factor for a successful marketing strategy because the effective purchase of a product constitutes the ultimate outcome of its success, showing that it responds well to customer needs or wants.

High-technology products are not exempt from this rule. On the contrary, IBM, Compaq, and Merck, for example, have built their success as much on the quality of their sales policy as on the value of their products, proving that the greatest technology is useless if it cannot be sold.

The initiative of Merck's sales people in 1990, for example, allowed the company to gain 10% in market share within one year. Merck manufactures "Zocor," an expensive drug used to treat extremely high levels of cholesterol, but its network of medical sales representatives succeeded in promoting this product with physicians for less serious medical conditions. This promotion was too detrimental to Fournier's "Lipanthyl," an existing product that was five times less expensive than "Zocor."

Furthermore, one may estimate that the distribution channels account for 25 to 40% of the retail price of goods and services in high-technology businesses (see Table 9.1) while the sales channel represents between 15 to 35% of the final sales price for industrial products. Consequently, distribution channels managed efficiently can have a significant impact not only on sales but also on profit margins.

However, if high technology is not excluded from building a strong sales strategy, its characteristics impose certain priorities and choices on the design of the distribution channels.

9.1 Selecting distribution channels for high-tech products

Most high-technology companies use their own sales forces to sell products directly to customers. However, companies might have to resort to other distribution channels in order to reach all the customers of a targeted market segment in the most efficient way. This comes at a time when new channels like the Internet and online services continue to emerge and new management tools, like data networks tracking in real time the inventories of all distributors in a market, have combined to speed up the evolution of more traditional channels. Today, for instance,

Table 9.1

Split Costs in Percentage of Sales Price for Consumer High-Technology Solutions. (*Source*: McKinsey, Eric Viardot.)

	Software	Laser Printers	PCs
Channel	25	30	40
Manufacturer value added	65	30	40
Raw material/components	10	40	30

value-added resellers are becoming more prominent in the distribution of electronic and telecommunication solutions. Selecting a distribution channel is very important because it can make or break a product since distributors are part of the reinforcing loop leading to increasing returns as seen in Chapter 2. Inasmuch as their revenues depend on the size of the market they can serve, they tend to concentrate on the solution that may have the most potential buyers. For instance, in addition to the application developers, distributors have been a major force behind the success of Microsoft Windows and the decline of Apple Computer. This choice must be continuously reevaluated in order to find the most efficient networks.

For instance, in France, as in the United Kingdom, cable TV companies are realizing that direct sales forces will stay pivotal up to the end of this century, even if retailers and direct marketing become increasingly substantial.

Five selection criteria can assist a marketing manager in his or her channel-design decisions: the size of the market, the cost of the distribution network, the type of product to be marketed, the degree of control on the distribution channels, and the channel's flexibility.

9.1.1 Channel-design decisions according to the size of the market

The size of the market and the variety in customer profiles often justify the use of indirect distribution channels so as to eliminate gaps in market coverage. The computer market, of which this is absolutely representative, has gone through four characteristic phases. During the first phase (the 1950s), the systems were sophisticated and potential customers were few; this corresponded to direct sales through the intermediary of sales engineers. From the 1970s on, the arrival of minicomputers and the increased number of users led to the development of external distribution channels, usually in the form of an original equipment manufacturer (OEM), which added specific applications to computers before the actual sale.

The development of microcomputers during the 1980s led to a greater use of distributors, who became the key success factors for Apple and Compaq. Similarly, the popularity of microcomputers brought about the development of direct marketing. Dell Computer was the first company to sell its computers directly by mail order without any physical intermediary and has since been imitated by a score of other firms.

Since the onset of the 1990s, large computer firms that want to reach a greater variety of market segments have to manage different marketing structures. These companies sell some of their products through authorized dealers, establish marketing agreements with distribution chains such as Computerland, and are in contact with dealers in used computers. Sales can also be made directly from computer to computer using electronic data interchange (EDI) or the Internet, which both are experiencing strong growth. EDI volume is estimated to expand by 25 to 40% annually in Europe and the United States. At the same time, traffic and transactions over the Internet World Wide Web (WWW), estimated today at $500 million at best, are developing steadily, while the number of commercial WWW sites has rocketed from 370 in June 1994, to 50,000 in January 1996, and more than 200,000 in June 1997.

For instance, DEC's WWW site on the Internet allows prospective business customers to search for products and services, review the specification of DEC machines, and contact sales representatives to place orders. Similarly, Oracle Corporation, the leading database software vendor, now distributes a new product over the Internet as well as through physical channels.

Other firms like Silicon Graphics, or Sun Microsystems, use the WWW to establish and maintain a relationship with their most important business customers. Furthermore, some new specialized distributors have now appeared on the Internet like Industry.Net or IBEX, which are electronically matching business buyers and sellers that also provide information and business services. In the consumer business, Dell Computer has implemented a direct order system through the Internet, a practice imitated by Apple Computer.

Such a trend will probably keep growing as the emergence of electronic commerce continues to build significant momentum. Supply is constantly increasing because of the development of infrastructure and services with companies such as Open Market who are offering hosting services for electronic commerce, which permit firms to outsource their electronic commerce activity if they desire. Simultaneously, the demand keeps expanding because consumer hesitation about using electronic commerce is lessening thanks to actions like AT&T's guarantee of credit card purchases over the Internet.

Finally, online markets provide better visibility of what consumers are buying, when they are buying it, and from whom they are buying it; best of all, they bring this information instantly to marketers.

Some firms such as NetCount and Inters are providing marketers with real-time information about what, when, and where customers are buying. They have created technologies enabling them to distinguish actual visits to a web site from mere "hits," which occur each time a file is manipulated. For example, a user entering one web page with three graphics icons stored as separate graphics files will show as four hits on that page while actually it was just one person accessing that page once. In a way, those firms may become the Nielsens of the Internet.

On the other side, this new customer visibility may be impeded by some privacy concerns. In the United States, Microsoft was compelled to halt its automatic downloading of information about user system configurations as part of the process of registering from Microsoft Network.

Similarly, Netscape had to make the "cookie technology" an optional feature and not an integrated one in its browser software; such a tool automatically takes information about user activities on the Internet and downloads them when the user accesses a web site. In France, getting electronic information on consumers or businesses is severely restricted by law: anyone always has the right to see the content of the information stored and may refuse to have this information used for business purposes, such as being listed on a customer database. Figure 9.1 summarizes this development of strategic choices and its consequences in terms of the organization. The only problem with running so many distribution channels is that they overlap on customer reach and, as a consequence, risk conflicting with each other. The solution for avoiding such a difficulty is to differentiate products and tailor margins to distinct retail channels, like Packard Bell has done with its PCs.

9.1.2 Channel-design decisions according to the cost of the distribution network

Besides the size of the market and its related volume of sales, the second selection criterion is obviously cost. Not only should the absolute value

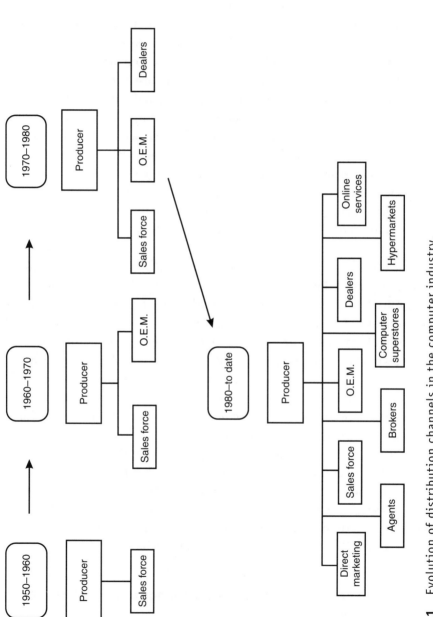

Figure 9.1 Evolution of distribution channels in the computer industry.

cost be considered but also the cost per customer in order to evaluate the profitability of different choices.

Actually, the use of a distributor means lower fixed costs than the use of a sales force; however, variable costs will increase more quickly because a distributor's payment represents a percentage of the total sales revenue. The estimated sales volume can indicate the most appropriate channel (see Figure 9.2).

Diadem, a French company that specializes in the manufacturing of graphics software, is a successful example of this approach. In less than three years it became one of the world's leaders because it decided to rely exclusively on a network of distributors. Diadem sells demonstration material to these distributors, who then assume the financial risks of the final sale in return for a significant margin. This flexible and extensive external structure has allowed Diadem to increase its market share very rapidly.

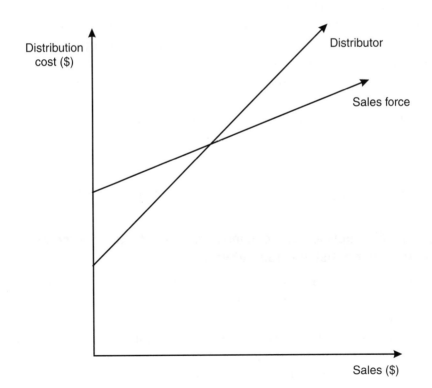

Figure 9.2   Selling or distributing? Profitability analysis.

9.1.3 Channel-design decisions according to the product characteristics

High-technology products can be divided into two categories: nonstandardized products and standard products. Nonstandardized products require a direct sales force. Because these products are manufactured on request for a particular customer, personal contact with the users is necessary.

Standard products justify the use of external distributors. These products have well-defined characteristics; products such as a computer memory or a standard microprocessor are sold in large quantities and at unit costs much lower than those for nonstandardized products, justifying the use of distributors.

For products that are neither entirely standard nor truly nonstandardized but rather in between these two categories, a marketing channel should be selected depending upon the technical complexity of the product and the need for customer service depending upon the distributor's ability. It is said that Dell started Dell Computer to sell PCs directly by phone to consumers after he strove to buy PCs from dealers who knew less about computers than he did. Today, Dell Computer provides powerful customized computers, technical support, and other services to an increasing number of advanced PC users directly by phone or the Internet.

On one side, if the distributor is not able to perform customer service, the product's or the technology's quality image can be seriously jeopardized, which in return can challenge an entire marketing strategy. On the other side, if a company does not have enough resources to provide any customer service, it should depend upon its distributors.

9.1.4 Channel-design decisions according to the degree of control over a distribution network

Some distributors are secretive, others are more "open" and willingly share their customer and price lists as well as any other information about customers.

Secretive distributors will not share any information and carry out their sales policy as they think best. This is the case, for example, with Japanese distributors in the chemical industry. When a distributor is successful, that distributor has a financial interest in being secretive and in handling its own marketing policy. However, it is potentially dangerous for a manufacturer to see a growing barrier between itself and its market because it would miss out on customer feedback. Furthermore, its technology can be copied by or through the distributor, which the manufacturer could fail to realize until the distributor cancels an agreement.

9.1.5 Channel-design decisions according to the flexibility of the distribution network

A distribution contract is often specifically for a fairly long period of time. A consumer electronics manufacturer could not easily change from a specialized sales force to direct sales through superstores.

However, recruiting and training a network of distributors takes time and requires an investment since this network cannot be put into effect immediately. In the high-technology-product world, product ranges follow each other at a high rate and market segments are constantly changing, which makes establishing a distributor network even more difficult.

In the microcomputer industry, distributors have replaced a traditional sales force but are now threatened by mail-order sales. The same holds true for the sales of facsimile machines; the traditional channels (such as Entreprise Générale de Téléphonie and France Telecom) have now been replaced by distributors who specialize in office automation. In the case of chemical molecules, the largest French companies have stopped their sales through dealerships and have acquired their own marketing networks that can more efficiently penetrate the North American market, for example: Rhone-Poulenc bought Rorer in the United States, and Merieux took over Connaught in Canada.

9.2 Managing distributors of high-tech products

The decision to sell products through a distributor is only one step in the process. A distributor must be selected, directed, and evaluated. Again, the characteristics of high technology impose slightly different criteria compared to those of more traditional products.

Every company that is looking for a distributor judges that distributor on its sales experience, financial situation, image toward customers of the target markets, the number and quality of its sales people, and the quantity and brands of its current product portfolio.

Moreover, since high-technology products have a high degree of innovation, a distributor must have unquestionable knowledge about a product to be able to respond to customer questions. Due to the frequent and rapid changes of high-technology products, a distributor must also be able to guarantee almost immediate availability in order to respond to demand at the right time. A distributor who sells technologically outdated products will see his customers go to competitors translating into lost sales. Usually, lost sales are largely underestimated. One computer manufacturer approximated its lost sales at 5 to 10% of total sales, eventually to realize that they were actually between 15 and 20%, almost two or three times its original estimate.

Furthermore, obsolescence is especially quick for some high-technology solutions with high variable costs, like computers or consumer electronics. Personal computers, for instance, may lose as much as 10% of their value each month; so after seven months, the value of a PC is more than halved. Thus, today major PC distributors have negotiated the right to return unsold products to the vendor at no cost.

Unquestionably, the best solution for restraining the impact of lost sales and obsolescence is to gauge them by running periodic customer and distributor surveys. Consequently, inventory and order management for high-technology products is obviously more sophisticated than that for standard products and is fairly similar to the management of fashion stores. For example, one high-tech company received first-month orders for its latest products surpassing its manufacturing capacity by more than 25%. It decided to adapt by increasing both component stock and production. However, three months later, orders plummeted, creating an enormous inventory. The product ended up being a flop. What happened was that tight initial capacities had actually boosted early demand for phony orders placed by distributors concerned about short supplies. Then, products did not move because the market was not buying, but the producer did not figure that out and wrongly decided to expand production on the sole basis of first impressions.

Finally, the high-technological content of these products calls for technical know-how and a professional organization. These two requirements are often important in assuring the quality of customer service.

Manufacturers who are looking to engage distributors often stumble on this last criterion because customer service entails different skills than sales.

However, customer service is a basic necessity for succeeding in high technology because customers must be assured of quality products that confirm their confidence in the manufacturing company. The best marketing plan for a highly technical product can be instantaneously ruined by a distributor whose customer service does not respond quickly and correctly to the frantic telephone calls of a customer demanding the repair of his or her VCR, software, or laser printer. Usually, the solution is to train technicians to make them more competent, but if their compensation is based on the quantity of services delivered rather than the quality, extra training may backfire and create a negative feedback cycle, as illustrated in Figure 9.3, because it erodes their working time and puts them under time pressure. Accordingly, technicians will make a slapdash diagnostic, falling short of detecting problems early and, hence, leaving customers more unsatisfied than before.

High-technology products require that distributors make use of more and better marketing, financial, and human resources in order to respond efficiently to these additional constraints of high technology.

Manufacturers, however, must also devote time to helping distributors assume these additional responsibilities. Every company must keep in mind that an intermediary is an independent company and more a customer representative than a manufacturer's "puppet." An intermediary is interested in selling products that customers will buy from it and, hence, in making it a profit. For example, a high-technology company like

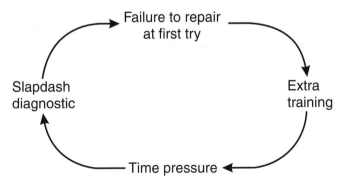

Figure 9.3   A negative feedback loop in distributors' training.

Hi-Shear Industries learned this the hard way. Originally, in the military aerospace business, Hi-Shear exploited its original technological know-how to build a new activity in automotive braking cable. Contrary to the military markets, automotive OEMs demand suppliers to significantly decrease their prices as long as volume is building. Thus, when Hi-Shear thought it had its distributors locked in the same way as its military customers and tried to increase its penetration prices, the distributors reacted strongly and almost put them out of this business. Thus, Hi-Shear had to adapt quickly to its new distribution channel.

A distributor is not instinctively sensitive to these requirements of technical knowledge, optimal product management, and quality of ser-vice but should be made aware of different incentive programs. A partnership should be set up with marketing objectives, inventory management, and promotional activities that are established by both parties, taking into account each other's needs.

It is the responsibility of the marketing or sales departments to monitor and manage distributors, organize training sessions for new products, present previews of new technologies, plan sales promotions, and verify that distributors' technical questions are answered by the company. This entire operation is usually secured by a contract in the form of a joint marketing plan (JMP) or common marketing plan (CMP), and it means that creating and maintaining a successful partnership requires resources. For example, in the beginning of the 1990s, Compaq was spending twice as much on promotions for its resellers as on advertising because its distribution strategy was considered a key success factor as well as a competitive advantage for gaining market share in the PC business.

The final step is to monitor distributor performance, and clearly sales quotas as the only criteria do not suffice in the high-technology industry. A marketing manager must monitor the level of inventory and its rotation, the quality of customer service operations, and the training level of sales people and must follow up on sales promotion campaigns. A marketing manager must also ensure that the distributor has correctly reported information on the customer, price, and product according to a previously determined format. This useful data could be needed to prepare new product launches. The best distributors can only be rewarded if they fulfill all criteria with an exceptional effort (see Figure 9.4).

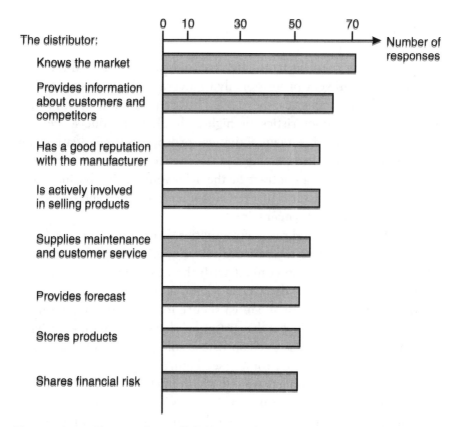

Figure 9.4 The perfect distributor for high-technology products. (*Source:* ADETEM, April 1990.)

9.3 Selling high-tech products

The majority of high-technology companies, and among them almost all companies that sell to organizations, use direct sales through their own sales force because of the limited number of customers in addition to the technical nature of the product.

However, this does not translate automatically into an extensive market coverage. For instance, in many high-tech companies, one may estimate that roughly 20% of personnel work in sales, of whom 25% are salespeople spending about 25% of their time face-to-face with customers. That means that such companies spend a little bit more than 1% of their time dealing with customers, and this does not include the time spent at customer locations by maintenance people, which may represent up to 8% of company time.

Consequently, to be truly effective and productive, a direct sales force must be run very professionally to leverage its various activities.

Basic sales principles can be applied but require some optimizations related to the characteristics of high-technology products. Personal selling consists of three main activities: prospecting, negotiation, and customer follow-up. Prospecting is performed for new customers; negotiation should lead to a contract or the achievement of a business goal; customer follow-up assures that the customer is satisfied and that a long-term relationship can be maintained.

In addition to these three main activities, every salesperson relies on support activities during the entire sales cycle; he or she must communicate in order to maintain contact with the customer; he or she must know how to manage all data received about customers, competitors, and the market; and he or she must secure logistics, from meetings to the installation of a product at the customer's location. All these activities are combined to form a sales chain whose sole purpose is to succeed in completely satisfying the customer (see Figure 9.5).

High-technology products are sold according to this general model. As we are going to see, early prospecting is necessary to understand, from the beginning, what the market wants. The high degree of innovation calls for teamwork during the negotiation but also during the rest of the entire sales cycle. The high-technological content requires a high level of service: the

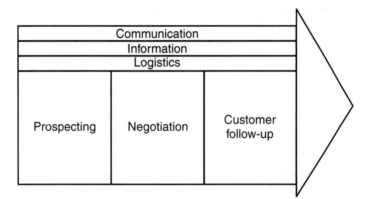

Figure 9.5 The six sales activities.

sale of a high-technology product does not end with the signing of a contract; installation, follow-up, and maintenance operations are also crucial. High technology also makes its mark on the salesperson's support activities. (For more details on selling high-tech products, see [1].)

9.3.1 Prospecting

Because high-technology products are very technical products, salespeople must start working with potential customers early on in order to influence their technical decision. This is even a greater necessity for systems that are subjected to a bidding process.

Whether dealing with the purchase of a sonar, a satellite, a robot, or a missile, a salesperson must identify these plans early on before the official bidding process starts and he or she must work with operational managers to guide them in their definition of technical standards. When the bidding process officially starts, it is often already too late. This explains why, for instance, when Brazil wanted to buy satellites, the product description more closely resembled Hughes Aircraft's American satellites than those manufactured by Aerospatiale.

One of the paradoxes of high technology is that new products succeed each other quickly even though each product needs a long preparation phase and has a longer life cycle due to a better production process. Even though each new model incorporates the latest novelties, the life of a satellite has not decreased: the life of a satellite now averages 13 years compared to a life of three to seven years, 10 years ago; and the sale's life cycle will last between 12 and 16 months before the final order is signed.

A salesperson must know how to manage this time lapse by finding in advance customers who might have a project (and a budget) to which he or she could respond. In order to do so, a salesperson must continuously look into the future and build a customer portfolio by analyzing each customer's and prospect's potential through the use of a qualification checklist (which will be discussed in the next section). This salesperson must sometimes even be able to refrain from selling if optimum requirements have not been met.

So the salesperson of high-technology products is not a simple order taker but a true marketing representative who understands customers, can anticipate their needs, and is able to propose suitable products.

9.3.1.1 Qualifying

Qualifying a customer is a means of being certain that the salesperson has all the necessary information to make a sale and to evaluate his or her chances of success along five criteria: the client's budget, needs, order and delivery schedule, decision-making process, and attitude toward competitors and suppliers. When any of the information in these five categories is missing, the sales representative must recontact the client in order to fill in the blanks. Negative responses represent additional difficulties in convincing the client to buy. Hence, it is only after this information has been collected that the salesperson can realistically evaluate his or her client portfolio and decide on plans of action.

Qualification is indispensable because it corresponds to the "right" questions that exceptional salespeople know how to ask. It is so effective that we often ask ourselves why it is not systematically used by all salespeople.

A checklist of qualification questions follows.

Budget

- How will the purchase be financed?

- Is the client ready to purchase or rent?

- Is the client creditworthy?

- Will the client accept our terms of payment?

Needs

- Does the prospect have a good idea of their needs?

- Do they welcome advice?

- Will a formal and official call for bids be made?

- Can other sales to the same client be foreseen?

Schedule

- Do we know the exact schedule of the project?

- Is the scheduled order date realistic?

- Is the scheduled delivery date realistic?
- Is the client's schedule in line with ours?

Decision-making process

- Are the more important decision makers in favor of the purchase?
- Is an advisor involved in the purchase decision?
- Do we know the decision-making process?
- Do we know who decides? The financier? The technician? The user? The consultant?

Us

- Do we really want to sell to this client on this market?
- Do we have the "right" products and solution?
- Are we a privileged supplier?
- What is our competitive edge?
- Do we have the support of some of the key decision makers?
- Do we have the references necessary to convince the client?

9.3.2 A teamwork approach

During the entire negotiation phase, the technological content of a product as well as the amount of the orders in question and the need to reassure the customer by answering all questions lead the salesperson of a high-technology product to call upon specialists. The salesperson must show leadership and organizational talents and be able to use either at any given time.

Consider the case of a sales engineer who sells supercomputers (see Figure 9.6). First, this person will call upon production engineers who can explain, with an emphasis on technical details, the manufacturing process and the product's components to the customer. The sales engineer will even organize one or more meetings with R&D engineers who work at different locations. These R&D engineers will explain to the customer, who has promised (in writing) not to disclose this information, the

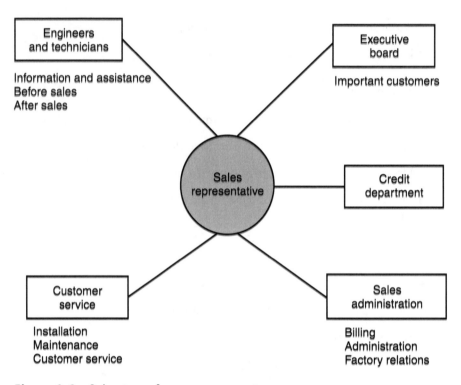

Figure 9.6   Sales team for a supercomputer.

new technologies that will be used for the design and manufacturing of this new computer.

The customer will then meet software specialists if he or she is concerned about the applications or programs that can be run on this machine. In this case, database specialists, AI experts, and management software program gurus (or molecular modeling professionals, according to customer needs) are called to the customer's location by the sales engineer who set up all the necessary meetings.

This computer demands certain specific installation requirements such as the minimum size of office space, heat-resistant insulation, and certain electrical standards. The sales engineer will organize meetings with the customer's building service at which installation specialists will answer questions and examine the location to determine if it is well suited to the machine.

The delivery waiting period now becomes an issue. Usually, the customer wishes to be able to use the computer as quickly as possible. A competitor has possibly already contacted him or her about the possibility of installing the material more quickly. The sales engineer asks an administrative manager who is in continuous contact with the company's factories to obtain the best delivery times for this machine.

All that remains is the question of financing. After receiving a price quote, the customer is interested in finding out about possible credit terms. If so, the sales engineer will organize a meeting with the manager of the branch that specializes in financing computers, who will detail the leasing and credit terms.

When a reassured and informed customer finally places an order, he or she will have spoken with at least a dozen different specialists but always under the watchful eye of the sales engineer. The sales engineer should be a true leader, capable of explaining to every "in-house" specialist what the future customer is expecting.

9.3.3 Customer follow-up

In order for the customer to enjoy the maximum benefits of a high-technology product's potential, he or she should have at his or her disposal training and technical assistance, followed by technical support for maintenance and repair. If not, there is the chance that the product will lose its appeal and its manufacturer will lose out. The customer who already felt uneasy about a technology that he or she did not always understand suddenly feels cheated.

One of the basic tasks of a salesperson is to know how to maintain the customer's confidence, even after the order has been signed. The salesperson must know how to cooperate with various customer services and, if necessary, take charge of these operations to assure that the company's different departments maintain an impeccable service quality.

However, the salesperson's job does not stop at this point. The salesperson must be able to develop customer loyalty by building a long-term relationship based upon trust. He or she must be perceived not as a salesperson but as an advisor who focuses on responding to customer needs and wants within the company's means. Therefore, the salesperson must keep in contact with customers.

This is not always the case, and a recent American study pointed out that, during a one-year period, almost 40% of current customers were never contacted (neither by phone nor in person) by the salespeople of the companies where they bought their products. Many salespeople forget their customer base, even though it could be rich in potential, and instead spend time on unsure prospects.

More than in any other industry, the sale of high-technology products requires a sales representative's consistency and professionalism to break down the barriers of uncertainty and hesitation and to help customers faced with innovation and technology.

To establish a reputation as an advisor, a salesperson must become a market specialist; he or she must understand the customer's business by making use of all available resources. In the computer industry, IBM has developed a strategic advising unit for customer service purposes. IBM's sales engineers can call on a "strategist" who will visit customers and meet with the board of directors about their strategic and development problems, competitive analysis, or intermediate planning. The objective is not to talk about computers, which is of little interest to these executives, but to see how the solutions from IBM—hardware, software, and services—can bring a competitive advantage to the company and make it even more profitable and competitive.

In addition, researchers in the R&D department of the salesperson's company can issue invitations for visits by researchers of potential customer organizations. Transfers of technical information and perspectives on future developments often arise at these types of meetings and can contribute to building trust and a productive business relationship.

Finally, a customer can function as a referral source and convince potential customers of his or her satisfaction with a purchase. Research shows that referred sales are a preferred sales method in high technology. A satisfied customer is the best spokesperson to convince a prospect of a slightly frightening technology. This spokesperson cannot be accused of being biased because, unlike the salesperson, he or she does not have a business interest in the operation.

9.3.4   Support activities

The importance of a technology also influences the support activities of a salesperson of high-technology products.

For communication purposes, the salesperson must translate the over-abundance of frequently very technical information in documentation into a language that is understandable to the customer.

Concerning information, the salesperson's knowledge is invaluable for the marketing department because the salesperson is in continuous contact with the market and represents the most significant source of information in the absence of truly reliable and updated market studies.

In the case of logistics, the salesperson is often the person who coordinates numerous and often complex operations concerning transportation, delivery, and product installation at customer's sites.

Every sales representative for high-technology products must spend time with existing customers to build their confidence in the company, to find new sales opportunities, and possibly to ask these customers to speak about their positive experience to new prospects. Figure 9.7 shows how much time spent face-to-face with the customer can increase sales in a software firm offering solutions to business customers.

Sales people can add to the amount of time spent with customers by using:

- Laptop computers and cellular phones to work outside of their offices;

- Automated systems for making proposals, price quotations, and order entries;

- Online company databases to directly answer technical or financial questions from customers or prospects.

In doing so, sales representatives increase the volume of sales calls and ameliorate the quality of each single call while decreasing its unit cost.

As a consequence, selling high-technology products often demands a high level of competency and, as a result, a higher profile and education compared to other industries. The company should take this type of activity into account when recruiting, managing, and evaluating its sales force. This means that the company must offer an attractive level of compensation to recruit interesting candidates. Then, the type of compensation must not only reflect results (orders) but also the need for quality relationships with customers and the desire to remain with the company on a long-term basis.

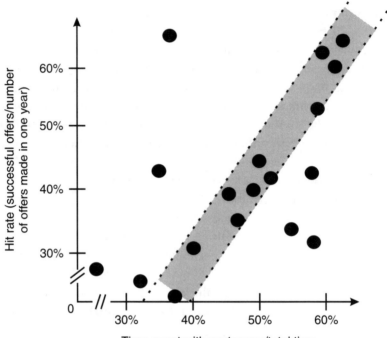

Figure 9.7 Impact on sales of the time spent face-to-face with customers for 18 sales representatives of a major telecommunications services firm. (*Source*: Interviews by Eric Viardot.)

Many high-technology companies have compensation systems with a fairly high percentage of fixed salary compared to commission (on the average, 80% fixed and 20% commission). Some companies even offer an income completely based upon salary so that salespeople are not tempted to sell just anything to assure themselves of an income at the end of the month.

Finally, salespeople must be continuously well-informed and trained about new products in order to present them intelligently to their prospects and customers and to correctly answer their questions. However, being well-informed about new products is not an easy task because product catalogues are often drastically changed in the high-technology industry due to the frequent launching of new products.

However, the rate at which new products are announced and the high degree of innovation of many high-technology products require a hefty investment in the training of salespeople, such as in the information systems business where companies invest between 10 and 15% of their salary budget on training, of which a large part is dedicated to their sales force. This high level of training costs can also be found in other high-technology sectors.

Besides, one of the roles of the marketing department is to supply the sales department with the necessary resources for this training (such as instructors, training manuals, product documentation, and cassettes) to ensure that the messages communicated to the salespeople match the marketing strategy.

9.3.5   After-sales market

Apart from improving service and support at the initial startup of machines or systems, industrial suppliers can earn more revenue and profit from after-sales activities.

In high-technology business more than in other industries, after-sales activity, that is, supplying spare parts and providing preventive and reactive maintenance for the installed base of customers, is very often a highly profitable business. Nowhere else can a firm so easily find a market where it usually has a commanding relative market share, while demand is stable and even predictable and entry barriers for competitors are high.

According to a survey by McKinsey, after-sales business accounts for 13% of revenues of electronic systems companies and 8% of revenues of electronic components companies. They contribute to an even bigger share of the total margin, representing 39% for electronic systems firms, and 17% for electronic components firms.

Furthermore, after-sales can generate three to four times the turnover of the original purchase during the solution's life cycle, especially for industrial equipment such as aircraft engines where after-sales represent 80% of the net present value versus 20% for original equipment. One must notice the opposite effect for aircraft, where after-sales account only for 30% of the net present value versus 70% for new equipment.

Though an increase of 1% in price and 1% in volume of after-sales can increase the return on sales by 3 to 5% and the profits by 30%, depending on the cost structure of a firm, McKinsey estimates that, on average, companies capture only about 20% of this market.

Even this 20% is seldom fully exploited, being priced in line with the cost of supplying the product or service rather than according to its value to the customer, which is usually much higher because it is measured by the cost consequence of its failure.

For instance, the average price of the spare parts order for digital telephone switchboards (PABX) is about $600. However, the cost of having phone lines shut down ranges from $10,000 per day for a business school to more than $600,000 for a direct marketing vendor like La Redoute in France or Land's End in the United States. In after-sales, the price is less an issue than consideration here; the key issues are reliability, swiftness of delivery, and availability of repair and maintenance services (see Figure 9.8).

Accordingly, after-sales products and services can and should be priced to value whenever it is possible, as seen in Chapter 7. In addition, after-sales solutions must be designed and marketed to keep out competitors—usually third-party maintenance specialists or customers' in-house maintenance units—because switching costs and convenient alternatives also have a strong influence on the value perceived by customers (see Figure 9.9). For example, a premium price can be charged for a critical component or service with no alternative on the market (pricing to value), but not for a simple part easily available close by (market price or cost + margin price).

The sales force should be in charge of the selling of after-sales solutions. Usually, most sales departments sell solutions directly connected

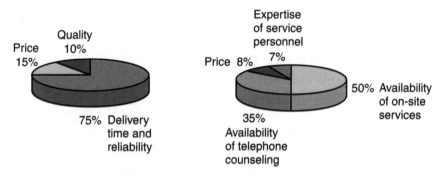

Percentage of respondents listing factor as highest priority

Figure 9.8   Key buying factors in after-sales for electronic components firms.

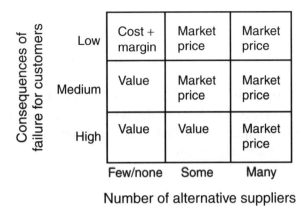

Figure 9.9 Various pricing tactics for after-sales solutions.

to the initial sale such as transport, installation, warranty, and training programs for a customer's maintenance personnel. However, experience shows that few sales people are interested in selling after-sales solutions during a product's operational life unless they have strong financial incentive to do so. They are more interested in selling new original equipment and services. Accordingly, one solution is to set up a sales forces dedicated to selling after-sales solutions, but because the after-sales unit is very often perceived as a competitor by the direct sales force, it must not overlap with the sales department when dealing with customers so as to avoid confusion and conflicts.

9.4 Chapter summary

Selecting distribution channels for high-technology products depends upon the size of the market, the cost of the distribution network, the product characteristics, the level of control on the network, and its flexibility.

Many high-technology products require distributors to make use of marketing, financial, and human resources that are superior to those needed for more traditional products. The marketing manager must therefore know how to select, manage, and evaluate distributors.

When a sales force directly sells high-technology products, preliminary prospecting is needed, followed by teamwork that facilitates a salesperson to call upon numerous specialists, and finally, an emphasis on customer follow-up in order to reassure them of a new technology. The importance of a technology similarly shapes the salesperson's support activities, for communication, as well as for information processing and logistics.

Selling high-technology products often demands a high level of competency and as a result a higher profile and education compared to other industries. The company should take this into account when recruiting, managing, and evaluating its sales force.

References

[1]   Kadish, J. E., *Global High-Tech Marketing*, Norwood, MA: Artech House, 1993.

10

The Position of Marketing Within High-Tech Companies

When a company decides to take a market-oriented approach, it focuses on customer needs and not on the appeal of a technology; in order to do so, it must have certain resources at its disposal. The company must define the internal organization of its marketing department and ensure the cooperation of all departments for complete customer satisfaction.

10.1   The position of the marketing department in a high-tech firm

The marketing philosophy can be translated three different ways for high-technology companies. The first is strategic marketing at the executive level where top management selects the areas in which the company will and will not compete (countries, market segments, technologies). The second translation is operational marketing where the marketing manager determines how (with which resources) the company will compete (these are the components of the marketing mix: product range, price, promotion, sales network, and distribution). The third is sales support marketing, either integrated or closely related to the sales force, which helps the sales force meet its goals. This support can help the sales force deal with competitor traps and hostile environments using resources such as sales promotions and sales presentations.

When putting the marketing philosophy into action, the marketing department has a different place in each organization depending upon the importance given to marketing by the company (see Figure 10.1).

Technology-driven companies assign the marketing responsibility to the sales manager. For years most of the French software service companies have been practicing a very basic type of marketing by simply exploiting business opportunities rather than actively executing a strategic plan; however, recently a slight market setback forced the most advanced computer service companies to become better organized in order to better understand their markets.

In most cases, high-technology companies with a marketing department give its director the same status as a sales manager. However, this situation presents functional difficulties and will require continuous coordination efforts, as will be explained later. Some companies regard sales (and rightly so) as only one aspect of marketing a product. These companies hold their marketing manager responsible for sales and put him or her in charge of all customer relations. In the computer industry, IBM has initiated this type of organization. Research shows that marketing's position in an organization changes with a company's development phases (see Figure 10.1).

A high-technology company that has been set up as a result of one successful innovative product must often quickly capitalize on its

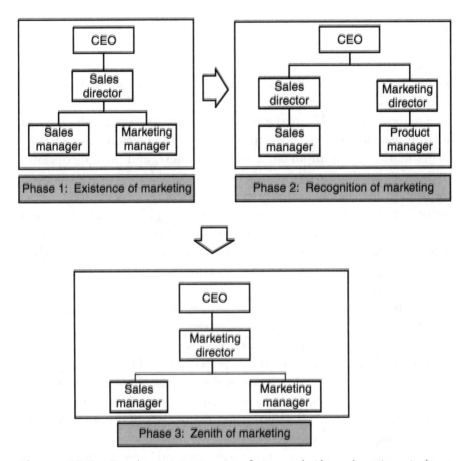

Figure 10.1 Development stages of a marketing department in a high-technology company.

technological breakthrough by increasing sales. The first goal of the new marketing department is to support the sales force with promotional tools such as leaflets, direct marketing, and attendance at trade shows. Company growth leads to the launching of new products and the development of advertising, promotion, and customer service activities. This growth often justifies a move to a different marketing structure, independent from the sales manager. This marketing structure lends itself more strongly to increasing sales.

However, this type of structure is often conflict-ridden. The sales department has essentially a short-term orientation; it must achieve its sales quota and obtain orders that translate into income for the company. This pressure on sales is even more pronounced because markets change very quickly in high technology. Faced with a decrease in sales, companies are tempted to react immediately by lowering prices, increasing the sales force, or introducing sales promotions.

On the other hand, a marketing department can have a wider view or horizon. Faced with a decrease in orders, it will question, for example, target markets, the importance of its products, and the appropriateness of the distribution channels, and will reconsider the overall marketing strategy in order to better respond to customer expectations. These opposite points of view often generate a "struggle" between sales and marketing. Sales will accuse marketing of its ivory tower at headquarters and its failure to understand anything about customer needs, while marketing will blame sales for its marketing myopia and its inability to step back from the field.

Another traditional conflict between sales and marketing in the high-technology industry concerns the use of research and development laboratories. In some companies, the sales force has immediate access to researchers from whom they can request customer presentations of new prototypes, for example. A research and development department often has two sides: a laboratory specialist, who is not familiar with competitors or manufacturing constraints, can easily be talked into giving sensitive or overly optimistic information regarding a new product release.

In reality, there is often a fairly long interval between the development of a prototype and the industrial product launch. If this information leaks to other customers or even to the press, the impact could be disastrous. This unintended slip-up will disrupt new product announcements and advertising plans that have been carefully prepared by the marketing department. Usually, the division head or company's managing director settles conflicts between sales and marketing, but if the number of these conflicts increase or if they become more serious, it will become necessary to acknowledge that marketing plays a strategic role in the company's future and that sales fall under the marketing department's responsibility.

Research shows that this type of organization limits the number of unexpected fluctuations and stresses the necessary symbiosis between the marketing department and the sales force for all operational marketing and sales support operations. This is the ultimate development stage of the marketing department. Technomed, a biomedical equipment company, is a prime example in this respect. From the start, it has made marketing a priority. It now has 18 employees in its marketing department out of a total 180 company employees; every product is managed by a product manager and an assistant manager.

On the other hand, Xerox's case is also quite significant. In May of 1985, it announced a new family of ten office products in order to compete with IBM, DEC, and Wang. Five years later, the expected breakthrough had still not been executed due to a lack of marketing and preparation of sales teams for the new markets. Not until January 1989 did worldwide marketing and sales activities consolidate.

10.2   The internal organization of the marketing department

The organization of a marketing department depends upon the size of the company's markets and its number of products. In some companies, the number of people working in the marketing department can be counted on one hand, but for large multinational companies personnel in marketing can exceed 10,000 worldwide.

The marketing structure must fit into the overall organization of the company while taking into account its management philosophy. A decentralized company will position the marketing department close to the sales force, whereas a centralized company will prefer its marketing department to be set up at headquarters; both cases can exist in high-technology companies.

Companies can decide to have a market-oriented or product-oriented internal organization. In the high-technology industry, the most often selected organization structures the sales force by market (geographically and by customer type) and assigns product managers for the most important products.

Some companies have organized their sales force and marketing by product. This approach is justified by the need to be familiar with products in order to sell them, especially if these products represent a major innovation. However, using a product-oriented approach could mean running the fairly large risk of losing touch with reality (market need).

IBM has experienced this type of problem. During the 1960s and 1970s, IBM structured its sales force by computer type; the main reason was the launching of a new, revolutionary model, the 360 system, which required special training for the sales force. In 1975, IBM had two organizations, one that sold mainframes and another that sold small business computers, peripherals, and typewriters.

Sales representatives from both groups quickly started competing against each other for a number of customers. As a result, customers became confused: Should they buy one large IBM computer or several smaller IBM systems? Because no clear answers were given, these customers often bought from other suppliers. In 1983, IBM finally decided to organize its sales force by customer type and separated large companies from the rest of the market and, in 1986, defined several geographic zones [1]. Since then, the organization has experienced several variations, but it remains market-oriented and is no longer product-oriented. Its organization, entitled "Go to Market," is even more customer-focused around 12 vertical "industries," such as communication, distribution, education, finance, and government. Each industry executive is responsible for revenue, profit, and customer satisfaction.

However, the high degree of innovation and the high rate of change that characterize high-technology products pose a problem in this type of organization. A salesperson who only sells to one type of customer must know the company's entire product range. In many cases, this means knowledge of several hundred product references. Because these product references are constantly changing, the salesperson must keep up with new products and product features and continuously update his or her product catalog.

In reality, most salespeople merely keep up with products that they already know well and that tend to sell and propose only those products to their customers. This behavior penalizes new products with which the sales force is less familiar and encourages a dangerous habit.

Large companies that sell a large number of products often employ product managers. Their role is to develop a product strategy (for which they are responsible), including a marketing plan and annual sales objectives. These product managers must keep the sales force and distributors excited about the product, organize advertising, and follow customer expectations to anticipate problems and capitalize on opportunities. They must also plan for product changes, together with other departments of the company, to better respond to the needs of different markets.

High-tech product managers, like their colleagues in more traditional companies, do not have any linear responsibility to other departments. They must convince these departments because they can never "force" their ideas. Therefore, they must have a solid technical education and field experience (with customers) in order to have significant credibility with researchers, manufacturing engineers, and the sales force.

The marketing department also performs sales support functions (for example, brochures and product documentation); communication (trade shows, media relations, advertising); and market studies, when necessary. In order to achieve all those activities, the marketers have to rely increasingly on information technologies (IT) for the following reasons.

First, IT help the marketer collect, screen, and analyze all the marketing-related information available before its introduction in the decision-making process. Of particular interest are the new datamining application softwares like Express from Oracle or Intelligent Miner from IBM. These application softwares coupled with large customers databases allow the marketer to identify market segments easily and quickly using various techniques like clustering, classification, association, and sequential buying patterns identification. Second, IT are also being used to enhance the support operation. Finally, IT may increase the value of service to customers. There is an explosion in the volume and variety of IT. See Table 10.1 for a list of some office-based IT currently available to marketers.

10.3 The necessary cooperation of the marketing department with other departments

To be efficient, the marketing department cannot stand alone and keep aloof from the rest of the company. Because its responsibility is to market products that fit customers' needs at the right time and with the right level

Table 10.1

Information Technologies for the Marketer.
(*Adapted from:* Powell, T., "Information: The Next Battleground,"
in *Handbook of Marketing for the Service Industries*, Carol Congram and
Margaret Friedman, AMACOM, 1991.)

Technology	Sample Application
Desktop publishing	Brochures, presentation
Imager (produces 35-mm slides)	Presentation
Projector (display PC screen)	Presentation
Electronic bulletin board	Customer/channel information
Spreadsheet	Media budgeting, sales forecasting, data analysis
Statistical software	Data analysis
Database manager	Customer list, mailings, lead management
Project manager	Planning and monitoring projects
Mailing list manager	Merge and purge mailing lists, test mailing
Computer-assisted telephone interviewing	Scripting of phone interviews, online data entries
Online database	Market research
CD-ROM	Market research, customer support
Datamining software	Segmentation

of quality, it has to work first with all the other departments, not only with R&D, but also with the manufacturing and the services departments.

10.3.1   Collaboration with research and development

In a 1984 issue of the *Harvard Business Review*, an article on the necessary connection between R&D and marketing as a key success factor for high-tech firms written by two specialists, William L. Shanklin and John K. Ryans, Jr., caused a considerable stir [2]. It is probably because there are so many walls, especially cultural walls, between marketing and research and development as listed in Table 10.2 that make them two different and separate worlds.

Table 10.2

Some Cultural Differences Between Marketing and Research and Development Professionals. (*Adapted from:* Griffin, G. A., and J. R. Hauser, "Integrating R&D and Marketing," *Journal of Product Innovation Management*, Elsevier, No. 13, 1996.)

Dimension	Marketing	R&D
Education	Business	Engineering, sciences
Training	General problem solving	Testing hypothesis
Time orientation	Short	Long
Professional orientation	Market and profit	Science and progress
Language	Product benefits and positioning	Product specification and performance

Marketing professionals usually have a business background. They are trained to combine data and intuition in order to answer general problems and to make profit-oriented business decisions, generally within a short time frame. They talk of markets, product benefits, and perceptual positioning for customers.

Conversely, research and development professionals generally have an engineering or sciences background. They are trained to generate and then test hypotheses in order to resolve technical problems and to promote scientific development on a long-term basis. They talk of product specifications and performance.

All these differences are frequently intensified by geography since research and development departments are located on an outside campus, while marketers are close to markets or at headquarters. This leads to less interpersonal activity and strengthens separate worlds of thought.

Numerous product failures, such as Machine Bull's GCOS 7 operating system for organizational use and Thomson's TO7 personal computer for consumer use, are the result of a disastrous lack of cooperation between the marketing and research and development departments. Also Ken Olsen was quoted as attributing his downfall at DEC, the company he founded, to a lack of communication between R&D and marketing.

On one hand, R&D needs marketing's market vision and guidance for the general direction of research. On the other hand, marketing needs R&D to invent products that correspond to the customer needs it has identified. Successful high-technology companies do not emphasize this necessary cooperation between their R&D and marketing organizations by chance.

On their own, these two departments are meaningless; together, they can perform miracles. Jean-René Edighoffer, vice president of Rhone-Poulenc, the French major chemical firm, stresses: "Without consistent market-oriented programs, research will go round in circles." However, this organizational link is often easier to discuss than to create. The initiative must come from upper management, which must affirm its priority and, as a result, must make available the necessary resources to materialize this link.

Larry Ellis, Oracle's founder, affirms that one of his main strategical intentions is to break down the barriers between R&D and marketing. Marketing managers and development managers report to the same product manager to facilitate this link between marketing and R&D, but the language or jargon used is often another barrier that separates departments. Oracle's employees use the same software engineering product "Case" that serves as a common language for product developers and marketing managers.

Using "Case," developers generate the software program and marketing generates the product documentation. As a result, a customer who reads Oracle's program documentation is more inclined to buy the product, which is not at all the case for all those software products with documentation written by technicians whose jargon turns off beginners and even informed amateurs. This cooperation between the two departments has as its goal to better satisfy customers; in 13 years Oracle increased in size (11 times) and has a revenue of over one billion dollars.

Moreover, for the most part, the time period preceding a new product announcement is filled with frequent communication between the R&D and marketing departments. Figure 10.2 summarizes the main movements related to the materialization of a new product.

At the onset, marketing gives the new product functional requirements that correspond to customer demand. Marketing will also indicate the desired time period for introducing this product to the market

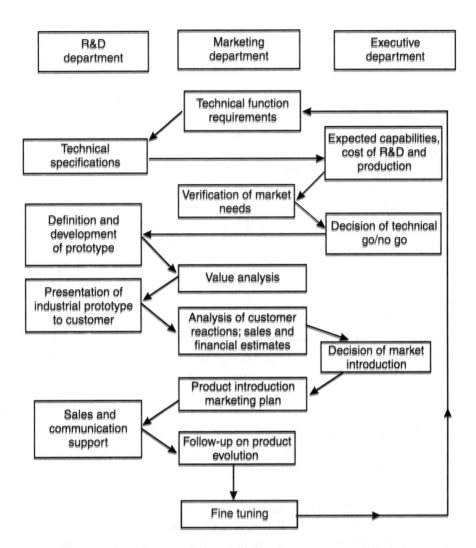

Figure 10.2 Links between R&D and marketing during a product's life.

and possibly a budget for product development costs and maximum manufacturing costs.

Based upon these indications, the R&D service—in connection with the manufacturing department—will develop the necessary technical specifications based upon technologies that exist within the company and those available on the market. However, dreams and realities lie far apart! Researchers can invent technical wonders, but they will come up against a certain number of physical constraints due to limitations in today's knowledge as well as financial limits.

The technical answer is approved by the marketing service if it believes that the proposed solution correctly corresponds to market expectations, even if the product differs from what was originally imagined. At this stage, all innovations that come directly from researchers are usually screened. Brilliant ideas (new products, new applications) must always be compared to customer expectations.

Taking into account these different elements, the company decides whether to continue with this product. If the project is accepted, the development service will build one or more prototypes to verify the consistency and feasibility of the technical selections. The characteristics of this prototype help marketing in performing a value analysis of this product using a certain number of representative customers and prospects.

If the value analysis appears positive, the development department will start working with the manufacturing department on the manufacturing of a prototype, which several customers are then asked to test. The marketing department will analyze customer reactions in order to measure the new product's rate of acceptance and to detect a possible need for (additional) modifications.

If the product is favorably received during testing, the marketing department will also prepare sales projections (revenue) and financial estimates (profit) that will justify the investments necessary for launching a new product.

At this stage, upper management must decide whether or not to put the product on the market. If it agrees to do so, the marketing department will finalize its marketing plan and prepare all necessary product-launching activities. Similarly, the manufacturing department will set up, in cooperation with product development engineers, a manufacturing process and assembly for the new product.

After the product has been marketed, the R&D department will appear again because it often plays an important role in communication; its researchers participate in conferences and write about the new products for professional journals. In certain cases, particularly for products in industrial markets, these researchers contribute to the sales effort by performing product demonstrations to convince customers. For example, Schlumberger Technologies, a major U.S.-French firm, sends its researchers out into the field 10% of their time.

Finally, marketing will continuously keep track of the product. User reactions will lead to possible new improvements and will be translated into functional specifications before being passed on to the R&D department. The product has now come full circle, and a new cooperative cycle begins.

This cooperation process varies from company to company. In some companies, the marketing department has the authority and necessary power to work with the research and development department. In other companies, this initiative comes from research's engineers who consult the marketing department to verify that they are on the right track and that their ideas truly correspond to a market need.

Some companies have adopted an extremely formal communication process between the two departments like the quality function deployment that was developed in Japan but is now widely used in western countries. Quality function deployment requires marketing and research and development to build a "house of quality" by clarifying and quantifying their assumptions and then translating them to one another through a relationship matrix. Such a process prevents misunderstandings and requires each group to explain their own thought world. Exchanging specifications and verification procedures requires formal documentation to ensure the consideration of all steps. Other companies prefer informal relations and encourage any form of communication. An electronics company even reorganized its office space so that product development engineers and marketing managers can work together more easily.

Ultimately, some firms try to integrate the two departments in various organizational structures such as permanent coordinating groups, matrix organizations, and project teams (which are less confusing and more efficient than a matrix structure). The goal is to stimulate cross-functional information; to improve the decision-making process, including conflict resolution; to decrease project uncertainties; and to shorten the time spent on new product development. Experience teaches that short project duration is more effective than long-term or permanent structure because the former improves integration without significantly diminishing the functional expertise of each team member.

The distance and isolation of these two departments could spell danger for high-technology companies. Traditionally, research laboratories are separated from the rest of a company so that researchers can devote their time to scholarly thoughts and be close to a university or other research centers. However, companies should not forget that technology in itself is worthless without customers.

In order to break down this ivory tower and prevent a company from getting lost in technomania, marketing people and researchers should work together. They should be grouped together by project managers or be joined in a task force.

10.3.2 Collaboration with manufacturing and customer service

More is at stake in high-technology companies: products must be launched very quickly. The first company in a market can usually demand a higher price, as its risk premium, and therefore a higher profit margin. On the other hand, companies that trail behind competitors and enter a market where prices have started to drop often end up in a financial disaster.

Don G. Reinertsen has calculated that introducing a laser printer six months late could lower cumulative profits by 30% (based upon a 20% annual market growth, a 12% annual price decrease, and a five-year product life cycle). On the other hand, a product development program that runs 30% over budget will only reduce cumulative profits by 2.3%.

John Doyle, vice president at Hewlett-Packard noted: "If we overspend by 50% on our engineering budget, but deliver on time, it impacts 10% on revenue. But, if we are late, it can impact up to 30% on revenues" [3]. A manager at Technology estimated that "a delay of six months when launching a product could cost two years of research."

The entire company should be ready to make a product launch a success—and this should be double-checked. Manufacturing problems can considerably contribute to a restrained product launch, even more so because new technologies involve more and more complex manufacturing constraints. In the manufacturing of DRAM computer memory chips, the number of process steps has increased from 230 in 1985 to 550 in 1990. Similarly, in the beginning of the 1980s, the manufacturing of photocopiers simply consisted of assembling the light source and a toner system with a mechanical system to move a piece of paper. Nowadays, copiers resemble computers and contain control hardware and software, panel displays, and organic photoreceptors.

This greater operational sophistication obviously requires a fundamental adaptation of the manufacturing department (including purchasing) and the customer service department. From the beginning, all departments in a company must work together even if their degree of involvement varies along the process. The manufacturing department must be included from the beginning of the prototyping phase in order to pinpoint possible difficulties in mass production and suggest improvements in product design. This cooperation can lead to precious time savings when compared with competitors who discover manufacturing problems only after a product launch has been carried out. In any case, it is also a guarantee of a better manufacturing quality.

Besides, in many high-technology businesses where product life cycles are short and demand is unpredictable, delivery performance is critical. When the delivery process is weak, it is usually because of a long lead time, which leads to distorted sales forecasts. When the manufacturing department does not respond quickly enough, the sales department overstates the customer's commitment or the size of its orders to build in a safety margin.

Consequently, production schedules and inventories do not match real demand and late changes have to be made to orders in the factory, adding more lead time to the process.

The solutions are not only an improvement of the sales forecast, but also in having various multifunction teams organized by segment of customers and products to effectively manage the order-to-payment process. The ultimate step is having a just-in-time production system like that of Dell Computer that builds most of its products on receipt of a customer order.

Furthermore, research engineers are usually preoccupied with technical product performance and marketing managers are often unaware of a product's malfunctioning and the amount of time necessary for repair, but these are the major reasons for the dissatisfaction of high-technology product users. So, installation and maintenance departments can also provide useful advice at the original steps of the development of a product. Because these departments have a good knowledge of problems due to their amount of customer contact, they will support simplicity and consistency during prototype development.

For Nintendo, the Japanese manufacturer of the most popular video games, customer service is a true marketing resource. More than 120 teenagers, called "game advisors," are available to give advice on the best way to play "Donkey Kong" or "Ninja Turtles." Weekly telephone calls number 50,000; these calls are analyzed to study the expectations of a very versatile group of young customers. Using this strategy, Nintendo came out with the most varied and most liked product range in an industry with more than 250 different games.

Finally, not only must products be launched very quickly, but, at the same time, they must have a very high quality. Accordingly, one new driving force to a better cooperation between the marketing department and the other departments (such as R&D, manufacturing, and customer service) is the ISO 9000 certification.

ISO 9000 is a European standard of quality management that has been adopted by more than 60 countries, including the United States, Canada, Japan, and all the members of the European Union. Philips Electronics, General Electric, British Telecom, DuPont, Dow, and even major software companies like Cap Gemini Sogeti or Sligos are certified and request suppliers to adopt ISO 9000. This standard provides a framework for telling clients the way a firm tests products, keeps records, fixes defects, and trains employees.

With more than 35,000 certificates issued worldwide, ISO 9000 is becoming an internationally recognized system, understandable to sellers and customers (much more than the American Malcolm Baldridge award). By putting the emphasis on quality and forcing companies to pass the certificate exam, the ISO 9000 drives a firm to reconsider the whole process of communication between the various departments involved in the design, production, and marketing of new products.

10.3.3 Organizing cooperation among departments

To ensure true team work between all departments, the issue is to move from a linear sequence where everyone works in his or her own field of expertise and transmits the results of his or her work to the next department to an integrated structure where everyone works together to propose quality solutions that respond to customer needs, as is shown in Figure 10.3.

In the model for traditional organizations in Figure 10.3, R&D generates new products and develops prototypes. Manufacturing purchases the required resources and produces the items that are then sold by marketing and installed and repaired by maintenance. In a high-tech organization, which is founded on customers, departments communicate with each other continuously during the entire product life cycle. Marketing is the preferred interface with the customer, which allows this type of organization to come up with new ideas for product improvement. A "just-in-time" and flexible production is needed but should guarantee high-quality and satisfying customer service.

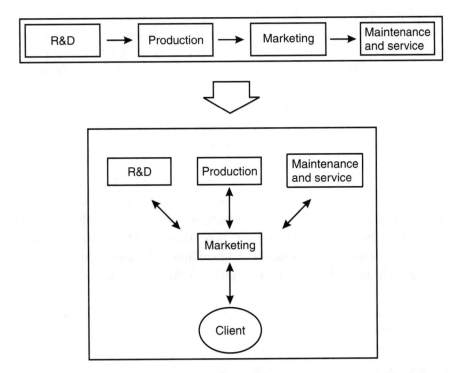

Figure 10.3 From a traditional organization to a multifunctional organization.

In order for this type of cooperation to succeed, the first step should be to establish relations between departments. However, research shows that successful companies go even further. These companies develop new products using integrated teams that consist of members from each department. Some teams even integrate outside suppliers and customers who become involved at a very early stage. Western Digital was one of the first companies to successfully implement this type of structure to develop disk storage controllers for computers.

The most profitable companies also set ambitious objectives for these multifunctional teams. When Canon was developing personal photocopiers, its objective was to invent a machine with a copy quality equal to IBM's office copiers that weighed less than 20 kilograms (the lightest machine on the market weighed 35 kilograms) and had a maximum price of $1,500 (compared to $3,000 for the lowest priced model on the market). Faced with such a demanding objective, the team researched all available opportunities in product and process design, manufacturing, marketing, and service. One of the key success factors was the development of a replaceable module that combined critical parts where previously several different parts were required; as a result, manufacturing and maintenance was simplified.

These successful high-technology companies also consider time as a major strategic variable to get the upper hand on their competitors, of which Northern Telecom's case is an example.

In 1987, faced with more and more aggressive competitors, Northern Telecom, a Canadian leader in telecommunications in the digital switch market, stated its objectives for success as follows: every new product, when specified by customers, had to be available within 12 months; improvements on existing products had to be made within a maximum of nine months; and to reduce inventory and costs, manufacturing cycle times had to be cut from several months to no more than two weeks.

In addition, instead of a continual cost reduction in the product's manufacturing costs (due to the learning curve effect), initial product costs could not be higher than 110% of the ultimate cost when producing at full capacity. Product documentation had to be available by the time the products themselves were released and had to undergo the same quality control, which had to satisfy the highest customer demands.

All these objectives share an emphasis on the optimal use of time. A multifunctional approach should be used to achieve this optimization of time. As Northern Telecom's President, Roy Merrills, emphasizes, "Since team members share ideas about what is commercially important or technically feasible or hard to manufacture while the product is on the drawing board, the functions resolve problems sooner and less expensively" [4]. The results have been spectacular. Between 1985 and 1989, Northern Telecom reduced its new product introduction interval by 20% to 50%, depending on the product. Similarly, inventory and manufacturing costs diminished by 20%. As a result, the average customer satisfaction grew from 100 in 1985 to 125 in 1989.

Today leading PC vendors are developing new products in 10 months when they needed more than double that time two years ago. To achieve such a dramatic result, they reconsidered their product development technology, as for instance, Compaq's design of application-specific integrated circuits (ASICs). Using electronic simulation software to eliminate the flaws in the conception of the circuits before making silicon prototypes, Compaq managed to cut development time by more than half by limiting the number of iterations between the computer maker and its chip suppliers.

Finally, profitable companies integrate even more technology by transferring their know-how from one product to another. For this reason, Thomson's new television sets and medical equipment contain very sophisticated acoustic units that were originally developed for sonar antisubmarine systems. Similarly, Canon has used the same miniaturized motors in its photolithography equipment, cameras, and copiers. These transfers require effective communication and cooperation between different project development teams as well as a certain work ethic.

Multifunctional project teams do not become successful overnight. By definition, these teams go against a company's traditional functional organization and can clash with an established company hierarchy. So, upper management's support is necessary to assure the success of project development teams. Executives must understand the importance of knowing how to manage innovation and to supervise both innovation and changes in the business environment with all departments in the company in a simultaneous and coordinated manner. This change is necessary to better respond to customer expectations and to surpass competitors.

Upper management must also plan for project team evaluation and motivation systems related to the assigned objectives such as improvements on market introduction intervals.

Nevertheless, the marketing department also plays a fundamental role in the acceptance of this multifunctional approach. As customer representatives responsible for customer interests, the marketing department is in the best position to play the role of intermediary and team coordinator, of which the main objective is to always better serve customer needs. Without waiting for upper management's impetus, the marketing department must take the initiative to organize this necessary cooperation between all departments in order to assure the success of its commercialization policy.

10.4   Chapter summary

The position of the marketing department in a company changes along with the company's growth stages. In the beginning, marketing starts off as a support of the sales force. When company growth leads to new products, marketing becomes independent from the sales department. This change can cause conflicts since these two departments have neither the same time horizon nor the same views on relations with the research and development department. Leading companies include sales within the responsibility of the marketing department.

Within the marketing department, the sales force should be organized by market instead of by product and with product managers for the most important products.

To be truly efficient, the marketing department must collaborate directly with the research and development department at all stages of product development, from prototyping to customer service. This collaboration must also involve manufacturing and customer service departments so as to shorten the time period necessary before product introduction and to increase the product quality.

This collaboration is one of the key success factors of the most profitable high-technology companies and must be supported by upper management. However, the marketing department plays an important role in its application because, as a representative of customers, it is in the best position to nurture multifunctional cooperation.

References

[1] Cespedes, F. V., "Agendas, Incubators and Marketing Organization," *California Review Management*, Fall 1990.

[2] Shanklin, W. L., and J. K. Ryans, "Organizing for High-Tech Marketing," *Harvard Business Review*, November–December 1984.

[3] Reinersen, D. G., "Whodunnit? the Search for New Product Killers," *Electronic Business*, July 1983, pp. 62–66.

[4] Merrils, R., "How Northern Telecom Competes On Time," *Harvard Business Review*, July–August 1989.

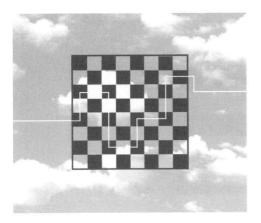

Appendix A:
Key Success Factors of a Marketing Department in a High-Tech Company

When asked for the key abilities that a marketing department must manage in order to be highly successful, experienced marketing managers of major high-tech firms gave the following answers (see Figure A.1):

1. Knowledge of customers and assessments of their future needs are the first priorities, which perfectly corresponds to the marketing department's objectives: the analysis of market needs. This first priority justifies marketing's existence and its credibility within the company.

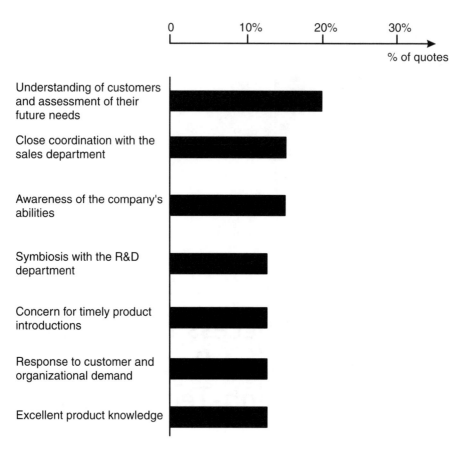

Figure A.1 Success factors of a marketing department in a high-technology company. (*Source:* Interviews by Eric Viardot.)

2. Close coordination with the sales department is a necessity. The sales force is the only informational source readily available in ever-changing markets. The sales force is in contact with customers whose impressions, opinions, and attitudes can be relayed to the marketing department. Finally, sales representatives participate in the execution of the marketing plan and are essential in the strategy's success. Marketing helps the sales force by supplying information on and training for new products. All these efforts must then be communicated to customers. For the two departments to work together efficiently, there should be no waste or loss of energy between them.

3. Awareness of the company's abilities is essential for the development of a realistic marketing strategy. Proposing new products is useless if the company does not have the necessary technical and financial abilities to materialize new products. Targeting a large number of markets with a sales force that is limited in size is also futile. Many examples of failed marketing strategies exist; these are failures due to a lack of needed resources.

4. Symbiosis with the research and development department is a necessity in the high-technology industry. Reasons for this symbiosis were explained in Chapter 10; marketing managers confirm that this cooperation must be part of the marketing team's day-to-day activities.

5. Concern for timely product introductions is imperative in an aggressive competitive environment with shortened product life cycles. The rules of the game are constantly changing; the first company in a market often comes away as the winner. In addition, a delay in a product's introduction usually has serious financial consequences that can increase the pressure on the marketing department to market products at the right place and time.

6. Response to customer and organizational demand is characteristic of the highly competitive and ever-changing high-technology industry. The marketing department must answer all questions quickly; if not, it will risk losing its credibility.

7. Excellent knowledge of the product is also necessary in order to establish credibility with the sales force, customers, and research and development, and manufacturing departments. In the high-technology industry, technology plays an important role, but it must be dedicated to meeting customer needs.

To bridge the gap between products and markets, the marketing department must understand in order both to translate customer demands into technical features and vice versa.

Appendix B:
The Marketing Plan

Because the high-tech business is highly volatile due to the breathtaking evolution of technology, the number of competitors and their moves, and market needs and attitudes, a marketing plan is very important for any marketing manager who wants to make a success of product management. A marketing plan is a systematic process that involves evaluating marketing opportunities and resources, determining marketing objectives, and developing a plan for implementation and control.

The strategic marketing plan, for three years or more, translates how managers perceive their marketing advantage, what objectives they want to achieve, their strategies to achieve them, the resources required, and the expected results. The operational marketing plan is the detailed scheduling and budgeting of the actions necessary for the achievement of the first year of the strategic marketing plan.

According to McDonald [1], the two principal benefits of a marketing plan are a greater profitability (than nonplanning companies over time) and improved productivity. These benefits stem from:

- Systematic identification of emerging opportunities and threats;

- Specification of sustainable competitive advantage;

- Improved communication between executives;

- Involvement of all levels of management in the process;

- More appropriate allocation of scarce resources;

- Consistency of approach throughout the organization;

- More market-focused orientation throughout the organization.

Items That Should Appear in a Strategic Marketing Plan

1. Executive summary.

2. Objectives:

    - Company mission;
    - Financial objectives;
    - Marketing objectives.

3. Marketing analysis:

    - Markets/products overview;
    - Marketing macroenvironment trends;
    - Competition situation;
    - Distribution situation.

4. SWOT analysis:

    - Strength and weaknesses of current marketing strategies;
    - Opportunities and threats;
    - Issues to be addressed.

5. Marketing strategies:

    - Segments;
    - Competitive advantage (by segment);
    - Positioning (by segment);

- Major decisions about all the elements of the marketing mix;
- Cooperation needed with the other departments.

6. Marketing action programs:

   - Marketing mixes by segment: product, price, promotion, and place;
   - Task and responsibilities.

7. Budget.

8. Controls and contingency plans.

The executive summary is a concise overview of the report for quick management skimming. It includes overall strategies, main conclusions, and key points of the marketing action programs. A table of contents must follow the executive summary.

Objectives give perspective to the report. They refer to the organization's mission statement, including the definition of the business and the contribution of the unit as well as its distinctive competence. The financial objectives are those expected from the business unit: return on investment, net profit, and cash flow.

Those financial objectives are translated in marketing objectives. A marketing objective is a statement of what is to be accomplished through marketing activities, in terms of gains in market share, sales volume, profitability per unit, degree of product introduction, and innovation. It must be stated in a measurable form ("increase market share by 10%") with a given time frame ("within the next 15 months") and internally consistent ("following the launching of our new product X").

The marketing analysis is the foundation of the marketing programs. The market/product overview helps the unfamiliar reader understand the marketing plan. It provides the necessary background about the market segments that are served as well as a brief summary of the past performance and history of the products on each of those segments.

Marketing analysis also includes a description and an evaluation of the major key macroenvironment trends, most specifically technological, economic, political, and legal. The competition situation introduces the major competitors described in terms of their size, goals, products, marketing strategies, and any other relevant characteristic. Initially, the distribution situation presents facts and data on the products split by channel the changing importance of each channel, in terms of volume and bargaining power (that is, the prices and trade conditions that are necessary to motivate them).

The SWOT analysis provides the rationale for the marketing strategy. On one hand, it identifies the strengths and weaknesses of current marketing strategies; on the other hand, it reviews the opportunities and threats of outside factors that can affect the future of the business. The results of the SWOT analysis define the main issues to be addressed in the plan.

The marketing strategies section presents a broad overview of the plan. It defines the targeted market segments and outlines the competitive advantage of the product on these segments as well as its positioning. It introduces strategic decisions about all the elements of the marketing mix, that is, the product strategy, the pricing strategy, the communication strategy, and the distribution strategy as well as the required needs of marketing research. Finally, it mentions the main avenues of cooperation with the other departments of the firm that are required to reach each of the targeted segments.

The marketing action program details precisely all the elements of the marketing mix and defines what is to be done, when, by whom, and how much it will cost. It lists all the activities that are required to implement the marketing plan and to achieve the marketing objectives. It is of key importance to check that all the tasks have been addressed and the responsibilities for action clearly identified.

The action plan translates into a supporting budget that looks like a profit-and-loss projected statement. On the revenue side are the forecasted sales volumes in unit and the average price; entries on the expense side include the cost of production, the cost of physical distribution, and all the costs of marketing: product development, advertising, distribution channel training and development, sales force training and compensation, and marketing research.

Finally, the controls section details the manner in which the performance of the plan will be measured as well as the schedule by which to monitor its progress by comparing results versus objectives. More specifically for the field of high-tech products, where the environment and markets change at breakneck speed, contingency plans that are designed for implementation in case of some specific adverse event, like a delay in new product launching because of technical problems or the earliest entry on the market of a new competitor, may be outlined.

References

[1]   McDonald, M. H. B., *Marketing Plans,* Oxford, England: Butterworth-Heinemann Limited, 1989.

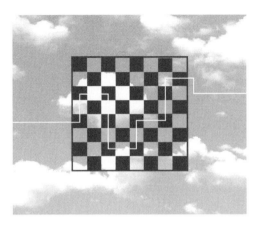

About the Author

Eric Viardot has a Ph.D. in management. He is a graduate of the HEC Business School, Paris, and the Institute of Political Sciences, Paris. After working for Digital Equipment, Dr. Viardot was a strategic consultant at Bain and Company. He is now a professor of marketing and strategy at Ceram Graduate Management Business School, Sophia Antipolis, France. He frequently advises general management in strategic and marketing decisions.

Index

For further information on these and other Artech House titles, including previously considered out-of-print books now available through our In-Print-Forever® (IPF®) program, contact:

Artech House
685 Canton Street
Norwood, MA 02062
Phone: 781-769-9750
Fax: 781-769-6334
e-mail: artech@artechhouse.com

Artech House
46 Gillingham Street
London SW1V 1AH UK
Phone: +44 (0)20 7596-8750
Fax: +44 (0)20 7630-0166
e-mail: artech-uk@artechhouse.com

Find us on the World Wide Web at:
www.artechhouse.com